Lecture Notes in Computer Science

T0255480

Lecture Notes in Computer Science

Lecture Notes in Computer Science

Edited by G. Goos and J. Hartmanis

175

André Thayse

P-Functions and Boolean Matrix Factorization

A Unified Approach for Wired,
Programmed and Microprogrammed Implementations
of Discrete Algorithms

Springer-Verlag
Berlin Heidelberg New York Tokyo 1984

Author

André Thayse
Philips & MBLE Associated S.A., Research Laboratory Brussels
Avenue Van Becelaere 2, Box 8, B-1170 Brussels, Belgium

CR Subject Classifications (1982): B.6, G.2

ISBN 3-540-13358-5 Springer-Verlag Berlin Heidelberg New York Tokyo
ISBN 0-387-13358-5 Springer-Verlag New York Heidelberg Berlin Tokyo

Printing and binding: Beltz Offsetdruck, Hemsbach / Bergstr.
2146 / 3140-543210

FOREWORD

By Sheldon B. Akers

Unlike most computer texts, this book can be recommended for both the hardware and the software specialist. Each should not only gain valuable insight into how his own discipline formally interacts with the other, but also each may well discover that the developed techniques have direct application to his particular problems and interests.

Dr. Thayse's basic approach has been to view the digital design process as that of "algorithm implementation". In this way he has been able to focus simultaneously on both the software and hardware aspects of the design process. Here, the results of his fruitful investigations are systematically and clearly presented.

This book's main contributions are twofold. First is the author's elegant and effective matrix formulation which provides a direct and meaningful bridge between many of the classical models of computation and the more mundane concerns of the logic designer. Second, and equally important, are the "implementation tools" which Dr. Thayse has developed. These include not only the powerful P-functions but also many other techniques based on his extensive background in switching theory and Boolean calculus.

This book makes an original, timely, and unifying contribution to the process of digital design.

Contents

Introduction.

In the early stages of the design of a digital system, one has to decide of the main features of the hardware architecture and of the software organization of this system. More precisely, one decomposes the system into subsystems which are either available as such or easier to design. This decomposition technique is fundamental and plays a key role from the lowest level of Boolean synthesis methods to the highest levels of systems hierarchy. Basically, the method rests upon our certainty that an appropriate cooperation between the exhibited subsystems will eventually yield the required system behaviour.

This decomposition process is important and it is worthwile to describe it more accurately. For this purpose, we shall consider our digital system as performing a *computation*, in the algebraic sense of this term (see e.g. Manna [1974]). The decomposition or synthesis of the system can then be viewed as the description of an *algorithm* able to produce the required computation results. By algorithm, we shall understand in the present text the combination of *computation primitives* by means of *acceptable constructs*. The *computation primitives* are usually called *instructions*, while the *acceptable constructs* are usually called *programs*. The instruction and program must be understood as abstract concepts. When an instruction is implemented, it is called a *gate* in a *hardware implementation*, an *instruction* in a *software* or *programmed implementation* and a *microinstruction* in a *microprogrammed implementation*.

When a program is implemented it is called a *logic network* in a *hardware implementation*, a *program* in a *software* or *programmed implementation* and a *microprogram* in a *microprogrammed implementation*.

By *synthesis of algorithm* we mean the *transformation* of *high-level instructions* (organized in a program which describes the algorithm) in terms of *low-level instructions* (organized in an equivalent program which describes the same algorithm). The formalism of the high-level instructions can be considered as the *informal description level* : it is the formalism in which the algorithm is currently described. The low-level formalism corresponds to the *materialization* or *implementation level* : it is the formalism which immediately leads to an implementation of the algorithm in a chosen technology (e.g. hardware, programmed or microprogrammed).

To the best of our knowledge, that way of viewing the structure of a digital system as spanned by an algorithm can be traced in its explicit form to the works of Glushkov [1965] and of Karp and Miller [1969]. It has, since then, been used fruitfully by a number of authors and it can be considered today as one of the most promising tools in education and in design methodology (see e.g. Keller [1970 , 1973 , 1974], Clare [1973], Mange [1979, 1980, 1981], Mange, Sanchez and

Stauffer [1982], Moalla, Sifakis and Zachariades [1976], Zsombor-Murray, Vroomen, Hudson, Le-Ngoc and Holck [1983], Moalla, Sifakis and Silva [1980], Davio, Deschamps and Thayse [1983a, 1983b], Davio and Thayse [1980], Thayse [1980, 1981, 1982, 1984a, 1984b]).

Glushkov's essential contribution was to show that, under appropriate conditions, an algorithm can be implemented as a synchronous sequential machine : the *control automaton*. The control automaton cooperates with a second synchronous sequential machine, the *operational automaton* which performs the data processing. For the purposes of the present text, it will be sufficient to assume that the operational automaton is made up of combinational switching circuits (the computation primitives) and of registers and that, at each algorithm step, it performs, according to the orders of the control automaton, some functional transfers such as the replacement of the contents of register R by a function f of the contents $[R_i]$ of registers R_i.

The Glushkov model of computation is a *synchronous model* : the execution of the various steps of the algorithm in the control automaton and the execution of the computations in the operational automaton are synchronized by a clock signal in order to avoid races and hazards. This synchronous cooperation between operational and control automata disappears in another model of computation : the *parallel program schema* which has been introduced by Karp and Miller [1969] and was later mainly developed by Keller [1970, 1972, 1973]. The parallel program schema can be viewed as a computation model whose aim is to control the evolution of a series of subsystems (sometimes called *processors*) which operate in a parallel way.

A parallel system is made-up of a series of independent subsystems which are working independently : it is not realistic to make hypotheses about the existence of a relation between the duration of the various operations in each of the subsystems. This leads us to consider the *asynchronism* as one of the fundamental characteristics of parallel systems, i.e. to adopt the hypothesis that the duration of the various operations is not known. A consequence of this hypothesis is that the elementary steps of the algorithm which is implemented in the control part (in the Glushkov as well as in the Karp and Miller model) can no longer be activated by a clock signal. A signal must be generated in the operational part which indicates the termination of an operation. The main interest of the asynchronous model lies in the fact that it allows us to take advantage of the own time duration of the various operations. The asynchronous computation model allows us to make a better use of the computation primitives and hence to improve the total computation duration for a given algorithm.

The introduction of the algorithm concept has the advantage of linking tightly the hardware and the software domains : the algorithm concept can indeed be considered as the basis for both hardware design and software implementation. With a given algorithm it is possible to associate a number of distinct materializations. Furthermore the separation between operational part and control part which appears as well in the Glushkov model of computation as in the parallel program schema of Karp and Miller allows us to concentrate on the control part the essential of the synthesis problem and this independently of the materialization which occurs in the operational part.

An adequate model for the representation and the synthesis of algorithms must allow us to maintain this separation between the operational part and the control part and to illustrate the cooperation which occurs between them. *The main purpose of the present text is to introduce an algebraic representation model which satisfies these items, to show how it encompasses and generalizes existing models and to relate it to a powerful mathematical theory, namely the theory of Boolean matrices, in order to take advantage of the results of matrix theory.*

For the representation of algorithms Glushkov [1970] adopted a type of instruction originally introduced by Mishchenko [1967]. In the present text we identify the Mishchenko's instruction with a *row-Boolean matrix*. We then discover that the transformation of the Glushkov synchronous model into the asynchronous Karp and Miller model requires the introduction of a new type of instruction that we identify to a *column-Boolean matrix*, which is nothing but the transpose of the Mishchenko's instruction. This identification between instructions and row and column-Boolean matrices suggests us to define a general type of instruction by means of a *rectangular Boolean matrix*. This matrix-instruction generalizes and encompasses both the Mishchenko's instruction and its transpose. Algorithms are then described by means of matrix-instructions whose entries are Boolean functions ; similarly elementary instructions such as *if then else, fork, join, do* etc. are described by means of matrices whose entries are the elementary predicates of the algorithm at hand. In the matrix vocabulary, *to synthesize an algorithm by means of elementary instructions reduces to factorize a matrix of Boolean functions as a product of elementary matrices of predicates.* The formulation of an algorithm and of an instruction in terms of matrices allows us to use the well known results of matrix calculus. We show e.g. that the implementation of an algorithm by means of the parallel schema model reduces to the realization of a matrix-instruction which activates the execution of operations and of another matrix-instruction which indicates the end of execution of the different operations that were activated ; these matrices may be derived from each other by a transposition operation. Since a factorization for a matrix is also a factorization for its transpose the two materializations of instructions can be derived from each other by a simple transposition operation.

The present text is basically made-up of a series of research results obtained these last years by the author in the domain of description and implementation of algorithms. The Glushkov and the Karp and Miller models are approached from a Boolean or a switching point of view. We show that the *Boolean calculus* and the *switching theory* which have merely been used in the past for the design of logical gate networks can also play a key role in the description and in the design of high-level computation models.

The text is organized into three parts. The fundamental steps of the proposed formulation for the description and the synthesis of algorithms are gathered in part I. The description of implementations as well as the algebraic developments which are less essential for the understanding of the analysis are gathered in parts II and III respectively.

The purpose of chapter 1 is the introduction of models for the *description* and the *implementation* of *algorithms*. We introduce a *matrix formalism* for the desciption of algorithms : this is the basic formalism which will be used through the text. The matrix formalism is used in connection with two computation models : the *synchronous Glushkov model* [1965] and the *asynchronous parallel program schema* of Karp and Miller [1969] . These two computation models are briefly introduced; a particular case of the parallel program schema, namely the *parallel flowchart* is also presented. The parallel flowchart, which is equivalent to the widely used *Petri net*, will be used in connection with the matrix formalism for the description and design of asynchronously implemented algorithms.

Chapter 2 is devoted to an introduction of the algorithm synthesis technique. Roughly speaking, the synthesis of an algorithm will be obtained by expressing *high-level instructions* in terms of *low-level instructions*. The high-level formalism can be considered as the *informal description level* : it is the formalism in which the algorithm is currently described. The low-level formalism corresponds to the *materialization level* : it is the formalism which immediately leads to an implementation of the algorithm. Both high-level and low-level instructions are described by means of Boolean matrices. The matrix formalism allows us to state the synthesis problem in the following way : *the synthesis of an algorithm reduces to the factorization of a matrix of Boolean functions (which corresponds to the high-level instruction) as a product of matrices of elementary predicates (which corresponds to low-level instructions).*

Interpretations are associated to matrix-instructions : we show that the rows and the columns of matrix-instructions can be *(and)-* or *(or)-interpreted*. There exist thus four interpretations for matrix-instructions, i.e. :

$$(\text{row; column})\text{-interpretation} = (\text{or; and})$$
$$= (\text{and; and})$$
$$= (\text{or; or})$$
$$= (\text{and; or})$$

The (or;and)-interpreted matrix-instructions are used in synchronous as well as in asynchronous implementations of algorithms : these instructions appear in both the Glushkov model of computation and in the parallel schema. The implementation of algorithms in an asynchronous way (parallel program schema) moreover requests the presence of (and;and)-interpreted matrix-instructions. The (or;or)- and the (and; or)-interpreted matrix-instructions are related to the description and to the analysis of non-deterministic models.

Since the present text is devoted to synthesis techniques for implementing deterministic algorithms, (or;and)- and (and;and)-interpreted matrix-instructions will unambiguously be called *(or)-* and *(and)- interpreted matrix-instructions* respectively.

The purpose of chapter 3 is the introduction of the mathematical tool that will be used further on for synthesizing algorithms or equivalently for factorizing Boolean matrices. The concept that will be used in the materialization of algorithms is that of *pair-of-functions* or *P-function*. The synthesis of high-level instructions in terms of low-level instructions is described by means of a *transformation between P-functions*.

Chapters 4,5 and 6 constitute the central chapters of this text : we introduce in these chapters computation methods for synthesizing matrix-instructions

We first introduce in chapter 4 a computation method for the synthesis of (or)-interpreted matrix-instructions with disjoint (or orthogonal) columns (the columns of a Boolean matrix $[f_{ij}]$ are said to be disjoint iff : $f_{ij}f_{ik} \equiv 0$ $\forall j \neq k$ and $\forall i$). In chapter 5 we state the additional computations which are needed for the synthesis of an (or)-interpreted matrix-instruction with non-disjoint columns. In chapter 6 we show how the theorems of chapters 4 and 5 can be interpreted in a dual way for the synthesis of (and)-interpreted matrix-instructions. Design examples are extensively developed in these chapters.

Chapters 7 constitutes a summary chapter which sums up in a synoptic way the synthesis schemes that were proposed in chapters 4,5 and 6. We present also in this chapter a global formulation of the *transposition principle* and of the *duality principle* which were stated in chapters 4,5 and 7. Finally chapter 7 is also a conclusion chapter for part I of this text.

One of the main purposes of part I is the introduction of a formalism (the Boolean matrix formalism) and of a calculus (the algebra of P-functions) which allows us to transform any high-level instruction in terms of low-level instructions. This transformation immediately leads to an hardware implementation of algorithms in terms of elementary logic primitives. To this *hardware implementation* is associated a *hardware description language* or *software description* of the control network. When the algorithm is described by means of (or)-interpreted matrix-instructions with disjoint columns the hardware description language coincides with a programming language (such as e.g. an algol-like language) and immediately leads to a *software implementation*. This is no longer the case when the algorithm description is performed by means of (or)-interpreted matrix-instructions with non-disjoint columns or by means of (and)- interpreted matrix instructions. The main purpose of part II is to derive the additional rules that are needed to transform a hardware description language into a programming language and to present the resulting programmed and microprogrammed implementations of algorithms. These additional rules are easily expressed in terms of *parallel flowcharts* or equivalently in terms of *Petri nets*.

Chapter 8 is devoted to the representation of instructions by means of parallel flowcharts. We also compare the fields of application of the parallel flowchart representation and of the P-function technique. The parallel flowchart and its associated vector addition system is a powerful tool for describing the connection between instructions and for analyzing their behaviour in order to show e.g. that they are organized into a *safe program configuration* ; the algorithm of P-functions is mainly a synthesis tool for implementing high-level instructions in terms of low-level instructions. Parallel flowcharts and P-functions are consequently design tools whose respective domains of application are complementary.

Chapter 9 is devoted to a comparison between synchronous and asynchronous implementations of instructions. We also introduce in this chapter the *feedback instructions* which are needed by the algorithm design when it is requested that several datas can be concurrently in progress (the program accepts new datas before the termination of the computations associated with the preceding datas).

Chapter 10 constitutes the basic chapter of part II. We derive in this chapter the additional rules which must satisfy the hardware description language of part I in order to become a *safe program*, i.e. an interconnection of instructions which constitute a *safe* or *correct programmed implementation*. In particular we show that a programmed implementation of an (or)- interpreted matrix-instruction is safe if and only if all its *join-or* instructions are degenerate instructions. Similarly, a programmed implementation of an (and)- interpreted matrix-instruction is safe if and only if it does not contain *fork* instructions.

Chapter 11 is devoted to microprogrammed implementation of safe programs, i.e. materialization of safe programs by means of large scale integrated components.

Chapter 12 is a conclusion chapter for part II of this book.

The P-functions were introduced in chapter 3 with respect to a formulation for the synthesis of algorithms. The purpose of part III is the study of the P-function as a mathematical tool associated with the concepts of Boolean function and of discrete function. The results of part III are twofold : some theorems and propositions whose proofs were presented in a rather informal way in parts I and II will rigorously be stated and some laws ruling P-functions will be extended; a number of new definitions and theorems will also be stated.

P-functions associated to Boolean functions are introduced in chapter 13. General transformation laws are stated : these transformation laws encompass and generalize the composition laws on P-functions that have been introduced in chapter 3. We also introduce the concept of *prime P-function* and we show that the instructions of an optimal program are characterized by the fact that their associated P-functions are prime P-functions. The concept of prime *P-function* plays thus with respect to *program synthesis* the same role as the concept of *prime implicant* with respect to *logical design*.

Multivalued or discrete functions i.e. functions having finite domain and codomain play a key role in various fields of computer science. Chapter 14 attempts to give a generalization of the theory of P-functions for discrete functions :

$$f : \{0,1,\ldots,m-1\}^n \to \{0,1,\ldots,m-1\} \ .$$

P-functions associated to discrete functions are defined and the laws ruling discrete P-functions are stated. We propose an interpretation of discrete P-functions in terms of program synthesis ; in particular we derive a realization method for programs using multivalued instructions as decision instructions. These decision instructions correspond to the *switch* instruction in *algol* and to the *case* instruction in *pascal*.

Chapter 15 is devoted to a study of the *vector extension* of P-functions and of their laws. P-functions whose domain functions are vectors were introduced in chapter 3 for the synthesis and the description of matrix-instructions. The algebraic properties and the interpretations of P-functions whose domain and codomain are vectors are investigated in this chapter. This chapter can be considered as a preliminary draft of a future research that will be performed in the field of computer science that has been investigated in this text.

The purpose of chapter 16 is to introduce some possible extensions of the theory of matrix-instructions. The material is presented in an unfinished and tentative form and must rather be considered as a preliminary draft of a future research work. A speech-recognition problem known as *isolated word recognition based on demisyllable segmentation* leads to a simple generalization of the concept of matrix-instruction and of its associated transposition principle. One introduces matrix-instructions having automata and Boolean functions as entries and shows how the peculiarities of the speech-recognition algorithms are reflected on the properties of the matrix-instructions.

Lausanne, August 1983

André Thayse

Part I : <u>A formalism and a computation method for the synthesis of algorithms</u>.

Chapter 1 : <u>Instructions and models of algorithm implementation</u>.

The purpose of chapter 1 is the introduction of models for *instructions* and for *algorithm implementation*.

We first introduce in section 1.1. the *matrix formalism* for the description of *instructions* : this formalism will then systematically be used through the text. Let us point out that by *instruction* we mean as well a *software* or *linguistic description* of computation primitives as their *hardware materialization* by means e.g. of logical components.

The computation models that will be used are the synchronous *Glushkov model* and the asynchronous *parallel program schema*. These computation models are introduced in a somewhat informal way in section 1.2. This informal description of the Glushkov model and of the parallel program schema is quite sufficient for the purpose of this text.

A formalisation of the Glushkov model and of the parallel program schema is briefly introduced in sections 1.3 and 1.4 respectively.

A particular case of the parallel program schema, namely the *parallel flowchart* is introduced in section 1.5. The parallel flowchart is equivalent to the widely used *Petri net*. The connection between parallel flowcharts (or Petri nets) and the computation models will more deeply be studied in chapter 8.

1.1. The basic formalism.

Algorithms are described by means of two types of instructions : *decision instructions* and *execution instructions*.

Decision instructions are e.g. the *if then else*, *fork* and *join* instructions. For a reason that will appear further on we shall adopt a *matrix notation* for describing instructions, the *if then else* instruction :

$$N \; \textit{if} \; x=0 \quad \textit{then goto} \; M_1 \quad \textit{else goto} \; M_2$$

is written as a row matrix, i.e. :

$$N \; [\; \bar{x} \quad x \;] \qquad\qquad (1)$$
$$ M_1 \quad M_2$$

In this formalism the row is associated to the instruction input label N while the columns are associated to the instruction output labels M_1 and M_2.

To the instruction (1) we associate a *transpose instruction* which we write :

$$M_1 \begin{bmatrix} \bar{x} \\ \\ M_2 \end{bmatrix} \begin{matrix} \\ x \end{matrix}$$
$$N$$

(2)

and which we interpret as follows :

as soon as the instruction label M_1 is reached and if x=0

or

as soon as the instruction label M_2 is reached and if x=1 go to the next instruction N.

The instruction (2) is the *then if* instruction or *transpose (if then else)*.

The *transpose (if then else)* instruction can also be interpreted in terms of two *if then else* instructions, i.e. :

$$M_1 \begin{bmatrix} \bar{x} & x \\ N & M_1 \end{bmatrix}$$

$$M_2 \begin{bmatrix} \bar{x} & x \\ M_2 & N \end{bmatrix}$$

These two row instructions can be gathered in a single matrix instruction written as follows :

$$\begin{matrix} M_1 \\ \\ M_2 \end{matrix} \begin{bmatrix} \bar{x} & x & 0 \\ \\ x & 0 & \bar{x} \end{bmatrix}$$
$$\begin{matrix} N & M_1 & M_2 \end{matrix}$$

This formalism can be interpreted by means of notations (1) and (2); it will be defined in a rigorous way in section 2.1.

We also point out that the *if then else* instruction is known in logic design as the *demultiplexer* gate while the *transpose (if then else)* instruction is known as the *multiplexer* gate (see section 4.1.4)

The instruction *fork* and its transpose the instruction *join* are written respectively :

$$N \begin{bmatrix} 1 & 1 \end{bmatrix}$$
$$\begin{matrix} M_1 & M_2 \end{matrix}$$

(3)

$$\begin{matrix} M_1 \\ M_2 \end{matrix} \begin{bmatrix} 1 \\ 1 \end{bmatrix}$$
$$N$$

(4)

their meaning is the following :

    : as soon as the instruction label N is reached go to the next instruction(s) M_1 and/or M_2 ;

    : as soon as the instruction label(s) M_1 and/or M_2 are reached go to the next instruction N

The *fork* and *join* instructions have two interpretations : an *(and)-interpretation* and an *(or)-interpretation*. We shall see later on that the (and)-interpretation will be used in the description of deterministic algorithms while the (or)-interpretation will be used in the description of non-deterministic problems. Observe that the matrix formalism (3), (4) is independent of the chosen interpretation.

    Execution instructions are of the *do* type ; the instruction :

$$N \quad do \ \sigma \ and \ go \ to \ M$$

is written :

$$N \ [\ \sigma \ ] \qquad\qquad\qquad (5)$$
$$M$$

To the decision instruction *do* we associate a transpose instruction *has been done* that we write

$$M \ [\ \tau \ ] \qquad\qquad\qquad (6)$$
$$N$$

and that we interprete as follows :

$$M \ as \ soon \ as \ \tau \ has \ been \ done \ go \ to \ N$$

The elementary execution instructions (5), (6) are 1×1 matrices, i.e. scalars; for sake of conciseness they will also be written respectively :

$$N \quad \sigma \quad M \quad ,$$
$$M \quad \tau \quad N \quad . \qquad\qquad (7)$$

    It will be convenient to gather decision and execution instructions into a single expression made-up of a decision and of an execution part. Let $f_1(x)$ and $f_2(x)$ be two functions of x ; we first consider instructions of the type :

$$N \quad \tau \ [\ f_1 \qquad f_2 \ ] \qquad\qquad (8)$$
$$\sigma_1 \qquad \sigma_2$$
$$M_1 \qquad M_2$$

that we interpret as follows :

as soon as the *end of execution* signal τ has been received we test the Boolean functions f_i ; we perform the commands σ_i corresponding to the functions f_i equal to 1 : these commands activate executions E_i. We go to the next addresses corresponding to the functions f_i equal to 1.

Since $f_i = 0,1,x$ or $\bar{x}$ the decision part of (8) can among others be of the form *if then else* or *fork*.

We have assumed that in the matrix representation of instructions the rows and columns were associated to input and output labels respectively, accordingly instruction (8) may also be written as a product of matrices, i.e. :

$$N \quad [\tau] \quad [f_1 \quad f_2] \quad \begin{bmatrix} \sigma_1 & 0 \\ 0 & \sigma_2 \end{bmatrix}$$
$$N' \quad M'_1 \quad M'_2 \qquad\qquad M_1 \quad M_2 \tag{9}$$

To instruction (8) we associate a transpose instruction which we write in the two following forms ;

$$\begin{array}{cc} M_1 & \tau_1 \\ M_2 & \tau_2 \end{array} \quad \begin{bmatrix} f_1 \\ f_2 \end{bmatrix} \tag{10}$$
$$\sigma$$
$$M$$

$$\begin{array}{c} M_1 \\ M_2 \end{array} \begin{bmatrix} \tau_1 & 0 \\ 0 & \tau_2 \end{bmatrix} \begin{bmatrix} f_1 \\ f_2 \end{bmatrix} \begin{bmatrix} \sigma \\ N \end{bmatrix} \tag{11}$$
$$M'_1 \quad M'_2 \quad N'$$

The interpretation of (10,11) derives from (2) and (4); (9) and (11) are *factorized* forms for (8) and (10) respectively.

Observe that elementary instructions are often formed by a decision and by an execution part ; for example the instruction *while do* , i.e. :

$$N \textit{ while } x=0 \textit{ do } \sigma \textit{ else go to } M$$

is written in the matrix formalism :

$$N \quad [\bar{x} \quad x]$$
$$\sigma \quad \lambda$$
$$N \quad M$$

where λ represents the *empty execution*.

The above instructions suggest us the introduction of a general kind of instruction, namely a *matrix instruction* that we write :

$$
\begin{array}{cc}
N_1 & \tau_1 \\
\vdots & \vdots \\
N_p & \tau_p
\end{array}
\left[
\begin{array}{ccc}
f_{11} & \cdots & f_{1q} \\
\vdots & & \\
f_{p1} & \cdots & f_{pq}
\end{array}
\right]
\qquad (12a)
$$
$$
\begin{array}{ccc}
\sigma_1 & \cdots & \sigma_q \\
M_1 & \cdots & M_q
\end{array}
$$

A definition and an interpretation of this matrix instruction will be given in section 2.1. Let us already point out that to any matrix instruction (12a) is associated a transpose matrix instruction written as follows :

$$
\begin{array}{cc}
M_1 & \tau'_1 \\
\vdots & \vdots \\
M_q & \tau'_q
\end{array}
\left[
\begin{array}{ccc}
f_{11} & \cdots & f_{p1} \\
\vdots & & \vdots \\
f_{1q} & & f_{pq}
\end{array}
\right]
\qquad (12b)
$$
$$
\begin{array}{ccc}
\sigma'_1 & \cdots & \sigma'_p \\
N_1 & & N_p
\end{array}
$$

1.2. The Glushkov model and the parallel program schema

Later on we shall assume that algorithms are described by sequences of decision and of execution instructions. We shall relate these instructions to two computation models widely used in practice, namely the *Glushkov model of computation* (Glushkov [1965, 1970], Glushkov and Letichevskii [1964]) and the *parallel program schema* (Karp and Miller [1969] , Keller [1973a, 1973b]).

The Glushkov model of computation is a *synchronous model* ; Glushkov's essential contribution was to show that under appropriate conditions an algorithm can be implemented as a synchronous sequential machine : the *control automaton*. The control automaton cooperates with a second synchronous machine : the *operational automaton* which performs the data processing such as register transfers. This cooperation is reflected in figure 1.a : the executions in the operational automaton are initiated by orders σ received from the control automaton where execution instructions of the form (5) are implemented. On the other hand, the operational automaton provides the control automaton with appropriate information about intermediate computation results. This information is provided under the form of Boolean variables x called *condition variables* which are elementary predicates of the decision instructions (1), (2). These instructions are implemented in the control automaton.

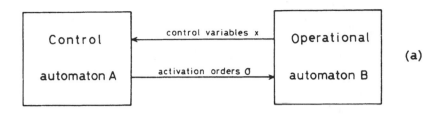

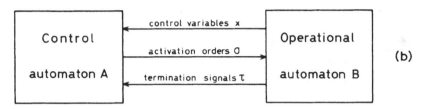

Figure 1 : (a) Glushkov model of computation or algorithmic
state machine
(b) Karp and Miller model of computation or
parallel program schema

The *parallel program schema* (or *Karp and Miller model*) can be considered as an *asynchronous Glushkov model* : the cooperation between the two automata is no longer driven by a clock but by the termination of the operations in execution. The main interest of an asynchronous model lies in the fact that it allows
us to take advantage of the own time duration of the various operations. The cooperation between automata in the Karp and Miller model is reflected in figure 1.b ;
in addition to the *condition variables* x and to the *commands* σ of figure 1a
we find the *end of execution signals* τ which are directed from the operational part
to the command part. As soon as the activated operations have been executed, the
signal τ allows the activation of the next operations.

We thus see that a synchronous implementation of algorithms needs
decision instructions (reflected by the connection x between automata) and *orders*
which initiate executions (reflected by the connection σ); an asynchronous implementation moreover requires *end of execution signals* (reflected by the connection τ).

The above informal description of the Glushkov model and of the Karp
and Miller model are sufficient for the purpose of this text ; a brief formal
description of these models is given in sections 1.3. and 1.4. respectively. Let
us note that Karp and Miller have also defined the *parallel flowchart*, which is a
special class of parallel schema having interesting properties. The parallel flowchart is equivalent to the widely used *Petri net*. It will briefly be introduced

in section 1.5. The Petri net will more thoroughly be studied in connection with computation models in chapter 8.

1.3. Formalisation of the Glushkov model.

The *operational automaton* of the Glushkov model can be described as the Moore automaton

$$B = < \Sigma, \Omega, Q^B, M^B, P^B >$$

where

(1) the input alphabet $\Sigma = \{\lambda, \sigma_1, \sigma_2, \ldots\}$ is the set of commands. It includes the empty command λ (no operation)

(2) the output alphabet $\Omega = \{\omega_1, \omega_2, \ldots\}$ is the set of minterms formed from the condition variables x ;

(3) Q^B, M^B, P^B represent as usual the state set, the transition function and the output function respectively. In particular, the transition function M^B associates with each command σ_i a transformation $(Q^B \rightarrow Q^B)$ of the state set Q^B. This transformation will be denoted σ_i without ambiguity.

On the other hand, the *control automaton* A, is the actual implementation of the computation algorithm. It performs in the following way : taking into account the present computation step (its own internal state) and formerly obtained computation results (its inputs, the condition variables), it decides   the next computation step (next state) and   the action to be performed (output command). Formally, the control automaton will thus be defined as the Mealy automaton :

$$A = < \Omega, \Sigma, Q^A, M^A, N^A > \quad ,$$

where the definitions are similar to those given for B.

Observe, however, that

(1) the input and output alphabets are interchanged between A and B ;

(2) the set Q^A of internal states identifies with the set of algorithm steps. From now on these steps will be called *instructions*.

To complete the definition of our model, we should now characterize the set of accepted instruction types. We shall accept matrix instructions which were already mentioned above (see (12)) and which will be defined in chapter 2. The *matrix instruction* tries to achieve two simultaneous goals :

(1) to cover as broad a class of instructions as possible as to provide the model with a maximum number of capabilities.

(2) to keep consistent with the automaton model and, more precisely to preserve the identity of the instructions and of the internal states. This will allow us to

design the control automaton by the standard procedures used for synchronous sequential circuits.

The interested reader may find more about the algebraic aspect of the Glushkov model of computation in the original papers by Glushkov([1965, 1970]), in the books by Davio, Deschamps and Thayse ([1983a, 1983b] or in the series of papers by Davio and Thayse [1980a, 1980b] , Thayse [1980] , Sanchez and Thayse [1981], Thayse [1981 a, 1981b, 1981c, 1982]).

1.4. Formalisation of the parallel program schema

A *parallel program schema* (see figure 2) consists of the cooperation of two automata :

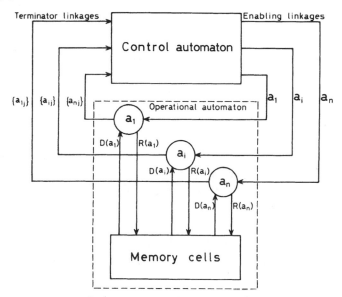

Figure 2 : Parallel program schema

(1) The *operational automaton* is made up by a number of automata symbolized by the operations a_i ; when an operation a_i is initiated, it obtains operands from the memory locations specified by $D(a_i)$, and when an operation a_i terminates, it places its results in the memory locations specified by $R(a_i)$ and selects an outcome a_{ij}. This outcome is introduced into the *control automaton* through the intermediate of the terminator linkages.

(2) The sequence of operations a_i, which may be computed concurrently, is enforced by the *control automaton*.

A parallel program schema can be regarded as a collection of primitive operations (the a_i' s) which depend on and affect memory locations. The operations communicate with a control automaton which provides the operational automaton with the set of the next operations to be initiated.

The model initially defined by Karp and Miller [1969] and later developed by Keller [1973] is based on this viewpoint and is specifically designed as a representation for programs in which several operations or several performances of any operation can be concurrently in progresss. The following definitions constitute a simplified version of some more elaborate concepts introduced by these authors.

The set of all natural numbers $\{0,1,2,...\}$ will be denoted by ω ; if A is a set, 2^A represents the set of all subsets of A.

Definition 1. An *operation set* $A = \{a_1, a_2, ... \}$ is a finite set of elements called *operations* , together with the following for each $a_i \in A$.

(1) a nonempty finite set of unique symbols $\sum(a_i) = \{a_{i1}, a_{i2}, ..., a_{i\,K(a_i)}\}$ called terminators of a_i ,

(2) a finite set $D(a_i) \subset \omega$ called the *domain* of a_i ,

(3) a finite set $R(a_i) \subset \omega$ called the *range* of a_i .

Further on, $\sum$, the alphabet, will denote the union of the $\sum(a_i)$ $\forall i$. Before giving the further definitions, we remark that an *operation set* is uninterpreted ; that is, it does not assign a particular meaning to its operations a_i. The only information given about operations is their associated domain and range locations in the memory. The papers by Karp and Miller [1969] and Keller [1973] are concerned with properties of parallel program schemata which hold true for all the interpretations placed on the operations. We next introduce the concept of interpretation and show how a schema together with an interpretation of its operations, defines computations.

Let M be a set of *memory locations*.

Definition 2. An *interpretation* I for memory locations M and for an operation set A is specified by :

(1) a function C associating with each element $i \in M$ a set $C(i)$ and an element
$$c_0 \in \underset{i \in M}{\times} C(i)$$
The set $C(i)$ consists of the possible contents of memory location i, and c_0 denotes the initial contents of memory M ;

(2) for each operations a_i, two functions :

$$F_{a_i} : \underset{i \in D(a_i)}{\times} C(i) \to \underset{i \in R(a_i)}{\times} C(i)$$

$$G_{a_i} : \underset{i \in D(a_i)}{\times} C(i) \to \{a_{i1}, a_{i2}, ..., a_{i\,K(a_i)}\}$$

The function F_{a_i} determines the result which operation a_i stores in memory upon its completion while the function G_{a_i} determines the outcome after a $K(a_i)$-way test has taken place ;

Definition 3. A *control* over an operation set A is a quadruple $F(Q,q_0,f,g)$ where

(1) Q is a countable set of states and $q_0 \in Q$ is the initial state ;

(2) $f : Q \times \sum \to Q$ is the partial state-transition function of the control automaton

(3) $g : Q \to 2^A$ is the enabling function or output function of the control automaton

A *parallel program schema* S (or simply a *schema*) is the three-tuple (M,A,F) ; a schema S together with an interpretation I for (A,M) may be called a *program* (S,I).

The following algorithm should complete the intuitive picture of how a program operates.

(1) The program starts with an instruction *begin* which puts the control automaton F in the initial state q_0 and assigns to the memory M its initial contents c_0 ;

(2) $g(q_0)$ is the set of operations which are enabled to be active, i.e. *computing* while the control is in state q_0.
Let $a_i \in g(q_0)$; the function F_{a_i} performs a transformation on the memory wherea G_{a_i} is a decision function which gives information about the memory to the control in the form of an element of the set $\{a_{i1}, a_{i2}, \ldots, a_{i\ K(a_i)}\}$;

(3) the control assimilates this information, and based upon it, allows a new state q_j of the automaton to be reached ; $g(q_j)$ are the set of operations enabled at this state;

(4) the program ends when a state q_ℓ is reached such that $g(q_\ell) = \phi$.

Labeled directed graphs may be used to represent schemata in the usual way (see e.g. Harrison [1965]). That is, nodes are labeled $(q,g(q))$ in correspondence with the states and enabled operations, and an arc is directed from q to q' with the labels q_{ij} iff $f(q,q_{ij}) = q'$.

The configuration of a program at any time during the performance of its operations is completely described by : c, the contents of memory and q, the state of the control ; the couple (c,q) at some point in time is called the *instantaneous description* of the program.

This configuration may change by changing the state of the control and/or altering the contents of the memory.

Implicit in the definitions presented above are two assumptions.

(1) Only one enabled operation may terminate at a time.

(2) An operation acts instantaneously.

Neither assumption has severe consequences from a practical point of view. Indeed, in case (1) it is generally not realistic to claim that the control mechanism can distinguish a simultaneous occurrence of two or more terminators.

In case (2), the action of an operation with a delay can be suitably modeled by the present formalism. To elaborate upon this, in Karp and Miller [1969] for example, extra notation was introduced to differentiate between the initiation of an operation, at which time the operation inspected its domain cells and began computation and termination of an operation at which time the operation changed its range cells and issued its terminator.

The notations used in this section 1.3 and in figure 2 are those of the original papers by Karp and Miller [1969] and by Keller [1973]. In order to remain consistent with the notations introduced in sections 1.1 for the instructions and in section 1.2 for the Glushkov model, the enabling linkages should be noted σ_i instead of a_i while the terminator linkages should be noted τ_{ij} instead of a_{ij}.

The interested reader may found more about the algebraic aspect of the parallel program schema in the papers by Karp and Miller [1969] and Keller [1973].

1.5. <u>A particular type of schema : the parallel flowchart.</u>

Karp and Miller have merely used the concept of parallel schema to discuss relationships among functional properties of schemata without being concerned about effective tests of these properties. In order to turning to questions concerning the existence of such tests, Karp and Miller restricted their attention to the *parallel flowchart*, a special class of schemata having interesting properties.

The fundamental step in the development of computation procedures is the introduction of a simple geometric structure called *vector addition system* and the introduction of an encoding which associates a vector addition system with each parallel flowchart.

First an attempt is made to provide the reader with insight into the definitions which will be used further on.

A *parallel flowchart* can be represented by a directed graph so defined :

(1) two types of nodes exist : nodes representing *operations* (the a_i's) and nodes representing *counters*, which control the enabling of the operations and certain integer values.

(2) edges connect the counter nodes with the operation nodes : if an edge is directed from a counter to an operation we call the first an *input counter* for that operation ; if an edge is directed from an operation to a counter this is called an *output counter*.

An operation is enabled if and only if the contents of all its input counters are positive. When the operation a_i occurs, the contents of all the input counters are decreased by 1 ; if the termination a_{ij} is selected, the contents of those output counters of a_i, which are connected to a_i by edges labelled a_{ij}, are increased by 1.

The following definitions constitute a simplified version of some more elaborate concepts which may be found in Karp and Miller [1969].

A *vector addition* system is a pair (d,W), where d is a r-dimensional vector of nonnegative integers and W is a finite set of r-dimensional integers vectors.

The *reachability set* R of a vector addition system (d,W) is the set of all the vectors of the form $d + \underline{w}_1 + \underline{w}_2 + \ldots + \underline{w}_s$ with $\underline{w}_i \in W$, such that $d + \underline{w}_1 + \ldots + \underline{w}_i \geqslant 0$, for $i=1,2,\ldots,s$.

Given a parallel flowchart with k counters and p tasks, let π_0 be a (k+p)-dimensional vector whose first k components represent the initial contents of the counter and the remaining p components are all equal to 0. The possible computations of the parallel flowchart can be described with the help of a (k+p)-dimensional vector addition system (d,W) so defined :

(1) $d_i = \pi_0(i)$ for $i=1,\ldots,k+p$

(2) W contains as many vectors as operation symbols a_i and termination symbols a_{ij} denoting by $\underline{w}_\sigma(h)$ the h-th components of a vector $\underline{w}_\sigma \in W$ corresponding to the event σ, the first k components are given by : if $\sigma = a_i$, $\underline{w}(h) = -1$ for all the components h corresponding to the counters decreased by a_i ;
if $\sigma = a_{ij}$, $\underline{w}(h) = +1$ for all the components h corresponding to the counters increased by a_{ij}
$\underline{w}_\sigma(h) = 0$ for all other components.
The remaining p components of $\underline{w}$ are given by :
if $\sigma = a_i$, $\underline{w}_\sigma(a_i) = +1$
if $\sigma = a_{ij}$, $\underline{w}_\sigma(a_{ij}) = -1$
$\underline{w}_\sigma(h) = 0$ for all other components.

d is called the *initial vector*, $\underline{w}_{a_i}$ are the *initiation vectors* (they correspond to the initiation of the operations), $\underline{w}_{a_{ij}}$ are the *termination vectors*.

The vector d is the initial state of the control of the program, and the vectors of the reachability set R are the different states through which the control of the program evolves in consequence of the initiation and the termination of the program operations. It should be noted that the algebraic properties of the vector addition system requires that a distinction must be made between initiation and termination of an operation a_i ; the initiation is denoted by the operation symbol a_i while the termination is denoted by the outcome a_{ij}. At every time, the reached vector π of R represents the contents of the counters and the operations presently in execution.

Analogies can again be drawn between certain proposed instructions for representing parallel sequencing in computer languages and certain capabilities of parallel flowcharts. For example, the *fork* instruction causes two or more operations to be initiated upon a given outcome. In flowcharts, this is achieved by having more than one +1 in a vector $\underline{w}_{a_{ij}}$ (i.e. having an outcome incrementing more than one counter). The *join* instruction causes the initiation of an operation when a set of preceding operations have all terminated with given outcomes. This corresponds to having a vector $\underline{w}_{a_i}$ with more than one -1 (i.e. an operation node is fed by more than one counter).

Chapter 2 : The synthesis of algorithms

Roughly speaking, the synthesis of an algorithm will be obtained by expressing *high-level instructions* in terms of *low-level instructions*. The low-level instructions are the *if then else, fork, join, do* instructions that are described in section 1.1 ; the high level instructions will be introduced in section 2.1. The high-level formalism may also be considered as the *informal description level* : it is the formalism in which the algorithm is currently described. The low-level formalism corresponds to the *materialization level* : it is the formalism which immediately leads to a realization of the algorithm.

Section 2.1. is devoted to the introduction of the high-level instructions, which are the *row-instruction (or generalized fork)*, the *column-instruction (or generalized join)* and the *matrix-instruction* which encompasses and generalizes the row and column instructions.

Interpretations are associated to high-level instructions. In section 2.2. we connect the various interpretations of the matrix-instructions to the possible organizations of the control and of the operational automata in the Glushkov and in the parallel program schema models.

The matrix formalism for low-level instructions is introduced in section 2.3.

An introduction to the program synthesis and to the program optimization problems is presented in section 2.4.

One of the examples that are extensively developed throughout the text is introduced in section 2.5.

2.1. High-level instructions

A *row instruction (or generalized fork)* is a decision instruction which we write :

$$N \begin{bmatrix} f_1 & f_2 & \cdots & f_q \\ M_1 & M_2 & \cdots & M_q \end{bmatrix} \quad , \quad f_i = f_i(\underline{x}) \tag{13}$$

and which we interpret as follows :
When arriving at the instruction N we first evaluate all the Boolean functions f_i of the predicates $\underline{x} = (x_1, x_2, \ldots, x_n)$; we then go to
- either *all* the next instructions M_i corresponding to the $f_i = 1$; ((*and*)-interpretation on the columns).
- or *one* of the next instructions M_i corresponding to the $f_i = 1$; ((*or*)-interpretation on the columns).

If the Boolean functions are disjoint, i.e. if $f_j f_k \equiv 0 \ \forall j \neq k$, the (or)- and the (and)-interpretations coincide. If the functions are non disjoint, the (and)-interpretation corresponds to a parallel initiation of tasks while the (or)-interpretation corresponds to a non-deterministic execution of a task. This will be illustrated further by means of examples. The condition variables x are the elementary predicates of the algorithm (or problem) described by instruction (13).

We associate to (13) a transpose instruction which is a column-instruction (or generalized join) ; we write this decision instruction as follows :

$$
\begin{array}{cc}
M_1 & \left[\begin{array}{c} f_1 \\ f_2 \\ \vdots \\ f_q \end{array} \right] \\
M_2 & \\
\vdots & \\
M_q & \\
& N
\end{array}
\tag{14}
$$

and we interpret it in one of the two following ways :

- we go to the next instruction N as soon as *all* the input labels M_i corresponding to f_i=1 have been reached ;
  ((and)-interpretation on the rows).

- we go to the next instruction N as soon as *one* of the input labels M_i corresponding to f_i=1 has been reached ;
  ((or)-interpretation on the rows).

The row-instruction (13) and the column-instruction (14) suggest us to define a *matrix instruction* which we write :

$$
\begin{array}{c}
N_1 \\
N_2 \\
\vdots \\
N_p
\end{array}
\left[
\begin{array}{cccc}
f_{11} & f_{12} & \cdots & f_{1q} \\
f_{21} & f_{22} & \cdots & f_{2q} \\
\vdots & & & \\
f_{p1} & f_{p2} & \cdots & f_{pq} \\
M_1 & M_2 & \cdots & M_q
\end{array}
\right]
\tag{15}
$$

The matrix-instruction (15) may be interpreted either as p row-instructions having identical output labels $\{M_i\}$ or as q column-instructions having identical input labels $\{N_j\}$. Since row-matrices have two interpretations on their columns and column matrices have two interpretations on their rows ((and)-interpretation, (or)-interpretation), the matrix-instruction (15) has four interpretations on its rows and columns, i.e. :

$$(\text{row};\text{column}) = \left.\begin{array}{l} (\text{or};\text{and})\text{-interpretation} \\ (\text{and};\text{and})\text{-interpretation} \end{array}\right\} \textit{deterministic instructions}$$
$$\left.\begin{array}{l} (\text{or};\text{or})\text{-interpretation} \\ (\text{and};\text{or})\text{-interpretation} \end{array}\right\} \textit{non-deterministic instructions}$$

Again it will be convenient to gather decision and execution components into a single matrix-instruction made-up of a decision and of an execution part. In view of (7) and (8) execution parts are added to the matrix decision instruction (15) in the following way :

$$
\begin{array}{cc}
N_1 & \tau_1 \\
\vdots & \vdots \\
N_p & \tau_p
\end{array}
\left[\begin{array}{ccc}
f_{11} & \cdots & f_{1q} \\
\vdots & & \vdots \\
f_{p1} & \cdots & f_{pq}
\end{array}\right]
\tag{16}
$$
$$
\begin{array}{ccc}
\sigma_1 & \cdots & \sigma_q \\
M_1 & \cdots & M_q
\end{array}
$$

Remember that the τ's are *end of execution signals* received from the operational part (see figure 1), the σ's are *commands* which are directed to the operational part and which enable new operations to occur while the f_{ij} are the *decision functions* implemented in the control automaton. The instruction (16) will also be written as a product of matrices,

$$
\begin{array}{c}
N_1 \\
\cdot \\
\cdot \\
\cdot \\
N_p
\end{array}
\left[\begin{array}{ccc}
\tau_1 & & \\
& \cdot & 0 \\
& & \cdot \\
0 & & \cdot \\
& & \tau_p \\
N'_1 & \cdots & N'_p
\end{array}\right]
\left[\begin{array}{ccc}
f_{11} & \cdots & f_{1q} \\
\cdot & & \cdot \\
\cdot & & \cdot \\
f_{p1} & \cdots & f_{pq} \\
M'_1 & \cdots & M'_p
\end{array}\right]
\left[\begin{array}{ccc}
\sigma_1 & & \\
& \cdot & 0 \\
& & \cdot \\
0 & & \cdot \\
& & \sigma_p \\
M_1 & \cdots & M_q
\end{array}\right]
\tag{17}
$$

Our main problem will be the synthesis of the central *decision matrix* of (17) i.e. :

$$
\begin{array}{c}
N'_1 \\
\vdots \\
N'_p
\end{array}
\left[\begin{array}{ccc}
f_{11} & \cdots & f_{1q} \\
\vdots & & \vdots \\
f_{p1} & \cdots & f_{pq}
\end{array}\right]
\tag{18}
$$
$$
\begin{array}{ccc}
M'_1 & \cdots & M'_q
\end{array}
$$

in terms of elementary instructions.

Observe that the matrix (18) gathers in a single expression a series of *fork* instructions followed by a series of *join* instructions : this is reflected by the following factorizations of (18) :

$$
\begin{array}{c} N'_1 \\ \vdots \\ N'_p \\ {} \end{array}
\begin{bmatrix} f_{11} & \cdots & f_{1q} \\ \vdots & & \\ \vdots & & \\ f_{p1} & \cdots & f_{pq} \\ \hline M'_1 & \cdots & M'_q \end{bmatrix}
=
\begin{array}{c} N'_1 \\ \vdots \\ N'_p \\ {} \end{array}
\left[\begin{array}{cccc}
f_{11} \cdots f_{1q} & & & 0 \\
& \cdots & & \\
0 & & f_{p1} \cdots f_{pq} & \\
N_{11} \cdots N_{1q} & \cdots & N_{p1} \cdots N_{pq}
\end{array}\right]
\left[\begin{array}{cccc}
f_{11} & & 0 & \\
& \ddots & & f_{1q} \\
0 & & & \\
& & \ddots & \\
f_{p1} & & 0 & \\
0 & & & f_{pq} \\
M'_1 & \cdots & M'_q &
\end{array}\right]
$$

$$(19a)$$

$$
\begin{array}{c} N'_1 \\ \vdots \\ N'_p \\ {} \end{array}
\begin{bmatrix} f_{11} & \cdots & f_{1q} \\ \vdots & & \vdots \\ \vdots & & \vdots \\ f_{p1} & \cdots & f_{pq} \\ \hline M'_1 & \cdots & M'_q \end{bmatrix}
=
\begin{array}{c} N'_1 \\ \vdots \\ N'_p \\ {} \end{array}
\left[\begin{array}{cccc}
f_{11} \cdots f_{1q} & & & 0 \\
& \cdots & & \\
0 & & f_{p1} \cdots f_{pq} & \\
N_{11} \cdots N_{1q} & \cdots & N_{p1} \cdots N_{pq}
\end{array}\right]
\left[\begin{array}{cccc}
1 & & 0 & \\
& \ddots & & 1 \\
0 & & & \\
& & \ddots & \\
1 & & 0 & \\
0 & & & 1 \\
M'_1 & \cdots & M'_q &
\end{array}\right]
$$

$$(19b)$$

$$
\begin{array}{c} N'_1 \\ \vdots \\ N'_p \\ {} \end{array}
\begin{bmatrix} f_{11} & \cdots & f_{1q} \\ \vdots & & \vdots \\ \vdots & & \vdots \\ f_{p1} & \cdots & f_{pq} \\ \hline M'_1 & \cdots & M'_q \end{bmatrix}
=
\begin{array}{c} N'_1 \\ \vdots \\ N'_p \\ {} \end{array}
\left[\begin{array}{cccc}
1 \cdots 1 & & & 0 \\
& \cdots & & \\
0 & & 1 \cdots 1 & \\
N_{11} \cdots N_{1q} & \cdots & N_{p1} \cdots N_{pq}
\end{array}\right]
\left[\begin{array}{cccc}
f_{11} & & 0 & \\
& \ddots & & f_{1q} \\
0 & & & \\
& & \ddots & \\
f_{p1} & & 0 & \\
0 & & & f_{pq} \\
M'_1 & \cdots & M'_q &
\end{array}\right]
$$

$$(19c)$$

In the matrix products (19), the additive law is the Boolean disjunction (that will be denoted "∨") while the multiplicative law is the Boolean conjunction (which is either denoted "∧", or more generally represented by the absence of symbol).

2.2. The interpretation of high-level instructions.

The *(or;and)-interpreted matrix instruction* may be considered as a composite instruction which gathers in a single formalism a series of *independent row-instructions*. The interest of this formalism lies in the fact that it leads to the simultaneous synthesis of several instructions. Since low-level instructions are used in the design of several high-level instructions, this technique involves a reduction of the number of low-level instructions present in the program. This technique allow us to reduce and to optimize the cost of programs (which may e.g. be reflected by the number of its instructions). A similar kind of design principle is well known in switching theory : it corresponds to the synthesis of multiple-input, multiple-output networks (see e.g. Davio, Deschamps and Thayse [1978]).

The synthesis technique used later on will also lead us to distinguish between matrix-instructions with *disjoint columns* which are characterized by the relations :

$$f_{ij} \, f_{ik} \equiv 0 \quad \forall j \neq k \ , \quad \forall i$$

and matrix-instructions with *non disjoint columns*.

To the matrix-instruction with disjoint columns corresponds a sequential organization of the control unit : since one and only one function f_{ij} is equal to 1 at a time, one and only one command σ_j may be active. If this command enables one operation in the operational automaton, we shall say that the organizations of both the control part and of the operational part are sequential (See figure 3a). If one operation is enabled at a time, the synchronous operation mode (Glushkov model) coincides with the asynchronous operation mode (parallel program schema). It may also occur that one command σ_j enables two or more operations in the operational automaton (multiple command). In this case the control automaton remains sequentially organized while some parallelism appears in the operational automaton. The cooperation between the two automata may be synchronous (figure 3b) or asynchronous (figure 3c).

To the matrix instruction with non-disjoint columns corresponds a parallel organization in the control unit which necessarily induces a parallel organization in the operational unit : since several functions f_{ij} may be equal to one at a time (for a fixed i) several commands σ_j may be activated simultaneously. Again the cooperation between the two automata may be synchronous (figure 3d) or asynchronous (figure 3e).

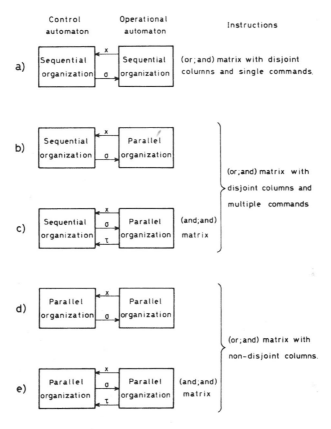

Figure 3 : Organizations for the control and for the
operational automata

Examples of the synthesis of (or;and)-matrix instructions will extensively be developed in the text. In section 2.5. we give an example (see also figure
4a) of an (or;and)-matrix-instruction with disjoint columns. It represents the elementary step of an algorithm which computes either the sum or the difference of two
numbers given by their binary representation. This algorithm is represented by a
(2×4)-matrix-instruction. The two rows of the matrix correspond to the activation
of the sum algorithm and of the difference algorithm respectively. Since the two
algorithms may not be activated simultaneously, the matrix is (or)-interpreted on
its rows. The four columns of the matrix correspond to the values (0,0),(0,1),(1,0)
and (1,1) which may take the sum component and the carry component of the result.
In section 5.3 we give an example of an (or;and)-matrix-instruction with non-disjoint columns (see also figure 4b). It represents a routing algorithm which selects
routes toward which messages entering at a switching node must be sent. This algorithm is represented by a (2×3)-matrix-instruction. The two rows correspond to two
possible priorities of the messages to be sent. Since the messages cannot have

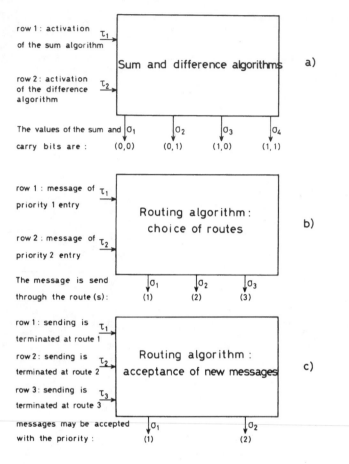

row 1 : activation of the sum algorithm τ_1

row 2 : activation of the difference algorithm τ_2

Sum and difference algorithms   a)

The values of the sum and carry bits are : σ_1 (0,0) σ_2 (0,1) σ_3 (1,0) σ_4 (1,1)

row 1 : message of priority 1 entry τ_1

row 2 : message of priority 2 entry τ_2

Routing algorithm : choice of routes   b)

The message is send through the route (s): σ_1 (1) σ_2 (2) σ_3 (3)

row 1 : sending is terminated at route 1 τ_1

row 2 : sending is terminated at route 2 τ_2

row 3 : sending is terminated at route 3 τ_3

Routing algorithm : acceptance of new messages   c)

messages may be accepted with the priority : σ_1 (1) σ_2 (2)

Figure 4 : Illustration of the use of (or)-interpreted and of (and)-interpreted matrix-instructions in algorithm design.

simultaneously the two priorities the matrix has (or)-interpreted rows. The three columns correspond to three possible routes toward which the messages may be sent We make an hypothesis which is classical for packet switched messages : for some conditions the message may be divided along two or three routes. It follows that the functions f_{ij}, which are requested to be 1 if a message with priority i must be sent along the route j, are no longer disjoint. For example, the solutions of the equation :

$$f_{i1} \, f_{i2} \, \bar{f}_{i3} = 1$$

characterize the values of the parameters for which a message with priority i may be sent along the routes 1 and 2.

The $(or;and)\text{-}interpreted\text{-}matrix\text{-}instructions$ are used to describe algorithms which are implemented in a synchronous or in an asynchronous way (see figures

3a-3e), i.e. according to the Glushkov model or to the parallel schema. The implementation of algorithms in an asynchronous way (parallel schema) moreover requests
the presence of *(and;and)-interpreted-matrix-instructions*. This kind of instruction
corresponds to the synthesis of a series of *independent column-instructions*. It is
associated to an asynchronous cooperation between the control automaton and the operational automaton (see figures 3c,3e). This kind of instruction may thus be viewed
as the extra instruction which is needed by the asynchronous cooperation of the automata. The (and;and)-instructions play the role of the synchronizing signal in synchronous cooperation ; when the cooperation is synchronous the next instruction in
the control part is activated by a clock pulse; when the cooperation is asynchronous
the next instruction in the control part is activated when all the enabled operation
in the operational automaton are finished. It is the (and;and)-matrix-instruction
which will indicate the termination of the enabled operations. Let us now indicate
why this type of instruction is necessarily (and;and)-interpreted. The activation of
the next execution σ_j^+ depends on the termination of a series of operations σ_i, σ_k,
..., σ_ℓ; it thus no longer only depends on the value of one function f_{ij} but it depends on the value of a series of functions f_{ij} and f_{kj} and ... and $f_{\ell j}$. This is
reflected by the (and)-interpretation on the rows of the matrix instruction. The connection between (and;and)-instructions and the asynchronous implementation mode of
algorithms will more deeply be investigated in chapter 9.

Again this kind of instruction may best be illustrated by continuing
the routing algorithm. A new message may be accepted at a routing node as soon as
the previous message has completely been sent. If e.g. the routes 1 and 2 were opened, we have to wait that the routes 1 and 2 have terminated their sending. The
rows of the (3×2) matrix instruction correspond in this case to the reception of
signals which indicate until activated routes have terminated the sending of the
message. As soon as the message has been sent a new message of priority 1 or 2 may
be accepted : this acceptance is ordered by the commands σ_1 and σ_2 which depend on
the matrix columns 1 and 2 respectively. We see that this (and;and)-interpreted-ma-
trix must be used in connection with the (or;and)-interpreted-matrix described in
figure 4b ; the input-output behaviour described by means of the (and;and)-interpre-
ted-matrix is schematized in figure 4c.

As a conclusion we can say that the (or;and) matrices are used in the
Glushkov model of computation while (or;and) and (and;and) matrices are used in the
parallel program schema. The distinction between matrices with disjoint and with
non-disjoint columns has merely been introduced for a computation technique point
of view : we shall see that the recognition of the disjoint character of the columns
allows the use of simplified design techniques (see chapter 4).

Note finally thay the (or;or) and (and;or) matrices are related to the
description and the analysis of non-deterministic models which will not be considered
in this text. Since the present text is devoted to synthesis techniques for imple-

menting deterministic algorithms, (or;and)- and (and;and)-interpreted→matrix-instruc-
tions will be called (or)-and (and)-interpreted-matrix-instructions respectively.

2.3. Low-level instructions

The low-level instructions are essentially the *if then else, fork, join, while do* instructions which were introduced in section 1.1. ; the predicates of the low-level instructions are the condition variables $\underline{x}$ of the Boolean functions $f_{ij}(\underline{x})$. In the synthesis problem we will be faced (see the example of section 2.5) with row-instructions having some common next labels, i.e. for example :

$$(N_1 \; \text{if} \; \bar{x}_i \; \text{then} \; N_{1i} \; \text{else} \; N_{2i}) : N_1 \begin{bmatrix} \bar{x}_i & x_i & 0 & 0 \\ N_{1i} & N_{2i} & N_{1j} & N_{2j} \end{bmatrix}$$

$$(N_2 \; \text{if} \; \bar{x}_j \; \text{then} \; N_{1j} \; \text{else} \; N_{2j}) : N_2 \begin{bmatrix} 0 & 0 & \bar{x}_j & x_j \\ N_{1i} & N_{2i} & N_{1j} & N_{2j} \end{bmatrix}$$

$$(N_3 \; \text{fork} \; (N_{1i}, N_{1j}, N_{2j}) \quad : N_3 \begin{bmatrix} 1 & 0 & 1 & 1 \\ N_{1i} & N_{2i} & N_{1j} & N_{2j} \end{bmatrix}$$

These instructions will then be gathered in a single matrix, i.e. :

$$\begin{array}{c} N_1 \\ N_2 \\ N_3 \end{array} \begin{bmatrix} \bar{x}_i & x_i & 0 & 0 \\ 0 & 0 & \bar{x}_j & x_j \\ 1 & 0 & 1 & 1 \end{bmatrix} \qquad (20)$$
$$\quad\; N_{1i} \quad N_{2i} \quad N_{1j} \quad N_{2j}$$

The matrices of the type (20) and their transpose play a key role in the synthesis of high-level instructions in terms of low-level instructions. This will appear in section 2.5 where it will be shown that the synthesis of an algorithm reduces to the factorization of matrices of the type (18) as product of elementary matrices of the type (20).

2.4. The synthesis and the optimization problems

The synthesis problem may be stated as follows ;
an algorithm being described in terms of high-level instructions, transform its des-cription in terms of low-level instructions.
The matrix formalism allows us to state the problem in the following way :

*factorize the (high-level) matrix-instruction (18) as a product of matrices (20)
whose rows and columns are in correspondence with low-level instructions.* These matrices have as entries boolean constants 0,1 and elementary predicates $\{x_i, \bar{x}_i\}$.

    The optimization problem may be stated in the following ways : Trans-
form high-level instructions describing an algorithm in terms of a minimal number
of low-level instructions (*optimal cost criterion*)
or :
Transform high-level instructions in terms of low-level instructions and minimize
the maximal (or mean) number of instructions between input and output labels (*optimal time criterion*).

    The optimization of the time criterion requests the factorization of a
matrix in terms of a minimal number of factors.

    Since each row and each column of a matrix instruction corresponds to
an elementary instruction the optimization of the cost criterion requests the factorization of a matrix as a product of matrices having the smallest dimensions.

    The synthesis and optimization problems will be solved by introducing
a theoretical tool associated to instructions : the algebra of P-functions (see chapter 3). This algebra will allow us to factorize a Boolean matrix of functions as a
product of matrices of elementary predicates.

2.5. Example 1

    We consider the synthesis of an algorithm which computes either the sum
or the difference of two numbers given by their binary representation. This algorithm
uses two binary digits x_1 and x_2, which are the bits of the first and of the second
number respectively, and a carry digit x_3 ; these inputs x_1,x_2,x_3 produce the outputs S_0,C_0,S_1,C_1 which are specified by the following Boolean functions :

$$S_0 = x_1 \oplus x_2 \oplus x_3 \qquad \text{(sum output)}$$
$$C_0 = x_1x_2 \vee x_2x_3 \vee x_1x_3 \qquad \text{(carry output for the sum)}$$
$$S_1 = x_1 \oplus \bar{x}_2 \oplus x_3 \qquad \text{(difference output)}$$
$$C_1 = x_1\bar{x}_2 \vee \bar{x}_2x_3 \vee x_1x_3 \qquad \text{(carry output for the difference)}$$

Note that the materialization of the algorithm producing (S_0,C_0,S_1,C_1) as outputs
and having (x_1,x_2,x_3) as inputs is known as a *Controlled Add/Substract cell* (CAS).

    Assume that according to the value of a parameter we want to evaluate
either the function (S_0,C_0) or the functions (S_1,C_1). This corresponds to the possibility of using the CAS cell either for the addition or for the difference; we have
to put in a 2-bit register [R] either $[S_0,C_0]$ or $[S_1,C_1]$. We verify that the algorithm describing the CAS input/output relationship is represented by the following
matrix instruction :

$$
\begin{array}{cc}
N_1 & \tau_1 \\
N_2 & \tau_2 \\
\end{array}
\left[
\begin{array}{cccc}
f_{11} & f_{12} & f_{13} & f_{14} \\
f_{21} & f_{22} & f_{23} & f_{24} \\
\sigma_1 & \sigma_2 & \sigma_3 & \sigma_4 \\
M_1 & M_2 & M_3 & M_4 \\
\end{array}
\right]
\tag{21}
$$

The meaning of the parameters in this matrix instruction is the following ; the elementary predicates of the problem are x_1, x_2, x_3 and the functions $f_i(x_1\ x_2\ x_3)$ are defined as follows :

$f_{11} = \bar{S}_0 \bar{C}_0 = \bar{x}_1 \bar{x}_2 \bar{x}_3$

$f_{12} = \bar{S}_0 C_0 = x_1 \bar{x}_2 x_3 \vee x_1 x_2 \bar{x}_3 \vee \bar{x}_1 x_2 x_3$

$f_{13} = S_0 \bar{C}_0 = \bar{x}_1 \bar{x}_2 x_3 \vee x_1 \bar{x}_2 \bar{x}_3 \vee \bar{x}_1 x_2 \bar{x}_3$

$f_{14} = S_0 C_0 = x_1 x_2 x_3$

$f_{21} = \bar{S}_1 \bar{C}_1 = \bar{x}_1 x_2 \bar{x}_3$

$f_{22} = \bar{S}_1 C_1 = \bar{x}_1 \bar{x}_2 x_3 \vee x_1 \bar{x}_2 \bar{x}_3 \vee x_1 x_2 x_3$

$f_{23} = S_1 \bar{C}_1 = \bar{x}_1 \bar{x}_2 \bar{x}_3 \vee x_1 x_2 \bar{x}_3 \vee \bar{x}_1 x_2 x_3$

$f_{24} = S_1 C_1 = x_1 \bar{x}_2 x_3$

τ_1, τ_2 means : the addition or the substraction algorithm may be initiated ;

$\sigma_1, \sigma_2, \sigma_3, \sigma_4$ means : put the value $(00), (01), (10), (11)$ in the output register respectively ; the first bit in the parentheses is the *sum bit* and the second bit is the *carry bit*. In order to separate the execution part from the decision part in the matrix instruction we first factorize the instruction (21) in the following form :

$$
\begin{array}{c}
N_1 \\
N_2 \\
\\
\end{array}
\left[
\begin{array}{cc}
\tau_1 & 0 \\
0 & \tau_2 \\
D_1 & D_2 \\
\end{array}
\right]
\left[
\begin{array}{cccc}
f_{11} & f_{12} & f_{13} & f_{14} \\
f_{21} & f_{22} & f_{23} & f_{24} \\
A_1 & A_2 & A_3 & A_4 \\
\end{array}
\right]
\left[
\begin{array}{cccc}
\sigma_1 & 0 & 0 & 0 \\
0 & \sigma_2 & 0 & 0 \\
0 & 0 & \sigma_3 & 0 \\
0 & 0 & 0 & \sigma_4 \\
M_1 & M_2 & M_3 & M_4 \\
\end{array}
\right]
\tag{22}
$$

We now verify that the central decision instruction of (22) may be factorized in the following form:

$$
\begin{array}{c} D_1 \\ D_2 \\ \\ \end{array}
\begin{bmatrix} f_{11} & f_{12} & f_{13} & f_{14} \\ f_{21} & f_{22} & f_{23} & f_{24} \\ \\ A_1 & A_2 & A_3 & A_4 \end{bmatrix}
=
\begin{array}{c} D_1 \\ D_2 \\ \\ \end{array}
\begin{bmatrix} x_2 & \bar{x}_2 \\ \bar{x}_2 & x_2 \\ \\ C_1 & C_2 \end{bmatrix}
\begin{bmatrix} \bar{x}_1 & 0 & x_1 \\ x_1 & \bar{x}_1 & 0 \\ \\ B_1 & B_2 & B_3 \end{bmatrix}
\begin{bmatrix} 0 & x_3 & \bar{x}_3 & 0 \\ \bar{x}_3 & 0 & x_3 & 0 \\ 0 & \bar{x}_3 & 0 & x_3 \\ \\ A_1 & A_2 & A_3 & A_4 \end{bmatrix}
\quad (23)
$$

To the factorization (23) corresponds the program of figure 5 made-up of *if then el-se* instructions. We verify that to each line of the matrices of (23) corresponds an *if then else instruction* ; to the columns made-up of two non-zero entries should correspond *transpose if then else instructions*. These transpose instructions have been omitted in figure 5 since they are *degenerate*. The degeneration of instructions will be studied in section 4.4. ; let us already mention that column instructions are degenerate iff the matrix instruction has disjoint columns; i.e. iff :

$$
f_{ij}\, f_{ik} \equiv 0 \qquad \forall j \neq k, \quad \forall i \qquad\qquad (24)
$$

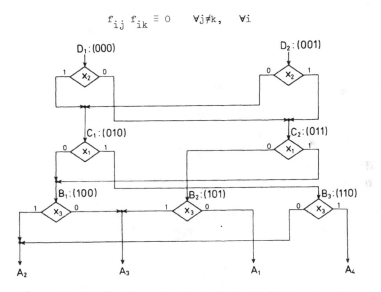

Figure 5 : Realization of a Controlled-Add-Substract cell

A systematic matrix factorization procedure will be developed in chapters 4,5 by making use of an *algebra of P-functions*. To this matrix factorization procedure will be associated an algorithm synthesis method.

The program realizing the matrix factorization (23) is obtained by reading the flowchart of figure 5 from top to bottom. If we now read the same flowchart from bottom to top we obtain a program which realizes the transpose of the matrix factorization (23). The relations between a program and its transpose will be studied in chapters 4 and 5.

Chapter 3 : <u>The formulation of algorithm synthesis in terms of P-functions</u>

      The purpose of chapter 3 is the introduction of the mathematical tool which will be used later on in this text for synthesizing algorithms or equivalently for factorizing Boolean matrices.

      We shall only introduce in this chapter the concepts, laws and relations which are strictly necessary for our goal : the synthesis and the optimization of algorithms. For the interested reader, a more complete algebraic treatment of the algebra of *P-functions* will be proposed in part III of this text.

      The concept which will be used in the materialization of algorithms is that of *pair-of-functions* or *P-function*.

      P-functions are introduced in a rather informal way in section 3.1 where the execution of an algorithm is described in terms of a transformation between P-functions.

      The executions of high-level instructions and of low-level instructions are described in terms of a transformation between P-functions in sections 3.2 and 3.3 respectively. In section 3.3 we introduce laws which act on pairs of P-functions; to each of these laws is associated the occurrence of an elementary instruction and of its transpose.

      The formalism for the synthesis of matrix-instructions by means of P-functions is introduced in section 3.4. It is the formalism which will be used in the further chapters of Part I of this text.

3.1. <u>P-functions associated to algorithms.</u>

      An algorithm A is described by means of sequences of decision and of execution instructions. To each instruction label we shall associate what we call a *P-function* or *pair-of-functions*, the left part or *domain* of the P-function will indicate what part of the algorithm has already been performed while the right part or *codomain* of the P-function will indicate what part of the algorithm remains to perform.

      An algorithm A may be described by means of one instruction, i.e. :

$$(begin) \quad do \quad A \ (end) \tag{25}$$

To the execution of instruction (25) we associate the *transformation between P-functions*:

$$(begin) : \langle t\lambda, A \rangle \underset{T^{-1}}{\overset{T}{\rightleftarrows}} \langle A; t\lambda \rangle : \ (end) \tag{26}$$

where λ is the *empty execution* and t the *predicate always true*. Clearly, when reaching the instruction *begin* nothing has already been done (λ) and the algorithm must be performed in any case (t) ; when reaching the instruction *end* , nothing remains to do (λ) and the algorithm has been performed in any case (t).

Let $\{t_i\}$ be operators which act on P-functions and which are associated with the elementary instructions at hand. The synthesis of an algorithm A by means of elementary instructions will reduce to finding a (minimal) sequence of transforma tions $\{t_i\}$ which realizes the transformation (26).

The direction of the transformation T was chosen from (*end*) to (*begin*) ; clearly an inverse transformation T^{-1} could be chosen from (*begin*) to (*end*). Note that the direction of the transformation is not related to the flow of the successive executions in the algorithm. We shall see later on that e.g. row-instructions are more easily synthesized by using (*end*) to (*begin*) transformations while column-instructions are more easily synthesized by using (*begin*) to (*end*) transformations.

Note also that the product $t\lambda$ in (26) means only the juxtaposition of an (empty) execution and of a predicate (always true) ; more generally the product $f\sigma$ means : σ will be executed if and only if f is 1. The product $f\sigma$ is a *pseudo-Boolean term* since it is the concatenation of a Boolean function with a non-Boolean factor. As a consequence some rules of pseudo-Boolean algebra will be used for the transformation of pseudo-Boolean expressions of the form :

$$\sum_i f_i \, \sigma_i$$

that will be encountered later on (for pseudo-Boolean algebra see e.g. Hammer and Rudeanu [1968] or Davio, Deschamps and Thayse [1978]).

Finally an expression such as :

$$\tau \: f \: \sigma$$

means : as soon as τ has been terminated, test the function f and activate σ if f is 1.

3.2. Transformations associated to high-level instructions

In order to illustrate the transformation (26), consider e.g. a row-instruction :

$$N \quad \tau \quad \begin{bmatrix} f_1 & \cdots & f_q \\ \sigma_1 & \cdots & \sigma_q \\ M_1 & \cdots & M_q \end{bmatrix}$$

whichwe factorize into the following matrix product in order to render obvious the separation between execution and decision instructions :

$$N \quad \begin{bmatrix} \tau \\ N' \end{bmatrix} \begin{bmatrix} f_1 \cdots f_q \\ M'_1 \cdots M'_q \end{bmatrix} \begin{bmatrix} \sigma_1 & & \\ & \ddots & 0 \\ 0 & & \ddots \\ & & \sigma_q \end{bmatrix} \tag{27}$$
$$M_1 \cdots M_q$$

In view of (26), to the instructions (27) are associated the following transformations between P-functions :

$$N : \langle \lambda t \; ; \; \tau(\textstyle\sum f_j \; \sigma_j) \rangle \tag{28a}$$

$$\uparrow t_\tau$$

$$N' : \langle \tau t \; ; \; \textstyle\sum f_j \; \sigma_j \rangle \tag{28b}$$

$$\uparrow T$$

$$M'_1 : \langle \tau f_1 \; ; \; \sigma_1 \; t \rangle \; , \ldots \; , \; M'_q : \langle \tau f_q \; ; \; \sigma_q t \rangle \tag{28c}$$

$$\uparrow t_{\sigma_1} \quad \cdots \qquad\qquad \uparrow t_{\sigma_q}$$

$$M_1 : \langle \tau f_1 \sigma_1 \; ; \; \lambda t \rangle \; , \ldots \; , \; M_q : \langle \tau f_q \sigma_q \; ; \; \lambda t \rangle \tag{28d}$$

The operators t_τ and t_σ as shown in (28) are shift operators associated to the occurrence of execution instructions ; if $\langle A\sigma \; ; \; B \rangle$ is a P-function, the application of the operator t_σ corresponds to the execution of σ , i.e. :

$$t_\sigma \; \langle A\sigma \; ; \; B \rangle \; = \; \langle A \; ; \; B\sigma \rangle \tag{29}$$

Since our main problem is the transformation of high-level instructions into low-level instructions, we shall consider further on only the transformation between (28b) and (28c) ; observe that the transformation (29) is associated to a low-level execution instruction. In order to be consistent with a pseudo-Boolean formalism, the transformation between (28b) and (28c) will be written in the following simplified form (obtained by putting $t=\tau=1$ in (28)) :

$$N' : \langle 1 \; ; \; \textstyle\sum f_j \; \sigma_j \rangle \xleftarrow{\;T\;} \begin{cases} \langle f_1 \; ; \; \sigma_1 \rangle : M'_1 \\ \quad \cdot \\ \quad \cdot \\ \quad \cdot \\ \langle f_q \; ; \; \sigma_q \rangle : M'_q \end{cases} \tag{30}$$

Observe that the transformation (30) does not make use of the interpretation of the
row-instruction. The transformation (30) synthesizes (or)-interpreted as well as
(and)-interpreted row-instructions. As it will be seen later on, the difference
between interpretations will appear when operations are associated to the vertices
of a graph (which is a design skeleton). Otherwise stated the transformation (30)
will design a graph which corresponds to an uninterpreted row-instruction ; the interpretation of an instruction is obtained by associating elementary operators to
the vertices.

As it will be seen, to the transformation (30) corresponds the factorization of the row-matrix

$$[f_1(\underline{x}),\ f_2(\underline{x})\ \dots\ f_q(\underline{x})]$$

in terms of elementary matrices of the form (20) whose entries are the elementary
predicates x_i of $\underline{x}$. Since a factorization for a matrix is also a factorization for
its transpose, the transformation (30) also corresponds to the synthesis of a
column-instruction, i.e. :

$$
\begin{array}{cc}
M'_1 & \tau_1 \\
\vdots & \vdots \\
M'_q & \tau_q
\end{array}
\left[
\begin{array}{c}
f_1 \\
\vdots \\
f_q
\end{array}
\right]
$$
$$\sigma$$
$$N'$$

Consider further the (or)-interpreted matrix-instruction :

$$
\begin{array}{cc}
N_1 & \tau_1 \\
\vdots & \vdots \\
N_p & \tau_p
\end{array}
\left[
\begin{array}{ccc}
f_{11} & \cdots & f_{1q} \\
\vdots & & \vdots \\
f_{p1} & \cdots & f_{pq}
\end{array}
\right]
\tag{31}
$$
$$
\begin{array}{ccc}
\sigma_1 & \cdots & \sigma_q \\
M_1 & \cdots & M_q
\end{array}
$$

that we also write in the form :

$$
\begin{array}{c}
N_1 \\
\vdots \\
N_p
\end{array}
\left[
\begin{array}{ccc}
\tau_1 & & \\
& \ddots & \\
& & \tau_p
\end{array}
\right]
\left[
\begin{array}{ccc}
f_{11} & \cdots & f_{1q} \\
\vdots & & \\
f_{p1} & \cdots & f_{pq}
\end{array}
\right]
\left[
\begin{array}{ccc}
\sigma_1 & & \\
& \ddots & \\
& & \sigma_q
\end{array}
\right]
\tag{32}
$$
$$
\begin{array}{cccccccc}
N'_1 & \cdots & N'_p & M'_1 & \cdots & M'_q & M_1 & \cdots & M_q
\end{array}
$$

Transformation (33)

(33a)

$$N_1 : \langle t\lambda \; ; \; \tau_1(\sum_i f_{1i}\sigma_i) \rangle$$
$$N_2 : \langle t\lambda \; ; \; \tau_2(\sum_i f_{2i}\sigma_i) \rangle$$
$$N_p : \langle t\lambda \; ; \; \tau_p(\sum_i f_{pi}\sigma_i) \rangle$$

$$\big\downarrow t_{\tau_1} \qquad \big\downarrow t_{\tau_2} \qquad \big\downarrow t_{\tau_p}$$

(33b)

$$N_1' : \langle t\tau_1 \; ; \; \sum_i f_{1i}\sigma_i \rangle$$
$$N_2' : \langle t\tau_2 \; ; \; \sum_i f_{2i}\sigma_i \rangle$$
$$N_p' : \langle t\tau_p \; ; \; \sum_i f_{pi}\sigma_i \rangle$$

$$\Big\downarrow T$$

(33c)

$$M_1' : \langle \sum_j \tau_j f_{j1} \; ; \; t\sigma_1 \rangle$$
$$M_2' : \langle \sum_j \tau_j f_{j2} \; ; \; t\sigma_2 \rangle$$
$$M_q' : \langle \sum_j \tau_j f_{jq} \; ; \; t\sigma_q \rangle$$

$$\big\downarrow t_{\sigma_1} \qquad \big\downarrow t_{\sigma_2} \qquad \big\downarrow t_{\sigma_q}$$

(33d)

$$M_1' : \langle (\sum_j \tau_j f_{j1})\sigma_1 \; ; \; t\lambda \rangle$$
$$M_2' : \langle (\sum_j \tau_j f_{j2})\sigma_2 \; ; \; t\lambda \rangle$$
$$M_q' : \langle (\sum_j \tau_j f_{jq})\sigma_q \; ; \; t\lambda \rangle$$

Transformation (34)

(34b)

$$
\begin{array}{cccccc}
 & \tau_1 & \tau_2 & \cdots & \tau_p & \\
N_1' :: \langle & 1 \;, & - \;, & \cdots \;, & - & ; \; \sum_i f_{1i}\sigma_i \rangle \\
N_2' :: \langle & - \;, & 1 \;, & \cdots \;, & - & ; \; \sum_i f_{2i}\sigma_i \rangle \\
N_p' :: \langle & - \;, & - \;, & \cdots \;, & 1 & ; \; \sum_i f_{pi}\sigma_i \rangle \\
\end{array}
$$

$$\Big\downarrow T = (T)^p$$

$$
\begin{array}{cccccc}
 & \tau_1 & \tau_2 & \cdots & \tau_p & \\
\langle & f_{11} \;, & \cdots \;, & f_{p1} & ; \; \sigma_1 \; \rangle & :: \; M_1' \\
\langle & f_{12} \;, & \cdots \;, & f_{p2} & ; \; \sigma_2 \; \rangle & :: \; M_2' \\
\langle & f_{1q} \;, & \cdots \;, & f_{pq} & ; \; \sigma_q \; \rangle & :: \; M_q' \\
\end{array}
$$

In view of (26) and of (28), to the instruction (32) are associated the transformations (33) between P-functions. Since our main problem is the transformation of a high-level decision instruction into low-level decision instructions, we shall consider the transformation between (33b) and (33c). In order to be consistent with a pseudo-Boolean formalism, the transformation between (33b) and (33c) is written in the form (34); the j-th column of the left part of the P-functions corresponds to a "minterm" in the τ_i's, i.e. :

$$\tau_j=1, \quad \tau_k=0 \; \forall k \neq j \quad .$$

This allows us to replace the transformation law T in (33) by the p-th power of the transformation laws T that are used for the synthesis of row-instructions.

Observe that we have used an (or)-interpretation of the matrix-instruction for the writing of the transformation (34). We shall see in chapter 6 that the synthesis of an (and)-interpreted-matrix-instruction may be deduced from the synthesis of an (or)-interpreted-matrix-instruction by using a *duality principle*. Moreover since a factorization of a matrix is also a factorization for its transpose the transformations (33) and (34) provide us also with syntheses for the two interpretations of the transpose of (31). In summary, the design skeleton that will be associated to the transformation (34) will provide us with four realizations, i.e. the realizations associated to the two interpretations of the matrix instruction $[f_{ij}]$ and of its transpose $[f_{ji}]$. If we now decide to consider also non-deterministic instructions, we shall see that the transformation (34) realizes a factorization or a graph to which may be assigned (and;and)-, (and;or)-, (or,and)- and (or;or)-interpretations : the design skeleton will provide us with eight materializations.

3.3. Transformations associated to low-level instructions.

Consider first an *(if then else)* instruction, i.e. :

$$N \; [\; \bar{x} \qquad x \;]$$
$$M_1 \qquad M_2$$

If $\langle g_1;h_1\rangle$ and $\langle g_2;h_2\rangle$ are the P-functions associated to the labels M_1 and M_2 respectively, we verify that the P-function associated to the label N is : $\langle \bar{x}g_1 + xg_2 ;$ $\bar{x}h_1 + xh_2\rangle$. An *(if then else)* instruction is a *decision instruction* : it executes nothing ; it is thus clear that if g_1 has been done and h_1 remains to do when reaching M_1 and that if g_2 has been done and h_2 remains to do when reaching M_2, then $\bar{x}g_1 + xg_2$ has been done and $\bar{x}h_1 + xh_2$ remains to do when reaching N. According to th notations of the preceding section the transformation associated to an *(if then else)* instruction is :

$$N_i \; : \; \langle \bar{x}_i g_1 + x_i g_2 \; ; \; \bar{x}_i h_1 + x_i h_2 \rangle \longleftarrow^{t_i} \begin{cases} \langle g_1 ; h_1 \rangle : M_1 \\ \\ \langle g_2 ; h_2 \rangle : M_2 \end{cases} \qquad (35)$$

For sake of conciseness we shall write this transformation in the following form :

$$\langle g_1 ; h_1 \rangle \; t_i \; \langle g_2 ; h_2 \rangle = \langle \bar{x}_i g_1 + x_i g_2 \; ; \; \bar{x}_i h_1 + x_i h_2 \rangle \qquad (36)$$

To the transformation (36) corresponds the matrix factorization :

$$N \begin{bmatrix} \bar{x}_i \, h_1 & x_i \, h_2 \\ M_1 & M_2 \end{bmatrix} = N \begin{bmatrix} \bar{x}_i & x_i \\ M'_1 & M'_2 \end{bmatrix} \begin{bmatrix} h_1 & 0 \\ 0 & h_2 \\ M_1 & M_2 \end{bmatrix} \qquad (37)$$

      The same transformation holds for a *transpose (if then else)* instruction ; it then also corresponds to the transpose of the matrix factorization (37). More precisely we shall associate to the transformation (35) an *(if then else)* instruction if N is an input label or a *transpose (if then else)* if M_1 and M_2 are input labels.

      Consider now a *fork* instruction, i.e.

$$N \begin{bmatrix} 1 & 1 \\ M_1 & M_2 \end{bmatrix}$$

If $\langle g ; h_1 \rangle$ and $\langle g ; h_2 \rangle$ are the P-functions associated to the labels M_1 and M_2 respectively, we verify that the P-function associated to the label N is $\langle g ; h_1 + h_2 \rangle$. We also verify that, since the *fork* instruction is a decision instruction, two P-functions with different codomains (i.e. : $h_1 \neq h_2$), may be connected through a *fork* if these two P-functions have identical domains (i.e. :g). We write this transformation :

$$\langle g ; h_1 \rangle \; \cup \; \langle g ; h_2 \rangle = \langle g ; h_1 + h_2 \rangle \qquad (38)$$

To the transformation (38) corresponds the matrix factorization (39)

$$N \begin{bmatrix} h_1 & h_2 \\ M_1 & M_2 \end{bmatrix} = N \begin{bmatrix} 1 & 1 \\ M'_1 & M'_2 \end{bmatrix} \begin{bmatrix} h_1 & 0 \\ 0 & h_2 \\ M_1 & M_2 \end{bmatrix} \qquad (39)$$

The same transformation holds for the *join instruction* which is a *transpose fork*: it then corresponds to the transpose of the transformation (39). Similar arguments show us that the transformation

$$\langle g_1;h\rangle \ \cup \ \langle g_2;h\rangle \ = \ \langle g_1 + g_2 \ ;h\rangle \qquad (40)$$

also corresponds to *fork* and *join* instructions. Observe finally that the transformation (38) is independent of the interpretations (or,and) of the *fork* and *join* instructions ; consequently the "+" operation in (38,40) is uninterpreted.

We shall see in next section that in the course of the transformation between systems of P-functions, a P-function (or equivalently an instruction label) may be used several times in order to generate several new P-functions. This corresponds to an *implicit law* (denoted Im) whose meaning is illustrated as follows. Assume that the P-function associated to the instruction label M_1 is used twice in order to generate two new P-functions associated to the instruction labels M and N respectively:

$$M_1 : \langle g_1;h_1\rangle \ t_i \ \langle g_2;h_2\rangle:M_2 = \langle \bar{x}_i g_1 + x_i g_2 \ ; \ \bar{x}_i h_1 + x_i h_2\rangle:M$$
$$M_1 : \langle g_1;h_1\rangle \ t_j \ \langle g_3;h_3\rangle:M_3 = \langle \bar{x}_j g_1 + x_j g_3 \ ; \ \bar{x}_j h_1 + x_j h_3\rangle:N \qquad (41)$$

To the transformation (41) corresponds the matrix factorization (42) :

$$
\begin{array}{c} M \\ N \end{array}
\begin{bmatrix} \bar{x}_i h_1 & x_i h_2 & 0 \\ \bar{x}_j h_1 & 0 & x_j h_3 \\ M_1 & M_2 & M_3 \end{bmatrix}
=
\begin{array}{c} M \\ N \end{array}
\begin{bmatrix} \bar{x}_i & x_i & 0 \\ \bar{x}_j & 0 & x_j \end{bmatrix}
\begin{bmatrix} h_1 & 0 & 0 \\ 0 & h_2 & 0 \\ 0 & 0 & h_3 \\ M_1 & M_2 & M_3 \end{bmatrix}
=
$$

$$
=
\begin{array}{c} M \\ N \end{array}
\begin{bmatrix} \bar{x}_i & x_i & 0 & 0 \\ 0 & 0 & \bar{x}_j & x_j \end{bmatrix}
\begin{bmatrix} 1 & 0 & 0 \\ 0 & 1 & 0 \\ 1 & 0 & 0 \\ 0 & 0 & 1 \end{bmatrix}
\begin{bmatrix} h_1 & 0 & 0 \\ 0 & h_2 & 0 \\ 0 & 0 & h_3 \\ M_1 & M_2 & M_3 \end{bmatrix}
\qquad (42)
$$

In view of the binary matrix in (42) we see that the *implicit law Im* corresponds to a *join* instruction and thus also to a *fork* instruction when applied to a transposed matrix. We can intuitively imagine the meaning of this implicit law as follows ; when an instruction label is used twice in the course of a program, this label and hence the associated P-function must be duplicated, i.e. :

$$Im \ \langle g;h\rangle \ = \ \langle g;h\rangle \ \cup \ \langle g;h\rangle \qquad (43)$$

The duplication involves a *fork* operation. If (43) is read from right to left, i.e.:

$$\langle g;h \rangle \cup \langle g;h \rangle = \langle g;h \rangle \qquad (44)$$

we recognize the *join* instruction (38). The transformation (41), or equivalently the factorizations (42) and its transpose are illustrated in figure 6.

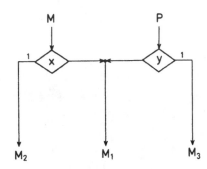

Figure 6 : <u>Realization of the implicit law Im</u>

In summary we have derived three laws on P-functions ; to each of these laws are associated an instruction and its transposed. This is summarized in Figure 7

Instructions

Laws	Instruction	Transpose Instruction
t_i	*if then else*	*then if*
U	*fork*	*join*
Im	*join*	*fork*

<u>Figure 7</u> : Correspondence between laws acting on
P-functions and instructions

3.4. The synthesis of matrix-instructions.

In view of section 2.3 we see that the synthesis of a matrix-instruction is obtained by transforming the system (34b) of P-functions into the system (34a), using the elementary transformation laws t_i, U and Im, the transformation (34) becomes :

$$
\left.
\begin{array}{l}
\langle 1\ ,\ldots,\ -\ ;\ \sum_i f_{1i}\sigma_i\rangle \\[2em]
\langle -\ ,\ldots, 1\ ;\ \sum_i f_{pi}\sigma_i\rangle
\end{array}
\right\}
\quad T =(\{t_i,U,Im\})^p \longleftarrow \quad
\left\{
\begin{array}{l}
\langle f_{11},\ \ldots\ ,\ f_{p1}\ ;\ \sigma_1\rangle \\[2em]
\langle f_{1q},\ \ldots\ ,\ f_{pq}\ ;\ \sigma_q\rangle
\end{array}
\right.
\tag{45}
$$

If the functions f_{ij} are disjoint (or orthogonal) with respect to the columns, i.e. if :

$$
f_{ij}\ f_{ik} \equiv 0\ ,\quad \forall j \neq k\ ,\quad \forall i
$$

we shall see that the transformation (45) leads to a simplified synthesis method : the union law U may be dropped in this case. Orthogonal or disjoint functions correspond to the important category of algorithms organized in a *sequential way*, i.e. without *parallel commands*.

The synthesis of matrix-instructions with disjoint columns will be considered in chapter 4 while the general case will be treated in chapter 5.

Chapter 4 : <u>The synthesis of (or)-interpreted matrix-instructions with disjoint</u>
<u>columns</u>

This chapter constitutes the central chapter of part I : we introduce a computation method for synthesizing an (or)-interpreted matrix-instruction with disjoint columns. In next chapter 5 we shall render obvious the additional computations which are needed for the synthesis of an (or)-interpreted matrix-instruction with non-disjoint columns. In chapter 6 we shall see how the theorems of chapters 4 and 5 can be adapted to the synthesis of (and)-interpreted matrix-instructions.

The general theory is introduced in section 4.1. ; it is the basic theorem of this section which will later on be generalized in chapters 5 and 6 for dealing with the synthesis of (or)-interpreted and (and)-interpreted matrix-instructions.

The theorem of section 4.1 is illustrated in section 4.2 by means of a classical design example : the synthesis of an addition-and-substraction cell (CAS-cell) working under different input-output constraints. This example is taken from the computer-arithmetic field (Hwang [1979]).

The problem of optimal synthesis of matrix-instructions is introduced in section 4.3. This optimization problem may be formulated as follows : among all the programs equivalent to a matrix-instruction (and which are derived from the theorem of section 4.1) select those satisfying a given optimality criterion . This optimality criterion may e.g. be a *cost criterion* (program made up with a minimal number of elementary instructions) or a *time criterion* (program with a minimal *execution time*).

In section 4.4. we consider the hardware implementation of matrix instructions. We also introduce a language for describing this hardware implementation. This language (made up of *if then else, fork, join, do* instructions) will be connected in part II (see chapter 10, 11)to programmed and microprogrammed realizations of matrix instructions. What we call *software description* in section 4.4 must be understood as a *language for describing a hardware implementation.*The *software implementation* of a matrix-instruction in terms of a *safe program* will be studied in chapters 10 and 11.

4.1. General theory

We assume that the matrix-instruction (31) has disjoint columns and that each row of the matrix covers the Boolean cube, i.e. :

$$f_{ij} \, f_{ik} \equiv 0 \ , \quad \forall j \neq k \ , \quad \sum_j f_{ij} \equiv 1 \ , \quad \forall i \tag{46}$$

The synthesis of matrix-instructions with disjoint predicates is based on the following theorem :

Theorem

Starting with the initial system of q P-functions :

$$
\left.\begin{array}{l}
<f_{11}, \ \cdots \ , \ f_{p1} \ ; \ \sigma_1> \\
\vdots \\
<f_{1q}, \ \cdots \ , \ f_{pq} \ ; \ \sigma_q>
\end{array}\right\} \quad \text{Initial system} \tag{47a}
$$

the iterative generation of P-functions by means of laws $(t_i)^p$
(where $(t_i)^p$ means the p-th componentwise extension of t_i, i.e. t_i applied to the p components of a vector) *produces in at least one way the ultimate system of p P-func tions :*

$$
\left.\begin{array}{l}
<1 \ , \ \cdots \ , \ - \ ; \ \sum_i f_{1i} \ \sigma_i> \\
\vdots \\
<- \ , \ \cdots \ , \ 1 \ ; \ \sum_i f_{pi} \ \sigma_i>
\end{array}\right\} \quad \text{Ultimate system} \tag{47b}
$$

To the transformation (47a) → (47b) is associated a program made-up of if then else instructions and realizing the matrix-instruction $[f_{ij}]$, $1 \leqslant i \leqslant p$, $1 \leqslant j \leqslant q$.

Proof

The proof derives from the fact that :

1) The complete Boolean cube is covered by the functions f_{ij}, i.e. :

$$
\sum_j f_{kj} \equiv 1 \quad \forall k
$$

so that after a sufficient number of operations t_i, which may be considered as consensus operations, the function "1" necessarily appears in any components of the left member (or domain) of the P-functions;

2) If a P-function has a "1" in its k-th left component, its right component (or codomain) is :

$$
\sum_j f_{kj} \ \sigma_j \ . \tag{48}
$$

This derives from the definition of P-function which states that to the domain "λt" , i.e. "1" in the formalism of the transformation (45), is associated the codomain (48).

3) The transformations t_i are associated to *if then else* instructions having the condition variables x_i as predicates □

4.2. Example 1 (continued)

Starting with the initial system (50a) of P-functions which is associated to the output labels (A_1, A_2, A_3, A_4) of the matrix-instruction (22), we apply iteratively the laws t_i $(1 \leqslant i \leqslant 3)$ in order to obtain the ultimate system (50b) of P-functions which is associated to the input labels (D_1, D_2) of the same matrix-instruction (22). Note that since the *domains* of the P-functions are the Boolean functions f_{ij} the operation "+" in the definition (36) of the law t_i is *interpreted* as the *Boolean disjunction* "∨", i.e. :

$$\langle g_1 ; h_1 \rangle \, t_i \, \langle g_2 ; h_2 \rangle = \langle \bar{x}_i g_1 \lor x_i g_2 \; ; \; \bar{x}_i h_1 + x_i h_2 \rangle \tag{49}$$

This remark is of little importance for the present example but will be meaningful for examples with non-disjoint columns.

The transformation to be performed is :

$$\left. \begin{array}{l} D_1 : \langle 1, - \; ; \; \sum_{1 \leqslant j \leqslant 3} f_{1j} \, \sigma_j \rangle \\[3mm] D_2 : \langle -, 1 \; ; \; \sum_{1 \leqslant j \leqslant 3} f_{2j} \, \sigma_j \rangle \end{array} \right\} \xleftarrow{\;(t_1, t_2, t_3)^2\;} \left\{ \begin{array}{ll} \langle f_{11}, f_{21} \; ; \; \sigma_1 \rangle : A_1 \\[2mm] \langle f_{12}, f_{22} \; ; \; \sigma_2 \rangle : A_2 \\[2mm] \langle f_{13}, f_{23} \; ; \; \sigma_3 \rangle : A_3 \\[2mm] \langle f_{14}, f_{24} \; ; \; \sigma_4 \rangle : A_4 \end{array} \right.$$

The sequence of operations encountered during the transformation (49) is detailed below. Observe that we have used for this transformation a *reduced law* t_i^r instead of t_i ; t_i^r is defined as follows :

$$\langle g_1 ; h_1 \rangle \, t_i^r \, \langle g_2 ; h_2 \rangle = \langle g_1(x_i = 0) \, g_2(x_i = 1) ; \; \bar{x}_i h_1 + x_i h_2 \rangle \tag{51}$$

A theoretical justification of the use of t_i^r will be given in part III ; the use of t_i^r will provide us with computational facilities that will appear later on.

$$\left. \begin{array}{l} A_1 = \langle \bar{x}_1 \bar{x}_2 \bar{x}_3, \; \bar{x}_1 x_2 \bar{x}_3 \; ; \; \sigma_1 \rangle \\[2mm] A_2 = \langle x_1 \bar{x}_2 x_3 \lor x_1 x_2 \bar{x}_3 \lor \bar{x}_1 x_2 x_3, \; \bar{x}_1 \bar{x}_2 x_3 \lor x_1 \bar{x}_2 \bar{x}_3 \lor x_1 x_2 x_3 \; ; \; \sigma_2 \rangle \\[2mm] A_3 = \langle \bar{x}_1 \bar{x}_2 x_3 \lor x_1 \bar{x}_2 \bar{x}_3 \lor \bar{x}_1 x_2 \bar{x}_3, \; \bar{x}_1 \bar{x}_2 \bar{x}_3 \lor x_1 x_2 \bar{x}_3 \lor \bar{x}_1 x_2 x_3 \; ; \; \sigma_3 \rangle \\[2mm] A_4 = \langle x_1 x_2 x_3, \; x_1 \bar{x}_2 x_3 \; ; \; \sigma_4 \rangle \end{array} \right\} \tag{50a}$$

$$B_1 = A_3 t_3^r A_2 = \langle x_1\bar{x}_2 \vee \bar{x}_1 x_2, \ \bar{x}_1\bar{x}_2 \vee x_1 x_2 \ ; \ \bar{x}_3\sigma_3 + x_3\sigma_2 \rangle$$

$$B_2 = A_1 t_3^r A_3 = \langle \bar{x}_1\bar{x}_2, \ x_1 x_2 \ ; \ \bar{x}_3\sigma_1 + x_3\sigma_3 \rangle$$

$$B_3 = A_2 t_3^r A_4 = \langle x_1 x_2, \ x_1\bar{x}_2 \ ; \ \bar{x}_3\sigma_2 + x_3\sigma_4 \rangle$$

$$C_1 = B_1 t_1^r B_3 = \langle x_2, \ \bar{x}_2 \ ; \ \bar{x}_1\bar{x}_3\sigma_3 + (\bar{x}_1 x_3 \vee x_1\bar{x}_3)\sigma_2 + x_1 x_3\sigma_4 \rangle$$

$$C_2 = B_2 t_1^r B_1 = \langle \bar{x}_2, \ x_2 \ ; \ \bar{x}_1\bar{x}_3\sigma_1 + (\bar{x}_1 x_3 \vee x_1\bar{x}_3)\sigma_3 + x_1 x_3\sigma_2 \rangle$$

$$D_1 = C_2 t_2^r C_1 = \langle 1,0 \ ; \ \bar{x}_1\bar{x}_2\bar{x}_3\sigma_1 + (x_1\bar{x}_2 x_3 \vee x_1 x_2\bar{x}_3 \vee \bar{x}_1 x_2 x_3)\,\sigma_2$$
$$+ (\bar{x}_1\bar{x}_2 x_3 \vee x_1\bar{x}_2\bar{x}_3 \vee \bar{x}_1 x_2\bar{x}_3)\sigma_3 + x_1 x_2 x_3\sigma_4 \rangle$$

$$D_2 = C_1 t_2^r C_2 = \langle 0,1 \ ; \ \bar{x}_1\bar{x}_2\bar{x}_3\sigma_1 + (\bar{x}_1\bar{x}_2 x_3 \vee x_1\bar{x}_2\bar{x}_3 \vee x_1 x_2 x_3)\sigma_2 +$$
$$+ (\bar{x}_1\bar{x}_2 x_3 \vee x_1 x_2\bar{x}_3 \vee \bar{x}_1 x_2 x_3)\sigma_3 + x_1\bar{x}_2 x_3\sigma_4 \rangle$$

$$(50b)$$

We finally observe that the obtention of the labels B_i, C_j and D_j corresponds to the extraction of the three matrices in the factorization (23) respectively ; this factorization was the following :

$$\begin{array}{c} D_1 \\ D_2 \\ \\ \end{array} \begin{bmatrix} f_{11} & f_{12} & f_{13} & f_{14} \\ f_{21} & f_{22} & f_{23} & f_{24} \\ A_1 & A_2 & A_3 & A_4 \end{bmatrix} = \begin{array}{c} D_1 \\ D_2 \\ \\ \end{array} \begin{bmatrix} x_2 & \bar{x}_2 \\ \bar{x}_2 & x_2 \\ C_1 & C_2 \end{bmatrix} \begin{bmatrix} \bar{x}_1 & 0 & x_1 \\ x_1 & \bar{x}_1 & 0 \\ B_1 & B_2 & B_3 \end{bmatrix} \begin{bmatrix} 0 & x_3 & \bar{x}_3 & 0 \\ \bar{x}_3 & 0 & x_3 & 0 \\ 0 & \bar{x}_3 & 0 & x_3 \\ A_1 & A_2 & A_3 & A_3 \end{bmatrix}$$

$$(23)$$

The program corresponding to the transformation : system (50a) → system (50b) is depicted in figure 5. If we start this program with the instruction labeled D_1 it computes the Sum and the Carry for the addition, while if we start it with the instruction labeled D_2 it computes the Sum and the Carry for the difference. The flow-chart of Figure 5 is written in (53) in terms of *if then else* instructions. For sake of conciseness and for a reason of *transposability* that will appear later on, we write the *if then else* instruction :

$$N \ \textit{if} \ x=0 \ \textit{goto} \ M_1 \ \ \textit{else go to} \ M_2$$

in the following way :

$$N(\bar{x} \ M_1 \ , \ x \ M_2) \qquad (52)$$

Using the notation (52) the program of figure 5 is written :

$$D_1 \ (\bar{x}_2 C_2, \ x_2 C_1)$$

$$D_2 \ (\bar{x}_2 C_1, \ x_2 C_2)$$

$$C_1 \ (\bar{x}_1 B_1, \ x_1 B_3)$$

$$C_2 \ (\bar{x}_1 B_2, \ x_1 B_1) \tag{53}$$

$$B_1 \ (\bar{x}_3 A_3, \ x_3 A_2)$$

$$B_2 \ (\bar{x}_3 A_1, \ x_3 A_3)$$

$$B_3 \ (\bar{x}_3 A_2, \ x_3 A_4)$$

The program (53) evaluates either the sum or the difference of two numbers ; in order to render obvious the capabilities of the P-function technique we slightly modify the program requirements : we want now to evaluate the sum and the difference (simultaneously) of two numbers.

Assume that the outputs of the CAS cell have to be put in a 4-bit register $[R] = S_0, C_0, S_1, C_1$. The CAS input/output relationship is specified by the following instruction (54) which is deduced either from the expressions of S_0, C_0, S_1, C_1 or from their tabular representation (see figure 8)

	x_1			
	0 0 1 0	1 0 0 1	0 1 1 0	1 0 0 0
x_3	1 0 0 1	0 1 1 1	1 1 0 1	0 1 1 0

x_2

Figure 8 : Karnaugh map

$$N \quad \tau \quad [f_1 \quad f_2 \quad f_3 \quad f_4 \quad f_5 \quad f_6] \tag{54}$$

$$\sigma_1 \quad \sigma_2 \quad \sigma_3 \quad \sigma_4 \quad \sigma_5 \quad \sigma_6$$

$$M_1 \quad M_2 \quad M_3 \quad M_4 \quad M_5 \quad M_6$$

$$f_1 = \bar{x}_1 \bar{x}_2 \bar{x}_3$$

$$f_2 = \bar{x}_1 \bar{x}_2 x_3 \lor x_1 \bar{x}_2 \bar{x}_3$$

$$f_3 = x_1 \bar{x}_2 \bar{x}_3$$

$$f_4 = x_1 x_2 \bar{x}_3 \lor \bar{x}_1 x_2 x_3 \tag{55}$$

$$f_5 = \bar{x}_1 x_2 \bar{x}_3$$

$$f_6 = x_1 x_2 x_3$$

The commands $\sigma_1, \sigma_2, \sigma_3, \sigma_4, \sigma_5, \sigma_6$ mean : put the values (0010),(1001),(0111),(0110), (1000),(1101) in the output register R respectively.

The synthesis is obtained by performing the following transformation (56) :

$$\text{(56b)} \qquad \text{(56)} \qquad \text{(56a)}$$

$$D : \langle 1 ; \sum f_j \sigma_j \rangle \xleftarrow{(t_1^r, t_2^r, t_3^r)} \begin{cases} \langle f_1 ; \sigma_1 \rangle : M_1 \\ \langle f_2 ; \sigma_2 \rangle : M_2 \\ \langle f_3 ; \sigma_3 \rangle : M_3 \\ \langle f_4 ; \sigma_4 \rangle : M_4 \\ \langle f_5 ; \sigma_5 \rangle : M_5 \\ \langle f_6 ; \sigma_6 \rangle : M_6 \end{cases}$$

The sequence of operations encountered during the transformation (56) is detailed below.

$$\begin{aligned} A_1 &= \langle \bar{x}_1 \bar{x}_2 \bar{x}_3 ; \sigma_1 \rangle , & A_2 &= \langle \bar{x}_1 \bar{x}_2 x_3 \vee x_1 \bar{x}_2 \bar{x}_3 ; \sigma_2 \rangle \\ A_3 &= \langle x_1 \bar{x}_2 x_3 ; \sigma_3 \rangle , & A_4 &= \langle x_1 x_2 \bar{x}_3 \vee \bar{x}_1 x_2 x_3 ; \sigma_4 \rangle \\ A_5 &= \langle \bar{x}_1 x_2 \bar{x}_3 ; \sigma_5 \rangle , & A_6 &= \langle x_1 x_2 x_3 ; \sigma_6 \rangle \end{aligned} \qquad (56a)$$

$$\begin{aligned} B_1 &= A_2 t_2^r A_4 = \langle \bar{x}_1 x_3 ; x_1 \bar{x}_3 ; \bar{x}_2 \sigma_2 + x_2 \sigma_4 \rangle \\ B_2 &= A_3 t_2^r A_6 = \langle x_1 x_3 ; \bar{x}_2 \sigma_3 + x_2 \sigma_6 \rangle \\ B_3 &= A_1 t_2^r A_5 = \langle \bar{x}_1 \bar{x}_3 ; \bar{x}_2 \sigma_1 + x_2 \sigma_5 \rangle \end{aligned}$$

$$\begin{aligned} C_1 &= B_3 t_1^r B_1 = \langle \bar{x}_3 ; \bar{x}_1 \bar{x}_2 \sigma_1 + \bar{x}_1 x_2 \sigma_5 + x_1 \bar{x}_2 \sigma_2 + x_1 x_2 \sigma_4 \rangle \\ C_2 &= B_1 t_1^r B_2 = \langle x_3 ; \bar{x}_1 \bar{x}_2 \sigma_2 + \bar{x}_1 x_2 \sigma_4 + x_1 \bar{x}_2 \sigma_3 + x_1 x_2 \sigma_6 \rangle \end{aligned}$$

$$D_1 = C_1 t_3^r C_2 = \langle 1 ; \sum_{1 \leqslant j \leqslant 6} f_j \sigma_j \rangle \qquad (56b)$$

The program corresponding to the above transformation is depicted in figure 9.

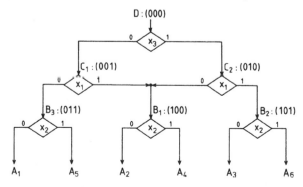

Figure 9: Program for computing the sum and the difference of two numbers.

In order to render obvious the capabilities of the P-function technique we again modify the program requirements : we want to evaluate one of the functions S_0, C_0, S_1, C_1 and to put the result in a 1-bit memory cell $[R]$. The CAS input/output relationship is specified by the following matrix-instruction :

$$
\begin{matrix}
N_1 & \tau_1 \\
N_2 & \tau_2 \\
N_3 & \tau_3 \\
N_4 & \tau_4 \\
\end{matrix}
\begin{bmatrix}
S_0 & \bar{S}_0 \\
C_0 & \bar{C}_0 \\
S_1 & \bar{S}_1 \\
C_1 & \bar{C}_1 \\
\end{bmatrix}
\quad\quad (57)
$$

$$
\begin{matrix}
\sigma_1 & \sigma_2 \\
M_1 & M_2 \\
\end{matrix}
$$

The meaning of the parameters in this matrix-instruction (57) is the following ; the functions S_0, C_0, S_1, C_1 were defined in section 2.2.4, i.e. :

$$S_0 = x_1 \oplus x_2 \oplus x_3 \qquad \text{(sum output)}$$
$$C_0 = x_1 x_2 \vee x_1 x_3 \vee x_2 x_3 \qquad \text{(carry output for the sum)}$$
$$S_1 = x_1 \oplus \bar{x}_2 \oplus x_3 \qquad \text{(difference output)}$$
$$C_1 = x_1 \bar{x}_2 \vee x_1 x_3 \vee \bar{x}_2 x_3 \qquad \text{(carry output for the difference)}$$

$\tau_1, \tau_2, \tau_3, \tau_4$ means : compute S_0, C_0, S_1, C_1 respectively ; σ_1, σ_2 means : put the value 1 or 0 in the output register R respectively.

The synthesis is obtained by performing the transformation (58) :

$$(58b) \qquad\qquad (58) \qquad\qquad (58a)$$

$$
\left.
\begin{matrix}
\langle 1, - , - , - ; S_0\sigma_1 + \bar{S}_0\sigma_2 \rangle \\
\langle -, 1 , - , - ; C_0\sigma_1 + \bar{C}_0\sigma_2 \rangle \\
\langle -, - , 1 , - ; S_1\sigma_1 + \bar{S}_1\sigma_2 \rangle \\
\langle -, - , - , 1 ; C_1\sigma_1 + \bar{C}_1\sigma_2 \rangle \\
\end{matrix}
\right\}
\xleftarrow{(t_1^r, t_2^r, t_3^r)^4}
\left\{
\begin{matrix}
\langle S_0, C_0, S_1, C_1 ; \sigma_1 \rangle \\
\langle \bar{S}_0, \bar{C}_0, \bar{S}_1, \bar{C}_1 ; \sigma_2 \rangle \\
\end{matrix}
\right.
$$

The sequence of operations encountered during the transformation (58) is detailed below :

$$
\left.
\begin{matrix}
A_1 = \langle x_1 \oplus x_2 \oplus x_3, \ x_1 x_2 \vee x_1 x_3 \vee x_2 x_3, \ x_1 \oplus \bar{x}_2 \oplus x_3, \ x_1 \bar{x}_2 \vee x_1 x_3 \vee \bar{x}_2 x_3 \ ; \sigma_1 \rangle \\
A_2 = \langle \bar{x}_1 \oplus x_2 \oplus x_3, \ \bar{x}_1 \bar{x}_2 \vee \bar{x}_1 \bar{x}_3 \vee \bar{x}_2 \bar{x}_3, \ x_1 \oplus \bar{x}_2 \oplus x_3, \ \bar{x}_1 x_2 \vee \bar{x}_1 \bar{x}_3 \vee x_2 \bar{x}_3 \ ; \sigma_2 \rangle \\
\end{matrix}
\right\}
\quad (58a)
$$

$$B_1 = A_1 t_3^r A_2 = \langle x_1 x_2 v \bar{x}_1 \bar{x}_2,\ x_1 \bar{x}_2 v x_1 x_2,\ x_1 \bar{x}_2 v \bar{x}_1 x_2,\ x_1 x_2 v \bar{x}_1 \bar{x}_2\ ;\ \bar{x}_3 \sigma_1 + x_3 \sigma_2 \rangle$$

$$B_2 = A_2 t_3^r A_1 = \langle x_1 \bar{x}_2 v \bar{x}_1 x_2,\ -\ ,\ x_1 x_2 v \bar{x}_1 \bar{x}_2,\ -\ ;\ \bar{x}_3 \sigma_2 + x_3 \sigma_1 \rangle$$

$$C_1 = B_1 t_1^r B_2 = \langle \bar{x}_2,\ -\ ,\ x_2,\ -\ ;\ (\bar{x}_1 \bar{x}_3 v x_1 x_3)\sigma_1 + (\bar{x}_1 x_3 v x_1 \bar{x}_3)\sigma_2 \rangle$$

$$C_2 = B_2 t_1^r B_1 = \langle x_2,\ -\ ,\ \bar{x}_2,\ -\ ;\ (x_1 \bar{x}_3 v \bar{x}_1 x_3)\sigma_1 + (x_1 x_3 v \bar{x}_1 \bar{x}_3)\sigma_2 \rangle$$

$$C_3 = B_1 t_1^r A_2 = \langle \bar{x}_2 \bar{x}_3,\ x_2,\ x_2 \bar{x}_3,\ \bar{x}_2\ ;\ \bar{x}_1 \bar{x}_3 \sigma_1 + (x_1 v x_3)\sigma_2 \rangle$$

$$C_4 = A_2 t_1^r B_1 = \langle x_2 x_3,\ \bar{x}_2,\ \bar{x}_2 x_3,\ x_2\ ;\ (\bar{x}_1 v \bar{x}_3)\sigma_1 + x_1 x_3 \sigma_2 \rangle$$

$$D_1 = C_1 t_2^r C_2 = \langle 1,0,0,0\ ;\ (x_1 \oplus x_2 \oplus x_3)\sigma_1 + (\bar{x}_1 \oplus x_2 \oplus x_3)\sigma_2 \rangle$$

$$D_2 = C_4 t_2^r C_3 = \langle 0,1,0,0\ ;\ (x_1 x_2 v x_1 x_3 v x_2 x_3)\sigma_1 + (\bar{x}_1 \bar{x}_2 v \bar{x}_1 \bar{x}_3 v \bar{x}_2 \bar{x}_3)\sigma_2 \rangle$$

$$D_3 = C_2 t_2^r C_1 = \langle 0,0,1,0\ ;\ (x_1 \oplus x_2 \oplus x_3)\sigma_1 + (x_1 \oplus x_2 \oplus x_3)\sigma_2 \rangle$$

$$D_4 = C_3 t_2^r C_4 = \langle 0,0,0,1\ ;\ (x_1 \bar{x}_2 v x_1 x_3 v \bar{x}_2 x_3)\sigma_1 + (\bar{x}_1 x_2 v \bar{x}_1 \bar{x}_3 v x_2 \bar{x}_3)\sigma_2 \rangle$$

(58b)

The program corresponding to the transformation : system (58a) → system (58b) is depicted in figure 10. It is also represented by the following factorization of the matrix (57) :

$$
\begin{array}{c}
D_1 \\ D_2 \\ D_3 \\ D_4
\end{array}
\begin{bmatrix}
S_0 & \bar{S}_0 \\
C_0 & \bar{C}_0 \\
S_1 & \bar{S}_1 \\
C_1 & \bar{C}_1 \\
\;A_1 & A_2
\end{bmatrix}
=
\begin{array}{c}
D_1 \\ D_2 \\ D_3 \\ D_4
\end{array}
\begin{bmatrix}
\bar{x}_2 & x_2 & 0 & 0 \\
0 & 0 & x_2 & \bar{x}_2 \\
x_2 & \bar{x}_2 & 0 & 0 \\
0 & 0 & \bar{x}_2 & x_2 \\
\;C_1 & C_2 & C_3 & C_4
\end{bmatrix}
\begin{bmatrix}
\bar{x}_1 & x_1 & 0 & 0 \\
x_1 & \bar{x}_1 & 0 & 0 \\
\bar{x}_1 & 0 & x_1 & 0 \\
x_1 & 0 & 0 & \bar{x}_1 \\
\;B_1 & B_2 & A_1 & A_2
\end{bmatrix}
\begin{bmatrix}
x_3 & \bar{x}_3 \\
\bar{x}_3 & x_3 \\
1 & 0 \\
0 & 1 \\
\;A_1 & A_2
\end{bmatrix}
\quad (59)
$$

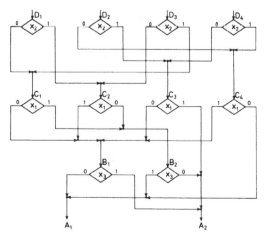

Figure 10 : Program for computing one of the functions S_0, C_0, S_1, C_1

4.3. An algorithm for generating optimal syntheses of matrix-instructions

There are clearly a high number of programs, made-up of elementary instructions which may represent a matrix-instruction : this corresponds to the possibility of factorizing a Boolean matrix in several different ways. Different programs
are e.g. obtained by taking different choices for the successive predicates to be
tested and by considering the possibility of having *reconvergent* or *degenerate join
instructions*. In the scheme of figure 5, the instruction B_1 is called *reconvergent*
since it may be reached through the intermediate of at least two (in this case C_1
and C_2) instructions and since it may never be reached through the intermediate of
these instructions *simultaneously* : we see in figure 5 that the information may
propagate from C_1 *or* from C_2 but never from C_1 *and* from C_2. This is a consequence
of having an (or)-interpreted matrix-instruction with disjoint columns, i.e. :

$$f_{ij} f_{ik} \equiv 0 \quad \forall i \quad \text{and} \quad \forall j \neq k .$$

As a consequence , the *join instruction* which reflects the reconvergence preceding
B_1 in figure 5 may be dropped or is *degenerate* .

There exists thus an optimization problem so far as the synthesis of programs is concerned. The main optimization criteria are the following ones :

(a) The maximal duration of a computation (*time duration*). This duration is reflected in the scheme of figure 5 by the maximal number of instructions between D_1 or
D_2 and any A_i.

(b) The number of instructions (*cost criterion*)

(c) Between all the programs having the shortest computation time find those having
a minimum number of instructions (*relative cost criterion*).

A general scheme for algorithms which have to generate optimal programs
(the optimality criterion will be stated precisely later   on) may be stated in
terms of P-functions as follows .

Step 1. *Give the list of all the P-functions ;*

Step 2. *Compute by using the composition laws t_i (or t_i^r), $1 \leqslant i \leqslant n$, all the P-
functions which may be obtained from the list of step 1 ;*

Step k. *Compute by using the composition laws t_i (or t_i^r), $1 \leqslant i \leqslant n$, all the P-
functions which may be obtained from those obtained at any preceding step.*

If the relative cost criterion is considered, the computation ends as soon as a step
k' is reached where the P-functions :

$$<-,-, \ldots , 1_j , - , - \ldots - ; \sum_i f_{ij}\sigma_i> \quad , 1 \leqslant j \leqslant q \tag{60}$$

appear : the presence of a "1" at the j-th place of the domain guarantees that the j-th row of the matrix-instruction is realized ("-" means indeterminate functions). If these P-functions are obtained in several ways at the step k', to each of these ways is associated a program which is optimal in time (since the step k' is the earliest step where these P-functions appear and since the maximal computation time of the program is k'-1). A cost comparison allows us then to detect the programs which are also optimal in cost. If the cost criterion is considered the computation ends as soon as a step k" is reached which contains only P-functions of the type (60). Again a cost comparison between all these programs leading to the ultimate P-functions (60) allows us to detect those having a minimal cost. If an optimal program is, e.g. obtained at a step k" > k', this program is optimal in cost but has a longer computation time than the programs derived at the step k'.

A rigorous justification of these algorithms will be given by means of the algebra of P-functions (see part III) ; some justifications may already be presented now.

First the generation of algorithms which satisfy either the cost criterion, or the relative cost criterion requires that the reconvergent instructions should be detected at each step of the computation. This goal is reached by starting the computation with the P-functions :

$$\langle f_{1j} , f_{2j} , \dots, f_{pj} ; \sigma_j \rangle \quad , \quad 1 \leqslant j \leqslant q \qquad (61)$$

Indeed, the solution of $f_{ij}(\underline{x})=1$ characterize the greatest domain where the command σ_j is activated. We moreover shall see (see section 13.1, theorems 1 and 2) that the maximal character of the domain function is preserved when the laws t_i or t_i^r are used. Since in a program, instructions may be merged only if they have the same domain functions, programs having the maximum number of reconvergent instructions are obtained from algorithms generating P-functions which have the greatest domain functions. This also will be stated in an algebraic way in part III (see chapter 13).

Later on in this section we shall exclusively consider the law t_i^r (see (51)). We shall see (section 13.1) that the use of this law (instead of the more general law t_i) eliminates only some types of non-simple programs (a program is *non-simple* if a predicate x_i may be tested several times during a computation, it is *simple* otherwise). The ease with which the law t_i^r can be used and the number of simplifications it allows provide a definite motivation for eliminating the law t_i when dealing with practical problems. We have seen in chapter 3 how the synthesis of a program could be interpreted in terms of generation of P-functions. We recall that a P-function is formed by a domain function and a codomain function. The synthesis is based on a computation law acting on the domain functions and on the codomain functions. We verify that when dealing with disjoint Boolean functions, the codomain function is used only for some verification purpose. In this respect, we shall in this section represent the P-functions by means of their domain function only.

The purpose of the present section is to derive a computation method allowing us to obtain the domain functions associated with an optimal program in the simpliest possible way. This method will consider in particular the following items.

(a) Elimination in an a priori way of the domain functions that cannot generate an optimal program.

(b) Elimination in the remaining domain functions of some terms that cannot generate an optimal program.

For the sake of clarity, an example will be developed.

Consider the two domain functions g_1 and g_2 ; let us write each of these functions as the disjunction of all its prime implicants and let us explicitly consider one of the variables x_i of $\underline{x}$:

$$g_j = \bar{x} \, g_j^0 \vee x_j \, g_j^1 \vee g_j^2 \, , \quad j=1,2 \tag{62}$$

where g_j^2 is the disjunction of the prime implicants of g_j independent of x_i and where $x_i^{(k)} \, g_j^k$ is the disjunction of the prime implicants of g_j dependent on $x_i^{(k)}$, k=0,1 (remember that $x_i^{(0)} = \bar{x}_i$ and $x_i^{(1)} = x_i$).

Consider the composition of g_1 and of g_2 by means of the law t_i, i.e. :

$$g = g_1 \, t_i \, g_2$$

$$= \bar{x}_i g_1 \vee x_i g_2 \vee g_1(x_i{=}0) \, g_2(x_i{=}1)$$

$$= \bar{x}_i(g_1^0 \vee g_1^2) \vee x_i \, (g_2^1 \vee g_2^2) \vee \qquad \text{(a)}$$

$$g_1^0 g_2^2 \vee g_1^2 g_2^1 \vee g_1^2 g_2^2 \vee \qquad \text{(b)} \qquad (63)$$

$$g_1^0 g_2^1 \qquad \text{(c)}$$

Part (a) of (63) is the contribution of the composition law t_i ; if we restrict ourselves to parts (b) and (c) of (63) the composition law considered is t_i^r which is able to generate any optimal simple program (see section 13.2). We show that the restriction of the law t_i^r to part (c) of (63) also generates all the simple optimal programs.

The P-function technique for generating (optimal) simple programs is based on the principle of obtaining new cube-functions at each step of the algorithm described below. These new cube-functions are contained in part (c) of (63) : the cubes g_1^2 and g_2^2 were already contained in g_1 and g_2 respectively.

Accordingly, the new cube-functions that may be generated by composition of g_1 with g_2 according to the law t_i^r are the prime implicants of the functions :

$$g_1^0 \; g_2^1 \text{ deriving from } g_1 \; t_i^r \; g_2 \;,$$

$$g_2^0 \; g_1^1 \text{ deriving from } g_2 \; t_i^r \; g_1 \;.$$

The above rule is systematically used in figure 11 where each of the variables x_i of $\underline{x}$ is successively considered.

The proposed algorithm is illustrated by means of example 1.

Algorithm (see also the transformation $(50a) \rightarrow (50b)$)

Step 1

The four domain functions given by the disjunction of their prime implicants are :

$$A_1 = \bar{x}_1\bar{x}_2\bar{x}_3, \; \bar{x}_1x_2\bar{x}_3$$

$$A_2 = x_1\bar{x}_2\bar{x}_3 \vee x_1x_2\bar{x}_3 \vee \bar{x}_1x_2\bar{x}_3, \; \bar{x}_1\bar{x}_2x_3 \vee x_1\bar{x}_2x_3 \vee x_1x_2x_3$$

$$A_3 = \bar{x}_1\bar{x}_2x_3 \vee x_1\bar{x}_2\bar{x}_3 \vee \bar{x}_1x_2\bar{x}_3, \; \bar{x}_1\bar{x}_2\bar{x}_3 \vee x_1x_2\bar{x}_3 \vee \bar{x}_1x_2x_3$$

$$A_4 = x_1x_2x_3, \; x_1\bar{x}_2x_3$$

In figure 11, $A_1,\ldots,A_4$ are successively written down with respect to the pairs of literals $\{\bar{x}_i,x_i\}$ $\forall i = 1,2,3$. In the entry $\{A_j,\bar{x}_i\}$ of figure 11 we place the coefficients of $\bar{x}_i$ of the prime implicants of A_j $(j=1\text{-}4)$. The coefficients correspond to the functions g_j^0 and g_j^1 of (63) (in (63) we have $j=1,2$).
The successive domain functions are generated in the following way : the B_1 in the entries $\{A_2,x_3\}$ and $\{A_3, \bar{x}_3\}$ of figure 11 means that the domain function B_1 is the product of the functions of these two entries. This function B_1 derives from the use of the predicate x_3 applied to A_2 and to A_3.

The evaluation of each of the possible products between the entries corresponding to the rows $A_1 \ldots A_4$ produces the domain functions B_1, B_2, B_3. For sake of conciseness only the products corresponding to the predicate x_3 have been used and labeled in figure 11. We easily verify in figure 11 that similar products could be derived by using the predicate x_1. The domain functions that could be derived from the consideration of the predicate x_2 are less interesting from the optimality criterion point of view : we verify that the products of these functions lead to domain functions with a smaller number of 1's in the Boolean cube. Remember also that the optimal synthesis of programs is related to the obtention of the greatest possible domain functions (see this section and section 13.2).

Step 2

Obtain (as in step 1) all the possible products corresponding to the rows $A_1\ldots A_4$, $B_1\ldots B_3$. The products produce the domain functions labelled C_1 and C_2. Again we observe that the products obtained in the columns $\{\bar{x}_1,x_1\}$ are better (from an optimality point of view) than those obtained in the columns $\{\bar{x}_2,x_2\}$.

	$\bar{x}_1$	x_1	$\bar{x}_2$	x_2	$\bar{x}_3$	x_3
$A_1 = \bar{x}_1\bar{x}_2x_3, \ \bar{x}_1x_2x_3$	$\bar{x}_2x_3, x_2x_3$		$\bar{x}_1x_3, 0$	$0, \bar{x}_1x_3$	$\bar{x}_1\bar{x}_2, \bar{x}_1x_2; B_2$	$\bar{x}_1\bar{x}_2 \vee \bar{x}_1x_2, \ \bar{x}_1\bar{x}_2 \vee \bar{x}_1x_2; B_1$
$A_2 = x_1\bar{x}_2x_3 \vee x_1\bar{x}_2\bar{x}_3 \vee x_1x_2\bar{x}_3, \ \bar{x}_1x_2\bar{x}_3 \vee x_1\bar{x}_2\bar{x}_3 \vee x_1x_2x_3$	$x_2x_3, x_2\bar{x}_3$	$\bar{x}_2x_3 \vee x_2x_3, \ \bar{x}_2\bar{x}_3 \vee x_2\bar{x}_3$	$x_1\bar{x}_3, x_1x_3 \vee \bar{x}_1\bar{x}_3$	$x_1\bar{x}_3 \vee \bar{x}_1\bar{x}_3, \ x_1\bar{x}_3$	$x_1\bar{x}_2, x_1x_2; \ B_3$	$x_1\bar{x}_2 \vee x_1x_2, \ x_1\bar{x}_2 \vee x_1x_2; B_1$
$A_3 = \bar{x}_1\bar{x}_2x_3 \vee x_1\bar{x}_2\bar{x}_3 \vee x_1x_2\bar{x}_3, \ \bar{x}_1x_2\bar{x}_3 \vee x_1x_2\bar{x}_3 \vee x_1x_2x_3$	$\bar{x}_2x_3 \vee x_2\bar{x}_3, \ x_2\bar{x}_3 \vee x_2x_3$	$\bar{x}_2\bar{x}_3, x_2\bar{x}_3$	$\bar{x}_1x_3, x_1x_3 \vee \bar{x}_1\bar{x}_3$	$x_1\bar{x}_3, x_1x_3 \vee \bar{x}_1x_3$	$x_1\bar{x}_2, x_1x_2, \ x_1\bar{x}_2 \vee x_1x_2; B_1$	$\bar{x}_1x_2, x_1x_2$ B_2
$A_4 = x_1x_2x_3, \ x_1\bar{x}_2x_3$		$x_2\bar{x}_3, \bar{x}_2x_3$	$0, x_1x_3$	$x_1x_3, 0$		$x_1x_2, x_1\bar{x}_2; B_3$
$B_1 = x_1\bar{x}_2 \vee x_1x_2, \ x_1\bar{x}_2 \vee x_1x_2$	$\bar{x}_2, x_2; C_1$	$\bar{x}_2, x_2; \ C_2$	$\bar{x}_1, x_1$	$\bar{x}_1, x_1$		
$B_2 = x_1\bar{x}_2, \ \bar{x}_1x_2$	$\bar{x}_2, x_2; C_2$		$\bar{x}_1, 0$	$0, \bar{x}_1$		
$B_3 = x_1\bar{x}_2, \ x_1\bar{x}_2$		$\bar{x}_2, x_2; C_1$	$0, \bar{x}_1$	$x_1, 0$		
$C_1 = \bar{x}_2, x_2$			$1,0; D_1$	$0,1; D_2$		
$C_2 = x_2, \bar{x}_2$			$0,1; D_2$	$1,0; D_1$		
$D_1 = 1,0$						
$D_2 = 0,1$						

Figure 11 : Tabular evaluation of P-functions

Step 3

The last step produces the domain functions $D_1=(1,0)$ and $D_2=(0,1)$.

The above algorithm with its tabular representation is quite sufficient for generating programs equivalent to matrix instructions. The obtention of
optimal programs (with lowest time duration or lowest cost) is grounded on the systematic obtention at each step of the greatest possible domain functions. A computer program using the theory of P-functions has been developed; this program automatically evaluates optimal realizations of matrix instructions. More about the optimization problems may be found in section 13.2.

4.4. Hardware implementations of matrix-instructions and an hardware description
     language.

The purpose of this section is the analysis of some properties of
hardware implementations of matrix-instructions with disjoint columns. The software description will be made-up from the *low-level instructions* defined in section
1.2. ; the hardware implementation will be made-up from the logical gates :
multiplexers , *demultiplexers* , *or-gates* , *and-gates* and *fanout connections* .
Special chapters will be devoted to *programmed* and *microprogrammed* implementations of matrix-instructions (see chapters 10 and 11).

The main characteristic of (or)-interpreted matrix-instructions with
disjoint columns is that there exists for any combination of the predicates x_i ,
one and only one *activated path* (i.e. where information may propagate in software
realizations or where electrical signals may propagate in hardware realizations)
between any *input label* and any *output label* . Indeed, the *(or)-interpretation*
on the rows of the matrix implies that the system is designed so that one and only
one row input may be reached at a time. Stated otherwise, the (or)-interpreted matrix-instructions are used to describe, by means of a single concept, algorithms
which cannot be activated simultaneously. The example 1 deals with an algorithm
which computes *either* the addition *or* the difference of two numbers : the matrix
instruction (21) and its realization (53) may never he used for evaluating simultaneously the addition *and* the difference of two numbers. The signals τ_1 and τ_2
in (21) may never be true simultaneously, i.e.:

$$\tau_1 \tau_2 - \phi$$

More generally an (or)-interpreted matrix instruction (16) is characterized by
disjoint *end of execution signals*, i.e. :

$$\tau_j \tau_k = \phi \qquad \forall j \neq k$$

Moreover since the boolean functions are disjoint for each row, i.e. :

$$f_{ij}\ f_{ik} \equiv 0 \qquad \forall i\ ,$$

the information on the signal propagates to one and only one output.

As a consequence, in the program, any instruction may be reached from one and only one preceding instruction. The *column-instructions* which are *join-instructions* or *transpose (if then else) instructions* may thus be dropped in the program : we say that *column-instructions* are *degenerate* in programs. This can again best be illustrated by means of example 1. Consider the first matrix of the factorization (23), i.e. :

$$
\begin{array}{c}
D_1 \\
D_2
\end{array}
\begin{bmatrix}
x_2 & \bar{x}_2 \\
\bar{x}_2 & x_2
\end{bmatrix}
\qquad\qquad (64)
$$
$$
\begin{array}{cc}
C_1 & C_2
\end{array}
$$

In view of the factorization (19) this matrix represents two row-instructions followed by two column instructions ; it may e.g. be factorized in the following ways in order to separate the row-instructions from the column-instructions :

$$
\begin{array}{c}
D_1 \\
D_2 \\
\ \\
\end{array}
\begin{bmatrix}
x_2 & \bar{x}_2 \\
\bar{x}_2 & x_2 \\
C_1 & C_2
\end{bmatrix}
=
\begin{array}{c}
D_1 \\
D_2 \\
\ \\
\end{array}
\begin{bmatrix}
\bar{x}_2 & x_2 & 0 & 0 \\
0 & 0 & \bar{x}_2 & x_2 \\
D_1' & D_1'' & D_2' & D_2''
\end{bmatrix}
\begin{bmatrix}
x_2 & 0 \\
0 & \bar{x}_2 \\
\bar{x}_2 & 0 \\
0 & x_2
\end{bmatrix}
\qquad (65)
$$
$$
\begin{array}{cc}
C_1 & C_2
\end{array}
$$

$$
=
\begin{array}{c}
D_1 \\
D_2 \\
\ \\
\end{array}
\begin{bmatrix}
x_2 & \bar{x}_2 & 0 & 0 \\
0 & 0 & \bar{x}_2 & x_2 \\
D_1' & D_1'' & D_2' & D_2''
\end{bmatrix}
\begin{bmatrix}
1 & 0 \\
0 & 1 \\
1 & 0 \\
0 & 1
\end{bmatrix}
\qquad (66)
$$
$$
\begin{array}{cc}
C_1 & C_2
\end{array}
$$

We extend the notation (52) in order to have simple representation of programs ; the row instruction N with two output labels M_1, M_2 is written :

$$N(f_1\ M_1\ ,\ f_2\ M_2) \qquad\qquad (67)$$

If $f_1=f_2=1$ (67) represents a *fork instruction* ; if $f_1=\bar{f}_2$ (67) represents an *if then else instruction*.

The column instruction with two input labels M_1, M_2 is written :

$$(f_1\ M_1,\ f_2\ M_2)\ N \tag{68}$$

If $f_1=f_2=1$ (68) represents a *join instruction* ; if $f_1=\bar{f}_2$ (68) represents a *transpose (if then else) instruction*. If necessary, the (or)-interpretation and (and)-interpretation are indicated.

With these notations the programs presented by the factorizations (65) and (66) are written in (69a) and (69b) respectively :

(69a)   (69b)

$$
\begin{array}{ll}
D_1(\bar{x}_2\ D_1'',\ x_2\ D_1') & D_1(\bar{x}_2\ D_1'',\ x_2\ D_1') \\[4pt]
D_2(\bar{x}_2\ D_2',\ x_2\ D_2'') & D_2(\bar{x}_2\ D_2',\ x_2\ D_2'') \\[4pt]
(\bar{x}_2\ D_2',\ x_2\ D_1')\ C_1 & (D_2',\ D_1')\quad C_1 \\[4pt]
(\bar{x}_2\ D_1'',\ x_2\ D_2'')\ C_2 & (D_1'',\ D_2'')\quad C_2
\end{array}
$$

Since instructions D_1 and D_2 may never be reached both in the same computation we verify that the column instructions in (69a, 69b) are degenerate and that the matrix (64) is represented by the two row instructions (70) :

$$
\begin{array}{l}
D_1\ (\bar{x}_2\ C_2\ ,\ x_2\ C_1) \\[4pt]
D_2\ (\bar{x}_2\ C_1\ ,\ x_2\ C_2)
\end{array}
\tag{70}
$$

Using the notations (7,67) we verify that the matrix instruction (21) is represented by the program (71a). This program corresponds to the factorization (23) and hence to the flowchart of figure 5. The input and output labels of this program are preceded and followed by arrows respectively.

An hardware realization of programs representing an (or)-interpreted matrix-instruction with disjoint columns may be deduced from its software description if we observe that to each elementary instruction corresponds a logical gate and that to each next instruction label corresponds a connection. The correspondance between instructions and logical gates is written down in figure 12 (see also figure 7).

(71a)　　　　　　　　　　　　(71b)

$$
\left.
\begin{array}{ccc}
\rightarrow & N_1 & \tau_1 & D_1 \\
\rightarrow & N_2 & \tau_2 & D_2
\end{array}
\right\} \text{execution} \left\{
\begin{array}{ccc}
D_1 & \sigma_1' & N_1 \rightarrow \\
D_2 & \sigma_2' & N_2 \rightarrow
\end{array}
\right.
$$

$$
\left.
\begin{array}{l}
D_1 \, (\bar{x}_2 \, C_2 \, , \, x_2 \, C_1) \\
D_2 \, (\bar{x}_2 \, C_1 \, , \, x_2 \, C_2) \\
C_1 \, (\bar{x}_1 \, B_1 \, , \, x_1 \, B_3) \\
C_2 \, (\bar{x}_1 \, B_2 \, , \, x_1 \, B_1) \\
B_1 \, (\bar{x}_3 \, A_3 \, , \, x_3 \, A_2) \\
B_2 \, (\bar{x}_3 \, A_1 \, , \, x_3 \, A_3) \\
B_3 \, (\bar{x}_3 \, A_2 \, , \, x_3 \, A_4)
\end{array}
\right\} \text{decision} \left\{
\begin{array}{l}
(\bar{x}_2 \, C_2 \, , \, x_2 \, C_1) \, D_1 \\
(\bar{x}_2 \, C_1 \, , \, x_2 \, C_2) \, D_2 \\
(\bar{x}_1 \, B_1 \, , \, x_1 \, B_3) \, C_1 \\
(\bar{x}_1 \, B_2 \, , \, x_1 \, B_1) \, C_2 \\
(\bar{x}_3 \, A_3 \, , \, x_3 \, A_2) \, B_1 \\
(\bar{x}_3 \, A_1 \, , \, x_3 \, A_3) \, B_2 \\
(\bar{x}_3 \, A_2 \, , \, x_3 \, A_4) \, B_3
\end{array}
\right.
$$

$$
\left.
\begin{array}{ccc}
A_1 & \sigma_1 & M_1 \rightarrow \\
A_2 & \sigma_2 & M_2 \rightarrow \\
A_3 & \sigma_3 & M_3 \rightarrow \\
A_4 & \sigma_4 & M_4 \rightarrow
\end{array}
\right\} \text{execution} \left\{
\begin{array}{ccc}
\rightarrow M_1 & \tau_1' & A_1 \\
\rightarrow M_2 & \tau_2' & A_2 \\
\rightarrow M_3 & \tau_3' & A_3 \\
\rightarrow M_4 & \tau_4' & A_4
\end{array}
\right.
$$

Laws	matrix instruction		transpose matrix instruction	
	elementary instructions	logical gates	elementary instructions	logical gates
t_i	if then else	demultiplexer	then if	multiplexer
Im	degenerate join	or-gate	degenerate fork	fanout

Figure 12 : Hardware and software primitives for the realization of an (or)-interpreted matrix-instruction with disjoint columns and of its transpose.

From the self-evident proposition in matrix theory :

Proposition 1.

A factorization for a matrix is also a factorization for its transpose
and from the realization of a matrix instruction we deduce a realization for the transpose matrix-instruction. Remember that to each matrix instruction we associate a

transpose instruction as follows :

$$
\begin{array}{cc}
N_1 & \tau_1 \\
\vdots & \vdots \\
N_p & \tau_p
\end{array}
\left[
\begin{array}{ccc}
f_{11} & \cdots & f_{1q} \\
\vdots & & \vdots \\
f_{p1} & \cdots & f_{pq}
\end{array}
\right]
\qquad
\begin{array}{cc}
M_1 & \tau_1' \\
\vdots & \vdots \\
M_q & \tau_q'
\end{array}
\left[
\begin{array}{ccc}
f_{11} & \cdots & f_{p1} \\
\vdots & & \vdots \\
f_{1q} & \cdots & f_{pq}
\end{array}
\right]
$$
$$
\begin{array}{ccc}
\sigma_1 & \cdots & \sigma_q \\
M_1 & \cdots & M_q
\end{array}
\qquad\qquad
\begin{array}{ccc}
\sigma_1' & \cdots & \sigma_p' \\
M_1 & \cdots & M_p
\end{array}
$$

Proposition 2 : <u>Transposition principle</u>

The realization of a transpose matrix instruction is deduced from the realization of the matrix instruction by transposing each instruction in a software model or by transposing each gate in a hardware realization, the connections remaining unchanged.

The correspondence between elementary instructions and their transpose and logical gates and their transpose is indicated in **figure** 12.

The notations (7,67) allow us to derive in a very easy way *transpose programs* describing *transpose matrix-instructions.*

Proposition 3 : <u>Transpose principle for software description</u>

If a matrix-instruction is described by a succession of elementary instructions that are successively read from top to bottom, each instruction being read from left to right, then the transpose matrix-instruction is described by the same program but which is now read from bottom to top, each instruction being read from right to left.

From the program (71a) describing the matrix-instruction (21) we deduce the program (72b) describing the transpose matrix-instruction. The program (71a) is read in the usual manner, i.e. from top to bottom, and from left to right. The program (71b) must be read from bottom to top; since we have reversed each instruction of (71a), the instructions of (71b) may also be read from left to right.

An interesting property may be deduced from proposition 2 if we restrict ourselves to *decision matrix-instructions*, i.e. matrix-instructions of the form :

$$
\begin{array}{c}
N_1 \\
\vdots \\
N_i \\
\vdots \\
N_p
\end{array}
\left[
\begin{array}{ccccc}
f_{11} & \cdots & f_{1j} & \cdots & f_{1q} \\
\vdots & & \vdots & & \vdots \\
f_{i1} & \cdots & f_{ij} & \cdots & f_{iq} \\
\vdots & & \vdots & & \vdots \\
f_{p1} & \cdots & f_{pj} & \cdots & f_{pq}
\end{array}
\right]
\qquad (72)
$$
$$
\begin{array}{ccccc}
M_1 & \cdots & M_j & \cdots & M_q
\end{array}
$$

From the definition of an (or)-interpreted matrix-instruction, we deduce that if the input label N_i is reached, then the output labels M_1, ..., M_j, ..., M_q are reached if the Boolean functions f_{i1}, ..., f_{ij}, ..., f_{iq} are equal to 1 respectively. Assume now that the matrix-instruction is realized by means of logical gates: if the logical value "1" is put on the N_i-th network entry and if the logical value "0" is put on the remaining network entries, then the network outputs M_1, ..., M_j, ..., M_q are equal to 1 if the Boolean functions f_{i1},...,f_{ij},...,f_{iq} are equal to 1 respectively; otherwise they are equal to 0. We shall say that the rows of the matrix (72) are available in a programmable way, i.e. to the input vector :

$$(N_1,...,N_i,...,N_p) = (0,...,1_i,...,0)$$

corresponds the output vector :

$$(M_1,...,M_j,...,M_q) = (f_{i1},...,f_{ij},...,f_{iq})$$

The following transposition principle immediately derives from proposition 2.

Proposition 4. Transposition principle for hardware implementation

If a synthesis of p×q Boolean functions is obtained as an interconnection of multiplexers, fanout connections and or-gates, then a transpose synthesis is derived by replacing the demultiplexers by multiplexers and by interchanging the fan-out connections and the or-gates. If the initial synthesis evaluates simultaneously all the Boolean functions of any row of a p×q matrix of functions, the different rows being available in a programmable way, then the transpose synthesis evaluates simultaneously all the Boolean functions of any column of this matrix, the different columns being available in a programmable way.

Figure 13 illustrates the two realizations which are deduced from the application of the transposition principle to the factorization (23) of the matrix instruction (21). Figures 13a and 13b use the graphical representations for one variable demultiplexer and multiplexer respectively. A demultiplexer of one command variable x is a logic gate with one input terminal y and two output terminals z_1 and z_2 realizing the functions :

$$z_1 = \bar{x}\, y \text{ and } z_2 = x\, y \qquad (73)$$

A mutliplexer of one command variable x is a logic gate with two input terminals y_1 and y_2 and one output terminal z realizing the function

$$z = \bar{x}\, y_1 \vee x\, y_2 \qquad (74)$$

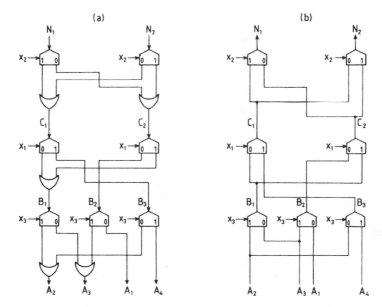

Figure 13. (a) Hardware realization of the program of figure 5 ;
(b) Hardware realization of the transpose program of figure 5.

Remark : *On some comparisons between the syntheses of matrix-instructions and of their transpose and between hardware and software realizations.*

The software realization of matrix-instructions has *degenerate join instructions* : this means that these instructions may be deleted without altering the program. The hardware equivalent of a *join* instruction is an *or-gate* which may not be deleted in the realization. To the *degenerate join* corresponds a *degenerate fork* in the transpose synthesis. Observe however that in this case the absence of a *fork* instruction corresponds more to a syntactic simplification in the writing than to the absence of an instruction. For example in the program (71b) the input label A_3 appears in two instructions, i.e. :

$$(\bar{x}_3 \, A_3 \, , \, x_3 \, A_2) \, B_1$$
$$(\bar{x}_3 \, A_1 \, , \, x_3 \, A_3) \, B_2$$

and the *fork* instruction does not explicitly appear in the program. In counter-part, the corresponding hardware implementation of the *fork* is a *fanout* connection which is well a degenerate gate. This illustrates the fact that the factorization of matrix-instructions and of their transpose leads to two unambiguously defined hardware descriptions. The software description of the transpose instruction requires more care in its representation. Let us however note that the draw-back inherent to the degenerate *fork* instruction can be circumvented by writing explicitly all the instructions, including the degenerate instructions, in the programs before transposing them.

The explicit writing of degenerate instructions is e.g. obtained by using the factorization scheme (19). We give in (75a) a program equivalent to (71a) but where the degenerate instructions are explicitly written down. This program is deduced from the factorization scheme (19a) applied to each of the matrices of the product (23) ; this ultimate factorization is written down in (76). The transpose of (75a) is written in (75b); this program does no longer contain degenerate *fork* instructions. Another equivalent program may be deduced from the factorization scheme (19b). It is written down in (77a) ; observe that the factorization scheme (19a) replaces the degenerate *join* instructions by *transpose (if then else)* while the factorization scheme (19b) replaces these degenerate *join* instructions by *(or)-interpreted join* instructions.

(75a)

$$
\begin{aligned}
&\rightarrow \ N_1 \qquad \tau_1 \qquad D_1 \\
&\rightarrow \ N_2 \qquad \tau_2 \qquad D_2 \\[4pt]
&D_1 \ (\bar{x}_2 \, D_1'' \, , \ x_2 \, D_1') \\
&D_2 \ (\bar{x}_2 \, D_2' \, , \ x_2 \, D_2'') \\
&(D_2' \, \bar{x}_2 \, , \ D_1' \, x_2) \quad C_1 \\
&(D_1'' \, \bar{x}_2 \, , \ D_2'' \, x_2) \quad C_2 \\
&C_1 \ (\bar{x}_1 \, C_1' \, , \ x_1 \, B_3) \\
&C_2 \ (\bar{x}_1 \, B_2 \, , \ x_1 \, C_2') \\
&(C_1' \, \bar{x}_1 \, , \ C_2' \, x_1) \quad B_1 \\
&B_1 \ (\bar{x}_3 \, B_1' \, , \ x_3 \, B_1'') \\
&B_2 \ (\bar{x}_3 \, A_1 \, , \ x_3 \, B_2') \\
&B_3 \ (\bar{x}_3 \, B_3' \, , \ x_3 \, A_4) \\
&(B_1' \, \bar{x}_3 \, , \ B_2' \, x_3) \quad A_3 \\
&(B_3' \, \bar{x}_3 \, , \ B_1'' \, x_3) \quad A_2 \\[4pt]
&A_1 \quad \sigma_1 \quad M_1 \ \rightarrow \\
&A_2 \quad \sigma_2 \quad M_2 \ \rightarrow \\
&A_3 \quad \sigma_3 \quad M_3 \ \rightarrow \\
&A_4 \quad \sigma_4 \quad M_4 \ \rightarrow
\end{aligned}
$$

execution / decision / execution

(75b)

$$
\begin{aligned}
&D_1 \qquad \sigma_1 \qquad N_1 \ \rightarrow \\
&D_2 \qquad \sigma_2 \qquad N_2 \ \rightarrow \\[4pt]
&(\bar{x}_2 \, D_1'' \, , \ x_2 \, D_1') \quad D_1 \\
&(\bar{x}_2 \, D_2' \, , \ x_2 \, D_2'') \quad D_2 \\
&C_1 \ (D_2' \, \bar{x}_2 \, , \ D_1' \, x_2) \\
&C_2 \ (D_1'' \, \bar{x}_2 \, , \ D_2'' \, x_2) \\
&(\bar{x}_1 \, C_1' \, , \ x_1 \, B_3) \quad C_1 \\
&(\bar{x}_1 \, B_2 \, , \ x_1 \, C_2') \quad C_2 \\
&B_1 \ (C_1' \, \bar{x}_1 \, , \ C_2' \, x_1) \\
&(\bar{x}_3 \, B_1' \, , \ x_3 \, B_1'') \quad B_1 \\
&(\bar{x}_1 \, A_1 \, , \ x_3 \, B_2') \quad B_2 \\
&(\bar{x}_3 \, B_3 \, , \ x_3 \, A_4) \quad B_3 \\
&A_3 \ (B_1' \, \bar{x}_3 \, , \ B_2' \, x_3) \\
&A_2 \ (B_3' \, \bar{x}_3 \, , \ B_1'' \, x_3) \\[4pt]
&\rightarrow \ M_1 \qquad \tau_1 \qquad A_1 \\
&\rightarrow \ M_2 \qquad \tau_2 \qquad A_2 \\
&\rightarrow \ M_3 \qquad \tau_3 \qquad A_3 \\
&\rightarrow \ M_4 \qquad \tau_4 \qquad A_4
\end{aligned}
$$

$$
\begin{array}{c} D_1 \\ D_2 \end{array}
\begin{bmatrix} f_{11} & f_{12} & f_{13} & f_{14} \\ f_{21} & f_{22} & f_{23} & f_{24} \\ A_1 & A_2 & A_3 & A_4 \end{bmatrix}
=
\begin{array}{c} D_1 \\ D_2 \end{array}
\begin{bmatrix} x_2 & \bar{x}_2 \\ \bar{x}_2 & x_2 \\ C_1 & C_2 \end{bmatrix}
\begin{bmatrix} \bar{x}_1 & 0 & x_1 \\ x_1 & \bar{x}_1 & 0 \\ B_1 & B_2 & B_3 \end{bmatrix}
\begin{bmatrix} 0 & x_3 & \bar{x}_3 & 0 \\ \bar{x}_3 & 0 & x_3 & 0 \\ 0 & \bar{x}_3 & 0 & x_3 \\ A_1 & A_2 & A_3 & A_4 \end{bmatrix}
$$

$$
\begin{array}{c} D_1 \\ D_2 \end{array}
\begin{bmatrix} x_2 & \bar{x}_2 \\ \bar{x}_2 & x_2 \\ C_1 & C_2 \end{bmatrix}
=
\begin{array}{c} D_1 \\ D_2 \end{array}
\begin{bmatrix} x_2 & \bar{x}_2 & 0 & 0 \\ 0 & 0 & \bar{x}_2 & x_2 \\ D_1' & D_1'' & D_2' & D_2'' \end{bmatrix}
\begin{bmatrix} x_2 & 0 \\ 0 & \bar{x}_2 \\ \bar{x}_2 & 0 \\ 0 & x_1 \\ C_1 & C_2 \end{bmatrix}
$$

(76)

$$
\begin{array}{c} C_1 \\ C_2 \end{array}
\begin{bmatrix} \bar{x}_1 & 0 & x_1 \\ x_1 & \bar{x}_1 & 0 \\ B_1 & B_2 & B_3 \end{bmatrix}
=
\begin{array}{c} C_1 \\ C_2 \end{array}
\begin{bmatrix} \bar{x}_1 & 0 & 0 & x_1 \\ 0 & x_1 & \bar{x}_1 & 0 \\ C_1' & C_2' & B_2 & B_3 \end{bmatrix}
\begin{bmatrix} \bar{x}_1 & 0 & 0 \\ x_1 & 0 & 0 \\ 0 & 1 & 0 \\ 0 & 0 & 1 \\ B_1 & B_2 & B_3 \end{bmatrix}
$$

$$
\begin{array}{c} B_1 \\ B_2 \\ B_3 \end{array}
\begin{bmatrix} 0 & x_3 & \bar{x}_3 & 0 \\ \bar{x}_3 & 0 & x_3 & 0 \\ 0 & \bar{x}_3 & 0 & x_3 \\ A_1 & A_2 & A_2 & A_4 \end{bmatrix}
=
\begin{array}{c} B_1 \\ B_2 \\ B_3 \end{array}
\begin{bmatrix} \bar{x}_3 & x_3 & 0 & 0 & 0 & 0 \\ 0 & 0 & x_3 & 0 & \bar{x}_3 & 0 \\ 0 & 0 & 0 & \bar{x}_3 & 0 & x_3 \\ B_1' & B_1'' & B_2' & B_3' & A_1 & A_4 \end{bmatrix}
\begin{bmatrix} 0 & 0 & \bar{x}_3 & 0 \\ 0 & x_3 & 0 & 0 \\ 0 & 0 & x_3 & 0 \\ 0 & \bar{x}_3 & 0 & 0 \\ 1 & 0 & 0 & 0 \\ 1 & 0 & 0 & 1 \\ A_1 & A_2 & A_3 & A_4 \end{bmatrix}
$$

$$(77a) \qquad\qquad\qquad\qquad (77b)$$

(77a)		(77b)
$\rightarrow\ N_1 \quad \tau_1 \quad D_1$	execution	$D_1 \quad \sigma_1 \quad N_1\ \rightarrow$
$\rightarrow\ N_2 \quad \tau_2 \quad D_2$		$D_2 \quad \sigma_2 \quad N_2\ \rightarrow$
$D_1\ (\bar{x}_2\, D_1'' ,\ x_2\, D_1')$		$(\bar{x}_2\, D_1'' ,\ x_2\, D_1')\, D_1$
$D_2\ (\bar{x}_2\, D_2' ,\ x_2\, D_2'')$		$(\bar{x}_2\, D_2' ,\ x_2\, D_2'')\, D_2$
$(D_2' ,\ D_1')\quad C_1$		$C_1\quad (D_2' ,\ D_1')$
$(D_1'' ,\ D_2'')\quad C_2$		$C_2\quad (D_1'' ,\ D_2'')$
$C_1\ (\bar{x}_1\, C_1' ,\ x_1\, B_3)$		$(\bar{x}_1\, C_1' ,\ x_1\, B_3)\, C_1$
$C_2\ (\bar{x}_1\, B_2 ,\ x_1\, C_2')$	decision	$(\bar{x}_1\, B_2 ,\ x_1\, C_2')\, C_2$
$(C_1' ,\ C_2')\quad B_1$		$B_1\quad (C_1' ,\ C_2')$
$B_1\ (\bar{x}_3\, B_1' ,\ x_3\, B_1'')$		$(\bar{x}_3\, B_1' ,\ x_3\, B_1'')\, B_1$
$B_2\ (\bar{x}_3\, A_1 ,\ x_3\, B_2')$		$(\bar{x}_3\, A_1 ,\ x_3\, B_2')\, B_2$
$B_3\ (\bar{x}_3\, B_3' ,\ x_3\, A_4)$		$(\bar{x}_3\, B_3' ,\ x_3\, A_4)\, B_3$
$(B_1' ,\ B_2')\quad A_3$		$A_3\quad (B_1' ,\ B_2')$
$(B_3' ,\ B_1'')\quad A_2$		$A_2\quad (B_3' ,\ B_1'')$
$A_1 \quad \sigma_1 \quad M_1$		$\rightarrow\ M_1 \quad \tau_1 \quad A_1$
$A_2 \quad \sigma_2 \quad M_2$	execution	$\rightarrow\ M_2 \quad \tau_2 \quad A_2$
$A_3 \quad \sigma_3 \quad M_3$		$\rightarrow\ M_3 \quad \tau_3 \quad A_3$
$A_4 \quad \sigma_4 \quad M_4$		$\rightarrow\ M_4 \quad \tau_4 \quad A_4$

Chapter 5 : <u>The synthesis of (or)-interpreted matrix-instructions</u>

It is the non-disjoint character of the columns in (or)-interpreted
matrix-instructions which generate the parallelism in both the control automaton
and the operational automaton. We state in this chapter the additional computations
(with respect to those described in chapter 4) which are needed for the synthesis
of an (or)-interpreted matrix-instruction with non-disjoint columns.

In section 5.1 we state the general theory which achieves and generalizes
the corresponding theory developed in section 4.1. for matrix-instructions with
disjoint columns.

Partially indeterminate matrix-instructions occur in the description of
many practical problems : these instructions are defined in section 5.2. and their
synthesis by means of P-functions is treated in the same section.

An example of synthesis of an indeterminate matrix-instruction is considered in section 5.3. We treat a classical problem of choice of routes at a computer network node.

In section 5.4 we consider the hardware implementation of matrix-instructions and their software description ; section 5.4. is the continuation of section
4.4. which dealt with similar questions in the restricted scope of (or)-interpre-
ted matrix-instructions with disjoint columns.

5.1. <u>General theory</u>

We no longer assume that the matrix-instruction (31) has disjoint columns
; as in chapter 4, we shall assume that each row of the matrix covers the Boolean
cube, i.e.

$$\sum_j f_{ij} \equiv 1 \quad \forall i \ .$$

The following theorem is a straightforward generalization of the theorem of section
4.1.

Theorem.

Starting with the initial system of q P-functions :

$$\left. \begin{array}{c} \langle f_{11} \, , \ \cdots, \ f_{p1} \, ; \, \sigma_1 \rangle \\ \cdot \quad \cdot \quad \cdot \\ \langle f_{1q} \, , \ \cdots, \ f_{pq} \, ; \, \sigma_q \rangle \end{array} \right\} \qquad \text{Initial system} \qquad (78a)$$

*the iterative generation of P-functions by means of laws $(t_i)^p$, U^p (where $(t_i)^p$
and U^p means the p-th componentwise extension of the laws t_i and U respectively)
produces in at least one way the ultimate system of p P-functions :*

$$\left.\begin{array}{l} <1 \ , \ \dots \ , - \ ; \ \sum_i f_{1i} \ \sigma_i> \\[6pt] \qquad \dots \\[6pt] <- \ , \ \dots \ , \ 1 \ ; \ \sum_i f_{pi} \ \sigma_i> \end{array}\right\} \qquad \text{Ultimate system} \qquad (78b)$$

To the transformation (78a) → (78b) is associated a program made up of if then else instructions, fork instructions and join-or instructions which correspond to the laws t_i, U and the implicit law Im respectively.

Proof

The above theorem holds for matrix-instructions with disjoint columns : it then reduces to the theorem of section 4.1.

Since :

$$\sum_i f_{ik} \equiv 1 \quad \forall k$$

it is always possible by using only the laws t_j ($1 \leqslant j \leqslant n$) to obtain P-function having a 1 in its k-th domain component; this P-function is of the form :

$$<-, \ \dots \ , \ 1_k, \ \dots \ , \ - \ ; \ h_j \subseteq \sum_i f_{ik} \ \sigma_i> \qquad (79)$$

Indeed, the functions f_{ik} being non-disjoint, only a subdomain of these functions is needed to cover the Boolean n-cube so that the codomain function h_j is included in $\sum f_{ik} \ \sigma_i$, i.e. :

$$h_j = \sum_i g_{ik}^j \ \sigma_i \ , \ g_{ik}^j \subseteq f_{ik} \quad \forall i,j,k.$$

The functions f_{ik} covering the Boolean cube, there exists a set of P-functions of the form (79) whose union produces the expected codomain function, i.e. :

$$\underset{j}{U} <\dots, \ 1_k \ ,\dots; \ h_j> = <\dots \ 1_k \ \dots; \ \sum_i (\sum_j g_{ik}^j) \sigma_i>$$

$$= <\dots \ 1_k \ \dots; \ \sum_i f_{ik} \ \sigma_i>$$

The proof of the theorem finally results from the correspondence between the operations on the P-functions and the elementary instructions as reflected by figure 7.

□

     Let us give a somewhat more informal description of the theorems of sections 4.1 and 5.1 and of their proofs.

     The theorem of section 4.1. assumes that the matrix has disjoint columns so that the obtention of a "1" in the k-th domain component necessarily requests the fact that the complete domain satisfying the relation

$$f_{ik} = 1 \ , \qquad \forall i \tag{80}$$

has been used in the "t_ℓ" operations. As a consequence the domain-functions (of the P-functions) are sufficient for the synthesis of matrix instructions.

The theorem of section 5.1. no longer assumes that the matrix has disjoin columns so that only a subdomain of (80) has been used in the "t_ℓ" operations. This subdomain is characterized by :

$$g_{ik}^j = 1 \ , \quad g_{ik}^j \subseteq f_{ik} \tag{81}$$

As a consequence the domain-functions (of the P-functions) are no longer sufficient for the synthesis of. matrix-instructions : the obtention of a "1" in the k-th compo-nent of the domain does not guarantee that the complete matrix-instruction has been synthesized. It is however always possible to obtain a series of subdomains whose union covers the domain (80); we so obtain a series of codomain functions satisfying the relation :

$$\underset{j}{\vee} \ g_{ik}^j = f_{ik} \ , \quad \forall i$$

The union of the corresponding P-functions :

$$\underset{j}{U} \ <1; \ \underset{i}{\sum} g_{ik}^j \ \sigma_i> = <1; \ \underset{i}{\sum} f_{ik} \ \sigma_i>$$

provides us with a realization for the matrix-instruction. Observe that it is the introduction of this union law which involves the presence of fork instructions in the matrix realization. As a consequence of the above considerations the algorithms for synthesizing matrix-instructions with non disjoint columns will use in their computations both the domain and the codomain functions of the P-functions and not only the domain functions as for the matrix-instructions with disjoint predicates

5.2. Partially indeterminate instructions.

A matrix-instruction is *partially indeterminate* if the Boolean functions $f_{ij}(\underline{x})$ are indeterminate in a subdomain of the Boolean cube. Assume e.g. that the subdomain of $\underline{x}$ characterized by the equation :

$$f^*(\underline{x}) = 1 \tag{82}$$

can never be reached. In switching theory we say that the solutions of equation (82) characterize the *do-not-care domain* of $\underline{x}$.

The synthesis of a matrix instruction $[f_{ij}(\underline{x})]$ with indeterminate domain characterized by $f^*(\underline{x})=1$ is based on the following theorem.

Theorem

Starting with the initial system of q P-functions :

$$
\left.
\begin{array}{l}
\langle f_{11} \vee f^* , \ldots , f_{p1} \vee f^* ; \sigma_1 \rangle \\
\quad \cdot \quad \cdot \quad \cdot \\
\langle f_{1q} \vee f^* , \ldots , f_{pq} \vee f^* ; \sigma_q \rangle
\end{array}
\right\} \quad \text{Initial system} \qquad (83a)
$$

the iterative generation of P-functions by means of laws $(t_i)^p$, υ^p, produces in at least one way the ultimate system of p P-functions :

$$
\left.
\begin{array}{l}
\langle 1 \quad , \quad \ldots \quad , - ; \sum_i f^*_{1i} \, \sigma_i \rangle \\
\quad \cdot \quad \cdot \quad \cdot \\
\langle - \quad , \quad \ldots \quad , 1 ; \sum_i f^*_{pi} \, \sigma_i \rangle
\end{array}
\right\} \quad \text{Ultimate system} \qquad (83b)
$$

with : $\qquad f_{ij}(\underline{x}) \leqslant f^*_{ij}(\underline{x}) \leqslant f_{ij}(\underline{x}) \vee f^*(\underline{x}) \qquad \forall i,j$.

To the transformation (83a) → (83b) is associated a program made up of if then else instructions, fork instructions and join-or instructions. This program is equivalent to the matrix instruction $[f_{ij}(\underline{x})]$ with indeterminate domain characterized by $f^*(\underline{x}) = 1$.

Proof

The proof directly derives from the theorem of section 5.1 and from the fact that :

$$
\underset{j}{\vee} \; (f_{ij} \vee f^*) \equiv 1 \qquad \forall i
$$

and that $f^*_{ij}(\underline{x})$ reduces to $f_{ij}(\underline{x})$ in the allowed domain of the predicates $\underline{x}$.

□

5.3. Example 2 : A routing problem

We consider the problem of choice of routes at a network node. The packet switched message arriving at node N for a destination node D may be routed along n possible routes which connect that node N to its n adjacent nodes respectively. We shall adopt the routine doctrine whereby it is possible to use multiple routes between selected source and destination nodes. The purpose of this technique is to cater for greater flows that can be carried by single routes. To achieve this routing process each node where multiple routes are proposed must specify

for each destination the fraction of traffic that is to leave the node by a particular route.

Let d_i be the time delay for a message to be transmitted from node N to
node D via its adjacent node D_i. Assume first that two nodes, say node 1 and node 2
are connected to node N ; we shall define the opening variable $x_{(i,j)}$ of the route
i with respect to the route j as follows :

$$x_{(i,j)} = 1 \text{ if } d_i + d < d_j \quad \text{or if } F_i = 1$$

$$= 0 \text{ otherwise} \tag{84}$$

In this definition, d is a threshold parameter which affects the value of the opening variable $x_{(i,j)}$; $(d_i+d < d_j)$ is the adaptative part of the opening variable :
it is the network which evaluates the values d_i and d_j and which periodically adapts
these values when the traffic is changing. The binary parameter F_i is the non-adaptative or external part of $x_{(i,j)}$: a route must have the possibility of being opened even if the time delay of the messages to be transmitted along this route is
very high. The opening variable satisfies the relation :

$$x_{(i,j)} = (d_i + d < d_j) \vee F_i \tag{85}$$

We have thus also :

$$\bar{x}_{(i,j)} = \bar{F}_i \, (d_j \leqslant d_i + d) \tag{86}$$

We decide that the route i $(1 \leqslant i \leqslant 2)$ must be opened if the Boolean function f_i
is 1 :

$$\begin{aligned} f_i &= x_{(i,j)} \vee \bar{x}_{(j,i)} \\ &= F_i \vee (d_i+d < d_j) \vee \bar{F}_j(d_i \leqslant d_j+d) \end{aligned} \tag{87}$$

We verify that in the configuration where N is connected with two adjacent nodes
N_1 and N_2, the two routes leading to these nodes must simultaneously be opened if
$f_1 f_2 = 1$, i.e. if :

$$f_1 f_2 = x_{(1,2)} \, x_{(2,1)} \vee \bar{x}_{(1,2)} \, \bar{x}_{(2,1)} \tag{88}$$

A straightforward induction rule allows us to evaluate the functions
$\{f_1, f_2, \ldots, f_n\}$ which characterize the node N algorithm when the latter is connected to n neighbouring nodes numbered $\{1, 2, \ldots, n\}$ respectively. We shall study the
synthesis of a decision algorithm for a node N connected to three adjacent nodes
N_1, N_2 and N_3. The functions f_i $(1 \leqslant i \leqslant 3)$ are defined as follows :

$$f_1 = (x_{(1,2)} \vee \bar{x}_{(2,1)}) \, (x_{(1,3)} \vee \bar{x}_{(3,1)})$$

$$f_2 = (x_{(2,1)} \vee \bar{x}_{(1,2)}) \, (x_{(2,3)} \vee \bar{x}_{(3,2)})$$

$$f_3 = (x_{(3,2)} \vee \bar{x}_{(2,3)}) \, (x_{(2,1)} \vee \bar{x}_{(1,2)}) \vee$$

$$(x_{(3,1)} \vee \bar{x}_{(1,3)}) \, (x_{(1,2)} \vee \bar{x}_{(2,1)})$$

(89)

These functions are derived from (87) ; they may be intepreted informally as follows :

f_1 = 1 if (route 1 is better than route 2) and if (route 1 is better than route 3) ;

f_2 = 1 if (route 2 is better than route 1) and if (route 2 is better than route 3) ;

We have decided that route 3 must be opened for weaker delay constructs, i.e. ;

f_3 = 1 if [(route 3 is better than route 2) and if (route 2 is better than route 1)] or if [(route 3 is better than route 1) and if [route 1 is better than route 2]

The delay constraints on route 3 are weaker since :

$$(x_{(3,2)} \vee \bar{x}_{(2,3)})(x_{(2,1)} \vee \bar{x}_{(1,2)}) \vee (x_{(3,1)} \vee \bar{x}_{(1,3)})(x_{(1,2)} \vee \bar{x}_{(2,1)})$$

$$\geqslant \quad (x_{(3,1)} \vee \bar{x}_{(1,3)})(x_{(3,2)} \vee \bar{x}_{(2,3)})$$

(90)

The Boolean functions f_1, f_2, f_3 are represented in the Karnaugh map of Figure 14a

Figure 14a : Karnaugh map

If f_i is the order for opening the route i, the instruction for opening the routes at node N is :

$$N \begin{bmatrix} f_1 & f_2 & f_3 \\ \sigma_1 & \sigma_2 & \sigma_3 \\ M_1 & M_2 & M_3 \end{bmatrix} \tag{91}$$

The synthesis of this instruction by means of the P-function calculus is depicted in Figure 14b. The tabular method implicitly contained in the computation of Figure 14b is a straightforward generalization of the method of section 4.3. which is illustrated in Figure 11.

The sequence of P-functions as obtained in the table of Figure 14b is also depicted by the transformation (92) ; for sake of conciseness we have replaced in Figure 14b as well as in (92) the Boolean variables $x_{(i,j)}$ by the symbol "ij".

$$\left. \begin{aligned} A_1 &= \langle f_1 ; \sigma_1 \rangle \\ A_2 &= \langle f_2 ; \sigma_2 \rangle \\ A_3 &= \langle f_3 ; \sigma_3 \rangle \end{aligned} \right\} \tag{92a}$$

$$B_1 = A_3 \, t^r_{13} \, A_1 = \langle 12 \vee \overline{21} \vee 32 \vee \overline{23} ; 13 \, \sigma_1 + \overline{13} \, \sigma_3 \rangle$$

$$B_2 = A_1 \, t^r_{31} \, A_3 = \langle 12 \vee \overline{21} \vee 32 \vee \overline{23} ; \overline{31} \, \sigma_1 + 31 \, \sigma_3 \rangle$$

$$B_3 = A_3 \, t^r_{23} \, A_2 = \langle 21 \vee \overline{12} \vee 31 \vee \overline{13} ; 23 \, \sigma_2 + \overline{23} \, \sigma_3 \rangle$$

$$B_4 = A_2 \, t^r_{32} \, A_3 = \langle 21 \vee \overline{12} \vee 31 \vee \overline{13} ; \overline{32} \, \sigma_2 + 32 \, \sigma_3 \rangle$$

$$B_{12} = B_1 \cup B_2 = \langle 12 \vee \overline{21} \vee 32 \vee \overline{23} ; (13 \vee \overline{31})\sigma_1 + (\overline{13} \vee 31) \, \sigma_3 \rangle$$

$$B_{34} = B_3 \cup B_4 = \langle 21 \vee \overline{12} \vee 31 \vee \overline{13} ; (23 \vee \overline{32})\sigma_2 + (\overline{23} \vee 32) \, \sigma_3 \rangle$$

$$C_1 = B_{34} \, t^r_{12} \, B_{12} = \langle 1 ; 12(13 \vee \overline{31})\sigma_1 + \overline{12}(23 \vee \overline{32})\sigma_2 + \\ [12(\overline{13} \vee 31) + \overline{12} \, (\overline{23} \vee 32)]\sigma_3 \rangle$$

$$C_2 = B_{12} \, t^r_{21} \, B_{34} = \langle 1 ; \overline{21}(13 \vee \overline{31})\sigma_1 + 21(23 \vee \overline{32}) \, \sigma_2 + \\ [\overline{21}(\overline{13} \vee 31) + 21(\overline{23} \vee 32)]\sigma_3 \rangle$$

$$C_{12} = C_1 \cup C_2 = \langle 1 ; f_1\sigma_1 + f_2\sigma_2 + f_3\sigma_3 \rangle \tag{92b}$$

From the transformation between the system (92a) of P-functions and the P-function (92b) we deduce the matrix factorization (93) and the program of Figure 15.

	$\overline{12}$	12	$\overline{21}$	21	$\overline{13}$	13	$\overline{31}$	31	$\overline{23}$	23	$\overline{32}$	32	U
$A_1=<f_1;\sigma_1>$		$13\vee\overline{31}$	$13\vee31$										
$A_2=<f_2;\sigma_2>$	$23\vee\overline{32}$			$23\vee\overline{32}$		$12\vee\overline{21}$ B_1	$12\vee\overline{21}$ B_2			$21\vee\overline{12}$ B_3	$21\vee\overline{12}$ B_4		
$A_3=<f_3;\sigma_3>$	$\overline{23}\vee32$	$\overline{13}\vee31$	$13\vee31$		$12\vee\overline{21}$ B_1			$12\vee\overline{21}$ B_3	$21\vee\overline{12}$ B_3			$21\vee\overline{12}$ B_4	
$B_1=<12\overline{21};\ 13.\sigma_1+\overline{13}.\sigma_3>$													B_{12}
$B_2=<12\overline{21};\ \overline{31}.\sigma_1+31.\sigma_3>$													B_{12}
$B_3=<21\overline{12};\ 23.\sigma_2+\overline{23}.\sigma_3>$													B_{34}
$B_4=<21\overline{12};\ \overline{32}.\sigma_2+32.\sigma_3>$													B_{34}
$B_{12}=<12\overline{21};\ (13\vee\overline{31})\sigma_1+(\overline{13}\vee31)\sigma_3>$		1 c_1	1 c_1										
$B_{34}=<21\overline{12};\ (23\vee\overline{32})\sigma_2+(\overline{23}\vee32)\sigma_3>$	1 c_2			1 c_2									
$C_1=<1;\overline{12}.(23\vee\overline{32})\sigma_2+12.(13\vee31)\sigma_1+[12.(\overline{13}\vee31)\vee12(\overline{23}\vee32)]\sigma_3>$													N
$C_2=<1;21.(\overline{13}\vee31)\sigma_1+21(23\vee\overline{32})\sigma_2+[21(13\vee31)\vee21(\overline{23}\vee32)]\sigma_3>$													N

$N= <1;f_1\ \sigma_1+f_2\ \sigma_2+f_3\ \sigma_3>$

Figure 14 b: Tabular evaluation of P-functions

$$C_{12} \begin{bmatrix} f_1 & f_2 & f_3 \\ A_1 & A_2 & A_3 \end{bmatrix} = C_{12} \begin{bmatrix} 1 & 1 \\ C_1 & C_2 \end{bmatrix} \begin{bmatrix} 12 & \overline{12} \\ \overline{21} & 21 \\ B_{12} & B_{34} \end{bmatrix} \begin{bmatrix} 1 & 1 & 0 & 0 \\ 0 & 0 & 1 & 1 \\ B_1 & B_2 & B_3 & B_4 \end{bmatrix} \begin{bmatrix} 13 & 0 & \overline{13} \\ \overline{31} & 0 & 31 \\ 0 & 23 & \overline{23} \\ 0 & \overline{32} & 32 \\ A_2 & A_2 & A_3 \end{bmatrix}$$

$$(93)$$

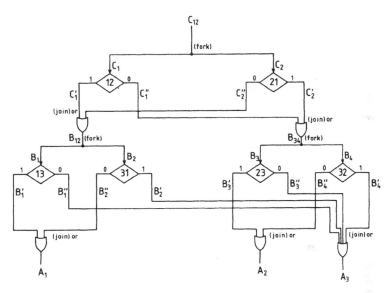

Figure 15 : <u>Implementation of the choice of routes</u>

Using the notation (67,68), the program of figure 15 is written :

$$
\begin{aligned}
&\rightarrow\ C_{12}\ (C_1,\ C_2) \\
&C_1\ \ (\overline{12}\ B_{34}\ ,\ 12\ B_{12}) \\
&C_2\ \ (\overline{21}\ B_{12}\ ,\ 21\ B_{34}) \\
&B_{12}\ (B_1,\ B_2) \\
&B_{34}\ (B_3,\ B_4) \qquad\qquad\qquad\qquad B_4\ (\overline{32}\ A_2,\ 32\ A_3) \\
&B_1\ \ (\overline{13}\ A_3\ ,\ 13\ A_1) \qquad\qquad A_1\ \ \sigma_1\ \ M_1\ \rightarrow \\
&B_2\ \ (\overline{31}\ A_1\ ,\ 31\ A_3) \qquad\qquad A_2\ \ \sigma_2\ \ M_2\ \rightarrow \\
&B_3\ \ (\overline{23}\ A_3\ ,\ 23\ A_2) \qquad\qquad A_3\ \ \sigma_3\ \ M_3\ \rightarrow
\end{aligned}
$$

$$(94)$$

We have deduced the transformation (92a)⟶(92b) and the factorization (93) from the computations of figure 14b; the *join* instructions are implicitly contained in the factorization (93) and in its software description (94). The *join* instructions explicitly appear in the program if the matrices of (93) are ultimately factorized according to the scheme (19b). To the factorization of the matrices of (93) :

$$
\begin{array}{c} C_1 \\ \\ B_{12} \ \ B_{34} \end{array}
\begin{bmatrix} 12 & \overline{12} \\ \overline{21} & 21 \end{bmatrix}
=
\begin{array}{c} C_1 \\ C_2 \\ C_1' \ \ C_1'' \ \ C_2' \ \ C_2'' \end{array}
\begin{bmatrix} 12 & \overline{12} & 0 & 0 \\ 0 & 0 & \overline{21} & 21 \end{bmatrix}
\begin{bmatrix} 1 & 0 \\ 0 & 1 \\ 1 & 0 \\ 0 & 1 \end{bmatrix}
\begin{array}{c} \\ \\ \\ B_{12} \ \ B_{34} \end{array}
$$

$$
\begin{array}{c} B_1 \\ B_2 \\ B_3 \\ B_4 \\ A_1 \ \ A_2 \ \ A_3 \end{array}
\begin{bmatrix} 13 & 0 & \overline{13} \\ \overline{31} & 0 & 31 \\ 0 & 23 & \overline{23} \\ 0 & \overline{32} & 32 \end{bmatrix}
=
\begin{array}{c} B_1 \\ B_2 \\ B_3 \\ B_4 \\ B_1' \ B_1'' \ B_2' \ B_2'' \ B_3' \ B_3'' \ B_4' \ B_4'' \end{array}
\begin{bmatrix} 13 & \overline{13} & 0 & 0 & 0 & 0 & 0 & 0 \\ 0 & 0 & 31 & \overline{31} & 0 & 0 & 0 & 0 \\ 0 & 0 & 0 & 0 & 23 & \overline{23} & 0 & 0 \\ 0 & 0 & 0 & 0 & 0 & 0 & 32 & \overline{32} \end{bmatrix}
\begin{bmatrix} 1 & 0 & 0 \\ 0 & 0 & 1 \\ 0 & 0 & 1 \\ 1 & 0 & 0 \\ 0 & 1 & 0 \\ 0 & 0 & 1 \\ 0 & 0 & 1 \\ 0 & 1 & 0 \end{bmatrix}
\begin{array}{c} \\ \\ \\ \\ \\ \\ \\ A_1 \ \ A_2 \ \ A_3 \end{array}
$$

corresponds the program (95) where the *join* instructions explicitly appear. These *join* instructions have also been indicated in the flowchart of figure 15. Remember that the program of figure 15 must be considered in the frame of an hardware description language. It may not be considered as a software realization ; the additional properties that must satisfy an hardware description language in order to become a safe program are studied in chapter 10.

$$
\begin{aligned}
&\rightarrow \ C_{12} \ (C_1, C_2) \\
&C_1 \ (\overline{12} \ \ C_1'' \ , \ 12 \ C_1') \\
&C_2 \ (\overline{21} \ \ C_2'' \ , \ 21 \ C_2') \\
&(C_1' \ , \ C_2'') \ B_{12} \\
&(C_2' \ , \ C_1'') \ B_{34}
\end{aligned}
$$

$$B_{12} (B_1 , B_2)$$

$$B_{34} (B_3 , B_4)$$

$$B_1 (\overline{13} \ B_1'' , 13 \ B_1')$$ (95)

$$B_2 (\overline{31} \ B_2'' , 31 \ B_2')$$

$$B_3 (\overline{23} \ B_3'' , 23 \ B_3')$$

$$B_4 (\overline{32} \ B_4'' , 32 \ B_4')$$

$$(B_1' , B_2'') \ A_1$$

$$(B_3' , B_4'') \ A_2$$

$$(B_1'' , B_2' , B_3'' , B_4') \ A_3$$

$$A_1 \quad \sigma_1 \quad M_1 \quad \rightarrow$$

$$A_2 \quad \sigma_2 \quad M_2 \quad \rightarrow$$

$$A_3 \quad \sigma_3 \quad M_3 \quad \rightarrow$$

To the programs (94) and (95) correspond transpose programs which are obtained by reading (94) and (95) from bottom to top and by reading each instruction from right to left.

The program (95), also described by the flowchart of figure 15 is optimal with respect to the number of *if then else* instructions : since each of the predicates $x_{(i,j)}$ of the problem appears in only one decision instruction, the number of these instructions is necessarily minimum.

It is also interesting to study the routing problem when the non-adaptative parts F_i of $x_{(i,j)}$ are all equal to zero. We then verify that due to the physical constraints of the problem the domains of the functions f_i have a large number of do-not-care conditions. Clearly $(d_2+d < d_1)$ and $(d_1+d < d)$ cannot occur simultaneously. This is reflected by the fact that the entries of the Boolean cube which are solutions of the equation :

$$x_{(1,2)} x_{(2,1)} = 1$$

contain do-not-care values. We verify that the domains of the Boolean cube where do-not-care conditions appear are characterized by the solutions of the following equations :

$$x_{(1,2)} \ x_{(2,1)} = 1$$

$$x_{(1,3)} \ x_{(3,1)} = 1$$

$$x_{(2,3)} \ x_{(3,2)} = 1$$

$$x_{(1,2)} \, x_{(2,3)} \, x_{(3,1)} = 1$$

$$x_{(1,3)} \, x_{(3,2)} \, x_{(2,1)} = 1$$

$$x_{(1,2)} \, x_{(2,3)} \, \bar{x}_{(1,3)} = 1$$

$$x_{(1,3)} \, x_{(3,2)} \, \bar{x}_{(1,2)} = 1$$

$$x_{(2,1)} \, x_{(1,3)} \, \bar{x}_{(2,3)} = 1$$

$$x_{(2,3)} \, x_{(3,1)} \, \bar{x}_{(2,1)} = 1$$

$$x_{(3,1)} \, x_{(1,2)} \, \bar{x}_{(3,2)} = 1$$

$$x_{(3,2)} \, x_{(2,1)} \, \bar{x}_{(3,1)} = 1$$

$$x_{(1,3)} \, \bar{x}_{(1,2)} \, \bar{x}_{(2,1)} \, \bar{x}_{(3,2)} \, \bar{x}_{(2,3)} = 1$$

$$x_{(3,1)} \, \bar{x}_{(1,2)} \, \bar{x}_{(2,1)} \, \bar{x}_{(3,2)} \, \bar{x}_{(2,3)} = 1$$

$$x_{(1,2)} \, \bar{x}_{(1,3)} \, \bar{x}_{(3,1)} \, \bar{x}_{(2,3)} \, \bar{x}_{(3,2)} = 1$$

$$x_{(2,1)} \, \bar{x}_{(1,3)} \, \bar{x}_{(3,1)} \, \bar{x}_{(2,3)} \, \bar{x}_{(3,2)} = 1$$

$$x_{(2,3)} \, \bar{x}_{(1,2)} \, \bar{x}_{(2,1)} \, \bar{x}_{(3,1)} \, \bar{x}_{(2,3)} = 1$$

$$x_{(3,2)} \, \bar{x}_{(1,2)} \, \bar{x}_{(2,1)} \, \bar{x}_{(3,1)} \, \bar{x}_{(1,3)} = 1$$

Let f^{*} the disjunction of the above cube-functions. The do-not-care conditions trans
form the Karnaugh map of Figure 14a into that of Figure 16a.

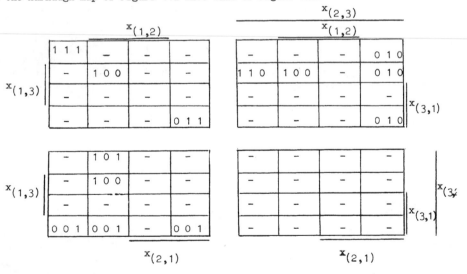

Figure 16a : Karnaugh map

The instruction (91) is replaced by the following one :

$$N \quad [(f_1 \vee f^*) \quad (f_2 \vee f^*) \quad (f_3 \vee f^*)]$$
$$\sigma_1 \qquad \sigma_2 \qquad \sigma_3$$
$$M_1 \qquad M_2 \qquad M_3$$

whose treatment by means of P-functions is depicted in Figure 16b. We verify that we obtain again the optimal solution that has already been obtained for the instruction (91). This result might be expected since the optimal solution of instruction (91) involved the occurrence of 6 decision instructions associated to the 6 predicates of the problem respectively. Moreover the do-not-care conditions do not allow us to drop any of these predicates ; otherwise stated the functions with do-not-care effectively depend on the 6 predicates.

5.4. The particularities of the implementation of matrix-instructions with non disjoint columns

We have seen in section 4.4. that the main characteristic of (or)-interpreted matrix-instructions was that there exists for any combination of the predicates x_i, one and only one *activated path* between any input label and any output label. As a consequence the column-instructions might be dropped in the program : we said that the columns-instruction were *degenerate*.

For matrix-instructions with non disjoint columns several activated paths may exist between an input label and any of the output labels. These information paths may present reconvergence in the course of the program so that the column-instructions which reduce to *join-or* instructions may no longer be dropped. Examples of *join-or* instructions corresponding to column-instructions are indicated in the program (95) and in its corresponding flowchart of figure 15.

The occurrence of the law U in the theorem of section 5.1. together with the non-degenerescence of the column-instructions make that the table of figure 12 which gives the correspondence between the implementation of the matrix instruction and the laws acting on P-functions must be replaced by the table of figure 17.

Laws	matrix-instruction		transpose matrix-instruction	
	elementary instructions	logical gates	elementary instructions	logical gates
t_i	if then else	demultiplexer	then if	multiplexer
Im	join-or	or-gate	fork	fanout
U	fork	fanout	join-or	or-gate

Figure 17 : Software and hardware primitives for the realization of an (or)-interpreted matrix-instruction and of its transpose.

	1̄2̄	12	2̄1̄	21	1̄3̄	13	3̄1̄	31	2̄3̄	23
						$B_1:\dfrac{12\vee\overline{21}}{32\vee\overline{23}}$	$\dfrac{12\vee\overline{21}}{32\vee\overline{23}}:B_2$	$B_2:\dfrac{12\vee\overline{21}}{32\vee23}$	$\dfrac{21\vee\overline{12}}{31\vee\overline{13}}:B_3$	$B_3:\dfrac{21\vee12\vee}{31\vee\overline{13}}$
					$B_1:\dfrac{12\vee\overline{21}}{32\vee\overline{23}}$					

$A_1 = \langle (12\vee\overline{21})(13\vee\overline{31}\vee23\vee\overline{32}) \vee (13\vee\overline{31})(\overline{32}\vee23); \sigma_1 \rangle$

$A_2 = \langle (21\vee\overline{12})(23\vee\overline{32}\vee13\vee\overline{31}) \vee (23\vee\overline{32})(31\vee\overline{13}); \sigma_2 \rangle$

$A_3 = \langle (31\vee\overline{13})(12\vee\overline{21}\vee32\vee23) \vee (32\vee\overline{23})(21\vee\overline{12}); \sigma_3 \rangle$

$B_1 = \langle 12\vee\overline{21}\vee32\vee\overline{23};\ 13\ \sigma_1 + \overline{13}\ \sigma_3 \rangle$
$B_2 = \langle 12\vee\overline{21}\vee32\vee\overline{23};\ \overline{31}\ \sigma_1 + 31\ \sigma_3 \rangle$
$B_3 = \langle 21\vee\overline{12}\vee31\vee13;\ 23\ \sigma_2 + \overline{23}\ \sigma_3 \rangle$
$B_4 = \langle 21\vee\overline{12}\vee31\vee\overline{13};\ \overline{32}\ \sigma_2 + 32\ \sigma_3 \rangle$

$B_{12} = B_1\, U B_2$

$B_{34} = B_3\, U B_4$

$B_{12} = \langle 12\vee\overline{21}\vee32\vee\overline{23};\ (13\vee\overline{31})\sigma_1 + (13\vee31)\sigma_3 \rangle$

$B_{34} = \langle 21\vee\overline{12}\vee31\vee1\overline{13};\ (23\vee\overline{32})\sigma_2 + (\overline{23}\vee32)\sigma_3 \rangle$

$C_1 = \langle 1;\ 12(13\vee\overline{31})\sigma_1 + \overline{12}(23\vee32)\sigma_2 + [12(13\vee31)\vee12(23\vee32)]\sigma_3 \rangle$

$C_2 = \langle 1;\ \overline{21}(13\vee\overline{31})\sigma_1 + 21(23\vee\overline{32})\sigma_2 + [\overline{21}(13\vee31)\vee21(\overline{23}\vee32)]\sigma_3 \rangle$

$C_{12} = \langle 1;\ (12\vee\overline{21})(13\vee\overline{31})\sigma_1 + (\overline{12}\vee21)(23\vee\overline{32})\sigma_2 + [((12\vee\overline{21})(13\vee31)\vee(\overline{12}\vee21)(\overline{23}\vee32)]\ \sigma_3 \rangle$

Figure 16b : Tabular evaluation of P-functions

79

	$\overline{32}$	32
$A_1 = \langle(12\text{v}\overline{21})(13\overline{31}\text{v}23\text{v}\overline{32})\text{ v }(13\text{v}\overline{31})(32\text{v}\overline{23}); \sigma_1\rangle$		
$A_2 = \langle(21\text{v}\overline{12})(23\overline{32}\text{v}13\text{v}\overline{31})\text{ v }(23\text{v}\overline{32})(31\text{v}\overline{13}); \sigma_2\rangle$	$21\text{v}\overline{12}\text{v}\\31\text{v}\overline{13}$:B$_4$	
$A_3 = \langle(31\text{v}\overline{13})(12\text{v}\overline{21}\text{v}32\text{v}\overline{23})\text{ v }(32\text{v}\overline{23})(21\text{v}\overline{12}); \sigma_3\rangle$		B$_4$: $21\text{v}\overline{12}\text{v}\\31\text{v}\overline{13}$
$B_1 = \langle12\text{v}21\text{v}32\text{v}\overline{23};\ 13\ \sigma_1+\overline{13}\ \sigma_3\rangle$		
$B_2 = \langle12\text{v}\overline{21}\text{v}32\text{v}\overline{23};\ \overline{31}\ \sigma_1+31\ \sigma_3\rangle$		
$B_3 = \langle21\text{v}\overline{12}\text{v}31\text{v}\overline{13};\ 23\ \sigma_2+\overline{23}\ \sigma_3\rangle$		
$B_4 = \langle21\text{v}\overline{12}\text{v}31\text{v}\overline{13};\ \overline{32}\ \sigma_2+32\ \sigma_3\rangle$		
$B_{12} = \langle12\text{v}\overline{21}\text{v}32\text{v}\overline{23};\ (13\text{v}\overline{31})\sigma_1+(\overline{13}\text{v}31)\sigma_3\rangle$		
$B_{34} = \langle21\text{v}\overline{12}\text{v}31\text{v}\overline{13};\ (23\text{v}\overline{32})\sigma_2+(\overline{23}\text{v}32)\sigma_3\rangle$		

Figure 16b : (Continued)

We verify that the propositions 2,3 and 4 of section 4.4. hold true for the matrix-instructions with non-disjoint columns.

The algorithm of section 4.3. for generating optimal syntheses of matrix instruction must be modified in the following way.

- At each step of the algorithm check for the presence of P-functions having identical domains, i.e. P-functions of the form :

$$\langle g;h_1 \rangle \ , \ \langle g;h_2 \rangle \ , \ \dots \ , \ \langle g;h_n \rangle$$

- Use the composition law U in order to replace these P-functions by the P-function $\langle g;h \rangle$ defined as follows :

$$\langle g;h \rangle = \bigcup_i \langle g;h_i \rangle$$
$$= \langle g; \sum_i h_i \rangle$$

The optimality criterions remain the same as in section 4.3. A new degree of freedom however appears in the algorithm : the *allowed degree of parallelism*. In a sequentially organized control automaton the degree of parallelism is 1: a single path is activated for the flow of information between each instruction input and output. In the example considered in section 5.3. the degree of parallelism is maximal : all the operations that can be performed in a parallel way are activated simultaneously. The parallelism is reflected by the non-disjoint character of the Boolean functions f_{ij} of the matrix instruction $\left[f_{ij} \right]$ and for a fixed i.

The degree 1 of parallelism and the maximal parallelism constitute two extremal cases : any intermediate degree of parallelism may be reached by choosing the initial P-functions in an appropriate way.

In summary an algorithm for deriving optimal programs may be stated as follows :

- The initial system of P-functions states the allowed degree of parallelism in the control part ;

- A straightforward extension (due to the introduction of the law U) of the tabular method of section 4.3 allows us to derive optimal programs.

The table of figure 16b illustrates the tabular method applied to example of section 5.3.

Chapter 6 : The synthesis of (and)-interpreted matrix-instructions

        The (and)-interpreted matrix-instruction is used in the description and the synthesis of algorithms according to the Karp and Miller model. It is the transformation of the Glushkov synchronous model into the asynchronous parallel program schema which requests the introduction of this new type of instruction ; (and)-interpreted matrix-instructions can be considered as the extra-instructions which play the role of the synchronizing clock signal.

        In section 6.1 we state how the synthesis methods which were developed in sections 5.1 and 5.2 for the synthesis of (or)-interpreted matrix-instructions may be adapted for the synthesis of (and)-interpreted matrix-instructions.

        A dual interpretation of the P-functions is represented in section 6.2. This dual interpretation allows a direct synthesis of (and)-interpreted instructions without resorting to the theory developed for (or)-interpreted instructions in chapters 4 and 5.

        An example is treated in section 6.3. It is the continuation of the routing problem that has been considered in section 5.3.

        In section 6.4. we consider the hardware implementation of (and)-interpreted matrix-instructions. Section 6.4. is the continuation of sections 4.4. and 5.4. which dealt with similar questions for (or)-interpreted matrix-instructions.

6.1. General theory

        The instruction that will be considered as the starting point for the generation of (and)-interpreted matrix-instructions is :

$$
\begin{array}{cc}
\begin{matrix} N_1 \\ \vdots \\ N_p \end{matrix} &
\begin{matrix} \tau_1 \\ \vdots \\ \tau_p \end{matrix} &
\left[\begin{matrix} f_1 \\ \vdots \\ f_p \end{matrix} \right] \\
& & \sigma \\
& & M
\end{array}
\tag{96}
$$

This instruction is (and)-interpreted, i.e. the command σ is performed and the next address M is reached as soon as *all* the signals τ_i corresponding to the functions f_i equal to 1 have been received.

        The matrix-instruction (97) :

$$
\begin{array}{ccc}
\begin{matrix} N_1 \\ \vdots \\ N_p \end{matrix} & \begin{matrix} \tau_1 \\ \vdots \\ \tau_p \end{matrix} & \begin{bmatrix} f_{11} & \cdots & f_{1q} \\ \vdots & & \vdots \\ f_{p1} & \cdots & f_{pq} \end{bmatrix} \\
& & \begin{matrix} \sigma_1 & \cdots & \sigma_q \end{matrix} \\
& & \begin{matrix} M_1 & \cdots & M_q \end{matrix}
\end{array}
\tag{97}
$$

may be considered as a series of q column-instructions having the same input labels N_j and termination signals τ_j.

Theorem

Starting with the initial system of q P-functions :

$$
\left.\begin{array}{c}
< f_{11} , \, \cdots , \, f_{p1} ; \sigma_1 > \\[2ex]
< f_{1q} , \, \cdots , \, f_{pq} ; \sigma_q >
\end{array}\right\} \text{Initial system} \tag{98a}
$$

the iterative generation of P-functions by means of the laws $(t_i)^p$, U^p *produces in at least one way the ultimate system of p P-functions*

$$
\left.\begin{array}{c}
< 1 \quad , \, \cdots , \, - \; ; \sum_i f_{1i} \, \sigma_i > \\[2ex]
< - \quad , \, \cdots , \, 1 \; ; \sum_i f_{pi} \, \sigma_i >
\end{array}\right\} \text{Ultimate system} \tag{98b}
$$

To the transformation system (98a) → *system (98b) is associated a realization of the (and)-interpreted matrix-instruction (97) made-up of transpose (if then else), join-and and fork instructions which correspond to the laws* t_i, *U and Im respectively.*

Proof.

The (or)-interpreted matrix-instruction (97) may be considered as realizing the p row-instructions that we write in the following symbolic form :

$$
N_j = \tau_j \left(\sum_i f_{ji} \, \sigma_i \right) \quad , \quad 1 \leqslant j \leqslant p \tag{99}
$$

The (and)-interpreted matrix-instruction (97) may be considered as realizing the q column-instructions that we write in the following symbolic form :

$$
M_i = \prod_j (\bar{f}_{ji} + \tau_j) + \sigma_i \quad , \quad 1 \leqslant i \leqslant q \tag{100}
$$

The instructions (99) were realized by factorizing the matrix $[f_{ij}]$ as a product of elementary matrices : in the matrix products the additive law is the disjunction while the multiplicative law is the conjunction. The transposed complemented matrix of Boolean functions $[\bar{f}_{ji}]$ is obtained from the factorization of $[f_{ji}]$ by :

1. Transposing the product of matrices ;
2. Replacing each matrix element by its complement ;
3. Using the conjunction as matrix additive law and the disjunction as matrix multiplicative law.

As a consequence a realization of (100) is obtained from a realization of (99) by :

1. Using a transpose interpretation of the laws
   (e.g. *if then else* → *transpose (if then else)* , *fork* → *join, join* → *fork*) ;
2. Complementing the condition variables x_i in the decision instructions ;
3. Changing the (or)-interpretation of the laws into an (and)-interpretation.

□

An important consequence of this theorem is that the theorem of section 5.1. may be used for the synthesis of (or)-interpreted as well as (and)-interpreted matrix-instructions. We have only to use a dual interpretation for the laws t_i, U and Im.

Theorem 5.1 was used for proving theorem 6.1.; a direct proof of theorem 6.1. requests the introduction of a new type of P-function. These P-functions and the corresponding proof of theorem 6.1 are shortly introduced in section 6.2. This section does not present new results and may eventually be dropped.

6.2. A dual system of P-functions

Consider the column-instruction :

$$
\begin{array}{cc}
N_1 & \tau_1 \\
\vdots & \vdots \\
N_p & \tau_p
\end{array}
\left[
\begin{array}{c}
f_1 \\
\vdots \\
f_p
\end{array}
\right]
$$
$$
\begin{array}{c}
\sigma \\
M
\end{array}
$$

that we factorize into the following matrix product in order to render obvious the separation between execution and decision instructions :

$$
\begin{array}{c}
N_1 \\
\vdots \\
N_p
\end{array}
\left[
\begin{array}{ccc}
\tau_1 & & 0 \\
& \ddots & \\
0 & & \tau_p
\end{array}
\right]
\left[
\begin{array}{c}
f_1 \\
\vdots \\
f_p
\end{array}
\right]
\left[
\begin{array}{c}
\sigma \\
M
\end{array}
\right]
\qquad (101)
$$
$$
N'_1 \cdots N'_p \qquad M'
$$

Since our main problem is the transformation of a high-level decision instruction into low-level decision instructions we shall consider the synthesis of the central decision matrix of (101), i.e. :

$$
\begin{array}{c}
N'_1 \\
\vdots \\
N'_p
\end{array}
\left[
\begin{array}{c}
f_1 \\
\vdots \\
f_p
\end{array}
\right]
\qquad (102)
$$
$$M'$$

In view of (26), to the realization of instruction (102) is associated the following transformation between P-functions :

(103a)   (103b)

$$
\left.
\begin{array}{l}
N'_1 \; : \; \langle \lambda \tau_1 \; ; \; \bar{f}_1 + \sigma \rangle \\
N'_2 \; : \; \langle \lambda \tau_2 \; ; \; \bar{f}_2 + \sigma \rangle \\
\vdots \\
N'_p \; : \; \langle \lambda \tau_p \; ; \; \bar{f}_p + \sigma \rangle
\end{array}
\right\}
\xrightarrow{T}
\langle \lambda \pi_i \, (\tau_i + \bar{f}_i) \; ; \; t\sigma \rangle : M'
$$

Consider further the (and)-interpreted matrix-instruction

$$
\begin{array}{cc}
N_1 & \tau_1 \\
\vdots & \vdots \\
N_p & \tau_p
\end{array}
\left[
\begin{array}{ccc}
f_{11} & \cdots & f_{1q} \\
\vdots & & \vdots \\
f_{p1} & \cdots & f_{pq}
\end{array}
\right]
$$
$$
\begin{array}{ccc}
\sigma_1 & \cdots & \sigma_q \\
M_1 & \cdots & M_q
\end{array}
$$

that we factorize into the following matrix product in order to render obvious the
separation between execution and decision instructions :

$$
\begin{array}{c}
N_1 \\
\vdots \\
N_p
\end{array}
\left[
\begin{array}{ccc}
\tau_1 & & 0 \\
& \ddots & \\
0 & & \tau_p
\end{array}
\right]
\left[
\begin{array}{ccc}
f_{11} & \cdots & f_{1q} \\
\vdots & & \vdots \\
f_{p1} & \cdots & f_{pq}
\end{array}
\right]
\left[
\begin{array}{ccc}
\sigma_1 & & 0 \\
& \ddots & \\
0 & & \sigma_q
\end{array}
\right]
\qquad (103)
$$
$$
\begin{array}{ccccccc}
N'_1 & \cdots & N'_p & M'_1 & \cdots & M'_q & M_1 \cdots M_q
\end{array}
$$

In view of (26), to the realization of the central decision matrix of (103) :

$$
\begin{array}{c}
N'_1 \\
\vdots \\
N'_p
\end{array}
\left[
\begin{array}{ccc}
f_{11} & \cdots & f_{1q} \\
\vdots & & \vdots \\
f_{p1} & \cdots & f_{pq}
\end{array}
\right] .
\qquad (104)
$$
$$
\begin{array}{ccc}
M'_1 & \cdots & M'_q
\end{array}
$$

is associated the transformation (105) between P-functions :

$$
\left.
\begin{aligned}
N_1' &: \langle \lambda \tau_1 \; ; \; \prod_i (\bar{f}_{1i} + \sigma_i) \rangle \\[4pt]
N_2' &: \langle \lambda \tau_2 \; ; \; \prod_i (\bar{f}_{2i} + \sigma_i) \rangle \\[4pt]
& \quad \cdot \; \cdot \; \cdot \\[4pt]
N_p' &: \langle \lambda \tau_p \; ; \; \prod_i (\bar{f}_{pi} + \sigma_i) \rangle
\end{aligned}
\right\}
\xrightarrow{\;T\;}
\left\{
\begin{aligned}
& \langle \lambda \prod_j (\tau_j + \bar{f}_{j1}) \; ; \; t \; \sigma_1 \rangle : M_1' \\[4pt]
& \langle \lambda \prod_j (\tau_j + \bar{f}_{j2}) \; ; \; t \; \sigma_2 \rangle : M_2' \\[4pt]
& \qquad\qquad \cdot \; \cdot \; \cdot \\[4pt]
& \langle \lambda \prod_j (\tau_j + \bar{f}_{jq}) \; ; \; t \; \sigma_q \rangle : M_q'
\end{aligned}
\right.
\tag{105}
$$

The above transformation (105) is to be compared with the dual transformation (33c) → (33b) that has been introduced in section 3.2.

The synthesis of instruction (104) is obtained by transforming the system (105a) of P-functions into the system (105b) of P-functions, using the laws $\perp_i$, ∩ and $(\text{Im})_d$ that are defined as follows :

$$
\langle g_1 ; h_1 \rangle \perp_i \langle g_2 ; h_2 \rangle = \langle (x_i + g_1)(\bar{x}_i + g_2); \; (x_i + h_1)(\bar{x}_i + h_2) \rangle
\tag{106}
$$

$$
\langle g_1 ; h \rangle \cap \langle g_2 ; h \rangle = \langle g_1 \, g_2 \; ; \; h \rangle
$$
$$
\langle g ; h_1 \rangle \cap \langle g ; h_2 \rangle = \langle g \; ; \; h_1 \, h_2 \rangle
\tag{107}
$$

The law $(\text{Im})_d$ is an implicit law which corresponds to a multiple use of the same P-function.

The laws $\perp_i$, ∩ and $(\text{Im})_d$ are dual laws with respect to the laws t_i, U and Im that were defined by means of the equalities (36), (38,40) and (43) respectively. From (43) we deduce :

$$
(\text{Im})_d \; \langle g \; ; \; h \rangle = \langle g \; ; \; h \rangle \cap \langle g \; ; \; h \rangle
\tag{108}
$$

In the synthesis of (and)-interpreted matrix-instructions, the laws $\perp_i$, ∩ and $(\text{Im})_d$ correspond to *transpose (if then else)*, to *join-and* and to *fork* instructions respectively.

In order to be consistent with a pseudo-Boolean formalism, the transformation between (105a) and (105b) is written in the form (110); the j-th column of the right part of the P-functions corresponds to a "maxterm" in the σ_i's, i.e. :

$$
\sigma_j = 0 \quad , \quad \sigma_k = 1 \quad \forall k \neq j \; .
$$

This allows us to replace the transformation T in (105) by the p-th power of the transformation laws T that are used for the synthesis of the row-instructions and of the column-instructions.

Transformation (109)

$$N_1 : \langle \lambda\, t;\ \tau_1 + \prod_i (\bar{f}_{1i} + \sigma_i) \rangle \quad \xrightarrow{\ t\tau_1\ } \quad N_1' : \langle \tau_1;\ \prod_i (\bar{f}_{1i} + \sigma_i) \rangle \quad \xrightarrow{\ T\ } \quad M_1' : \langle \bigwedge_j \prod_j (\tau_j + \bar{f}_{j1});\ t\sigma_1 \rangle \quad \xrightarrow{\ t\sigma_1\ } \quad M_1 : \langle \prod_j (\tau_j + \bar{f}_{j1}) + \sigma_1;\ \lambda t \rangle$$

$$N_2 : \langle \lambda\, t;\ \tau_2 + \prod_i (\bar{f}_{2i} + \sigma_i) \rangle \quad \xrightarrow{\ t\tau_2\ } \quad N_2' : \langle \tau_2;\ \prod_i (\bar{f}_{2i} + \sigma_i) \rangle \qquad M_2' : \langle \bigwedge_j \prod_j (\tau_j + \bar{f}_{j2});\ t\sigma_2 \rangle \quad \xrightarrow{\ t\sigma_2\ } \quad M_2 : \langle \prod_j (\tau_j + \bar{f}_{j2}) + \sigma_2;\ \lambda t \rangle$$

$$\vdots$$

$$N_p : \langle \lambda\, t;\ \tau_p + \prod_i (\bar{f}_{pi} + \sigma_i) \rangle \quad \xrightarrow{\ t\tau_p\ } \quad N_p' : \langle \tau_p;\ \prod_i (\bar{f}_{pi} + \sigma_i) \rangle \qquad M_q' : \langle \bigwedge_j \prod_j (\tau_j + \bar{f}_{jq});\ t\sigma_q \rangle \quad \xrightarrow{\ t\sigma_q\ } \quad M_q : \langle \prod_j (\tau_j + \bar{f}_{jq}) + \sigma_q;\ \lambda t \rangle$$

Transformation (110)

	σ_1	σ_2	$\dots$	σ_q				σ_1	σ_2	$\dots$	σ_q	
$N_1' : \langle \tau_1;$	$\bar{f}_{11},$	$\bar{f}_{12},$	$\dots$	$\bar{f}_{1q} \rangle$		$\xrightarrow{\ T = (\mathbb{T})^q\ }$	$M_1' : \langle \bigwedge_j \prod_j (\tau_j + \bar{f}_{j1});$	$0,$	$1,$	$\dots$	$1 \rangle$	$:: M_1'$
$N_2' : \langle \tau_2;$	$\bar{f}_{21},$	$\bar{f}_{22},$	$\dots$	$\bar{f}_{2q} \rangle$			$M_2' : \langle \bigwedge_j \prod_j (\tau_j + \bar{f}_{j2});$	$1,$	$0,$	$\dots$	$1 \rangle$	$:: M_2'$
$\vdots$							$\vdots$					
$N_p' : \langle \tau_p;$	$\bar{f}_{p1},$	$\bar{f}_{p2},$	$\dots$	$\bar{f}_{pq} \rangle$			$M_q' : \langle \bigwedge_j \prod_j (\tau_j + \bar{f}_{jq});$	$1,$	$1,$	$\dots$	$0 \rangle$	$:: M_q'$

The transformations (109) and (110) should be compared with the transformations (33) and (34) of section 3.2 respectively. More generally the formalism of the present section should be compared with the formalism of section 3.2: a duality relation exists between these two formalisms.

6.3. Example 2 (continued)

Again we consider the problem of choice of routes at a (computer) network node. At a message reception and if the network is ready to send ($\tau=1$) we test the values of the Boolean functions (88) : f_1, f_2, f_3, which are associated to the 3 routes connected to the node respectively. According to the values of the delays associated to the routes, the i-th route will be opened (the order σ_i is transmitted) if $f_i=1$ or closed if $f_i=0$. Several routes may be opened ($f_i f_j=1$) and the message is then divided according these routes (multiple-routes hypothesis). At the end of the message sending process along route i (end of process characterized by $\tau_i=1$) the node is ready to send a message again. The program described by the above algorithm is :

$$
N \qquad \tau \quad \begin{bmatrix} f_1 & f_2 & f_3 \\ \sigma_1 & \sigma_2 & \sigma_3 \\ M_1 & M_2 & M_3 \end{bmatrix} \qquad (111a)
$$

$$
\begin{matrix} M_1 & \tau_1 \\ M_2 & \tau_2 \\ M_3 & \tau_3 \end{matrix} \begin{bmatrix} f_1 \\ f_2 \\ f_3 \end{bmatrix} \qquad (111b)
$$
$$
\sigma
$$
$$
N'
$$

The instruction (111a) corresponds to instruction (90) which has already been synthesized in section 5.3 (see the program (95) and the corresponding flowchart of figure 16).The instruction (111b) is an (and)-interpreted column-instruction. It derives from instruction (111a) by a transposition operation. According to the theorem of section 6.1 the program which realizes (111b) in terms of *transpose (if then else)*, *fork* and *join-and* instructions is simply obtained by reading the programs (95) (or the flowchart of figure 15) from bottom to top, each instruction being read from right to left.

A realization of the instruction (111a) has been proposed in figure 15. From this realization we deduce the hardware realization of the program (111a, 111b) : it is depicted in figure 18 (The rectangles in figure 18 are counters or

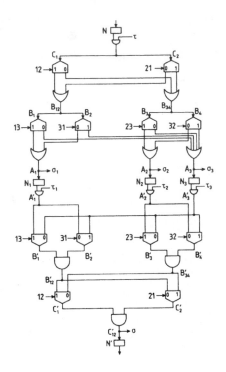

<u>Figure 18</u>. Hardware implementation of the routing program

RS flip-flops the use of which is indicated in chapter 9).

We terminate this example by illustrating the use of the transpose system of P-functions which has been introduced in section 6.2.

The synthesis of the instruction (111b) has been obtained by using the system (112) :

$$A_1 = \langle f_1 \; ; \; \sigma_1 \rangle$$
$$A_2 = \langle f_2 \; ; \; \sigma_2 \rangle \tag{112}$$
$$A_3 = \langle f_3 \; ; \; \sigma_3 \rangle$$

as initial system of P-functions and the laws t_i and U. The functions (89) allow us to write the system (112) in terms of the elementary predicates of the problem, i.e.

$$A_1 = \langle f_1 = (12 v \overline{21}) \, (13 v \overline{31}) \; ; \; \sigma_1 \rangle$$
$$A_2 = \langle f_2 = (21 v \overline{12}) \, (23 v \overline{32}) \; ; \; \sigma_2 \rangle \tag{113}$$
$$A_3 = \langle g_3 = (12 v \overline{21}) \, (\overline{13} v 31) v (21 v \overline{12}) \, (\overline{23} v 32) \; ; \; \sigma_3 \rangle$$

We shall now obtain the synthesis of instruction (111b) by using the system

$$A_1 = \langle \bar{f}_1 \; ; \; \tau_1 \rangle$$
$$A_2 = \langle \bar{f}_2 \; ; \; \tau_2 \rangle \qquad\qquad (114)$$
$$A_3 = \langle \bar{g}_3 \; ; \; \tau_3 \rangle$$

as initial system of P-functions and the laws $\bot_i$ and $\cap$.

$A_1 = \langle \overline{12.21 \vee 13}.31 \; ; \; \tau_1 \rangle$

$A_2 = \langle \overline{21.12 \vee 23}.32 \; ; \; \tau_2 \rangle \qquad\qquad (115a$

$A_3 = \langle (\overline{12.21 \vee 13.\overline{31}})(\overline{21.12 \vee 23.\overline{32}}) \; ; \; \tau_3 \rangle$

$B_1 = A_3 \bot_{13} A_1 = \langle \overline{12.21.23.\overline{32}} \; ; \; (\overline{13} + \tau_1)(13 + \tau_3) \rangle$

$B_2 = A_1 \bot_{31} A_3 = \langle \overline{12.21.23.\overline{32}} \; ; \; (31 + \tau_1)(\overline{31} + \tau_3) \rangle$

$B_3 = A_3 \bot_{23} A_2 = \langle 12.\overline{21}.13.\overline{31} \; ; \; (\overline{23} + \tau_2)(23 + \tau_3) \rangle$

$B_4 = A_2 \bot_{32} A_3 = \langle 12.\overline{21}.13.\overline{31} \; ; \; (32 + \tau_2)(\overline{32} + \tau_3) \rangle$

$B_{12} = B_1 \cap B_2 = \langle \overline{12.21.23.\overline{32}} \; ; \; (\overline{13}.31 + \tau_1)(\overline{31}.13 + \tau_3) \rangle$

$B_{34} = B_3 \cap B_4 = \langle 12.\overline{21}.13.\overline{31} \; ; \; (\overline{23}.32 + \tau_2)(23.\overline{32} + \tau_3) \rangle$

$C_1 = B_{34} \bot_{12} B_{12} = \langle 0 \; ; \; (12 + (\overline{23}.32 + \tau_2)(23.\overline{32} + \tau_3))(\overline{12} + (\overline{13}.31 + \tau_1)$
$\qquad\qquad (13.\overline{31} + \tau_3)) \rangle$

$C_2 = B_{12} \bot_{21} B_{34} = \langle 0 \; ; \; (\overline{21} + (\overline{23}.32 + \tau_2)(23.\overline{32} + \tau_3))(21 + (\overline{13}.31 + \tau_1)$
$\qquad\qquad (13.\overline{31} + \tau_3)) \rangle$

$C_{12} = C_1 \cap C_2 = \langle 0 \; ; \; (\bar{f}_1 + \tau_1)(\bar{f}_2 + \tau_2)(\bar{g}_3 + \tau_3) \rangle \qquad\qquad (115b$

6.4. Implementations of (and)-interpreted matrix-instructions and of their transpose.

The *complement* of a matrix of Boolean functions is a Boolean matrix where each of the Boolean functions have been replaced by their complement, i.e.

$$\overline{\begin{bmatrix} f_{11} & \cdots & f_{1q} \\ \vdots & & \\ f_{p1} & \cdots & f_{pq} \end{bmatrix}} = \begin{bmatrix} \bar{f}_{11} & \cdots & \bar{f}_{1q} \\ \vdots & & \\ \bar{f}_{p1} & \cdots & \bar{f}_{pq} \end{bmatrix} \qquad\qquad (116)$$

If a factorization of a Boolean matrix is formed by a product of matrices with the disjunction "∨" as additive law and the conjunction "∧" as multiplicative law,then we call *dual factorization* a factorization formed by a product of matrices with the conjunction "∧" as additive law and the disjunction "∨" as multiplicative law.

The proof of the theorem 6.1. was grounded on the following property of Boolean matrices :

Proposition 1.

A factorization for a Boolean matrix is also a dual factorization for its complement.

From proposition 1 we deduce the following proposition for the realization of an (and)-interpreted matrix-instruction.

Proposition 2. Duality principle

The realization of and (and)-interpreted matrix-instruction is deduced from the realization of an (or)-interpreted matrix-instruction by giving a dual interpretation to each instruction in a software model or by giving a dual interpretation to each gate in a hardware realization, the connection remaining unchanged.

Clearly the change of interpretation transforms the or-gate into an and-gate. The change of interpretation of a multiplexer is obtained by interchanging the disjunction and the conjunction and by changing the polarity of the control variable x in the relation (74), i.e. :

$$or\text{-}multiplexer \quad : \quad z = \bar{x}\, y_1 \vee x\, y_2 \tag{117a}$$

$$and\text{-}multiplexer \quad : \quad z = (x \vee y_1)(\bar{x} \vee y_2) = \bar{x}\, y_1 \vee x\, y_2 \tag{117b}$$

We see that an and-multiplexer is nothing but an or-multiplexer : it does not constitute a different gate concept. We say that the *or-multiplexer concept* coincides with the *and-multiplexer concept* : it will simply be called *multiplexer* as before.

The change of interpretation of a demultiplexer is obtained by interchanging the disjunction and the conjunction and by changing the polarity of the control variable x in the relation (73) , i.e. :

$$or\text{-}demultiplexer \quad : \quad z_1 = \bar{x}\, y \quad , \; z_2 = xy \tag{118a}$$

$$and\text{-}demultiplexer \quad : \quad z_1 = x \vee y \quad , \; z_2 = \bar{x} \vee y$$

The *(or)-demultiplexer* and the *(and)-demultiplexer* are two different concepts and should be distinguished when necessary.

We verify that the propositions 2,3 and 4 of section 4.4. hold true for (and)-interpreted matrix-instructions. We have only to replace the (or)-inter-

preted logical gates in these propositions by (and)-interpreted elementary instructions and by (and)-interpreted logical gates respectively.

The correspondence between the laws on P-functions, the elementary
instructions and the logical gates as depicted by the table of figure 17 remains
also true providing the (or)-interpretations on instructions and gates are replaced by (and)-interpretations on instructions and gates.

The *programmable availability* of the rows and columns in a p×q matrix
of Boolean functions which appears in proposition 4 of section 4.4. must also be
interpreted in a dual way. Proposition 4 states that the rows of decision matrix :

$$
\begin{matrix}
N_1 \\
\vdots \\
N_p
\end{matrix}
\begin{bmatrix}
f_{11} & \cdots & f_{1q} \\
\vdots & & \vdots \\
f_{p1} & \cdots & f_{pq}
\end{bmatrix}
$$
$$
\quad M_1 \quad \cdots \quad M_q
$$

are available in a programmable way. This means in the present case that to the
input vector :

$$(N_1, \ldots, N_i, \ldots, N_p) = (1, \ldots, 0_i, \ldots, 1)$$

corresponds the output vector :

$$(M_1, \ldots, M_j, \ldots, M_q) = (\bar{f}_{i1}, \ldots, \bar{f}_{ij}, \ldots, \bar{f}_{iq}) .$$

Chapter 7. <u>A summary and the conclusions of part I</u>

        The purpose of this chapter is to present in a synoptic way the main results of chapters 4,5 and 6. The synthesis scheme that has been proposed in these chapters for realizing any type of matrix-instruction is subsumed in section 7.1. We present also in this section a global formulation of the transposition principle and of the duality principle.

        An example which illustrates the synthesis of any possible interpretation for a matrix-instruction is given in section 7.2.

        A short conclusion for part I is written down in section 7.3.

7.1. <u>A synthesis procedure for the realization of matrix instructions</u>

        The synthesis scheme that has been proposed in chapters 4,5 and 6 for realizing any type of matrix instruction may be summarized as follows :

- The theorem 4.1. provides us with a synthesis method for realizing *(or)-interpreted matrix-instructions with disjoint columns* by means of *if then else* and *join* instructions (which are both (or)-interpreted).

- The theorem 5.1., which derives from the theorem 4.1. by the introduction of a law U, provides us with a synthesis method for realizing *(or)-interpreted matrix-instructions* by means of *if then else* , *join* (which are both (or)-interpreted) and *fork* instructions ;

- The theorem 5.1. and the transposition principle of section 4.4. provide us with a synthesis method for realizing the *transpose of (or)-interpreted matrix-instructions* in terms of *then if* (which is the transpose of the *if then else*), *fork* and *join* instructions.

- The theorem 5.1., the transposition principle of section 4.4. and the duality principle of section 6.4. provide us with a synthesis method for realizing *(and)-interpreted matrix-instructions* by means of *if then else, join* (which are both (and)-interpreted) and *fork* instructions and for realizing the *transpose of (and) interpreted matrix-instructions* in terms of *then if, fork* and *join* instructions.

This synthesis scheme is depicted in Figure 19.

        It will be seen in part II of this text (Chapter 9) that the realization of algorithms according to the synchronous Glushkov model of computation involves the materialization of *(or)-interpreted-matrix-instructions*. The realization of algorithms according to the asynchronous Karp and Miller model of computation requests that to the materialization of each (or)-interpreted matrix-instruction will be associated the materialization of the *transpose (and)-interpreted matrix-instruc-*

tion. In view of figure 19 these two materializations are obtained from the use of theorem 5.1. and of the duality and the transpose principles.

A hardware interpretation of the synthesis procedure and of the duality and transpose principles may be stated in the following form. *If a synthesis of a (p×q) matrix of Boolean functions* $[f_{ij}]$ *is obtained as an interconnection of or-demultiplexers, or-gates and fanout connections, then :*

- *a dual synthesis of a (p×q) matrix of Boolean functions* $[\bar{f}_{ij}]$ *is obtained by replacing the or-demultiplexers and the or-gates by and-demultiplexers and and-gates respectively.*

- *a transpose synthesis of a (q×p) matrix of Boolean functions* $[f_{ij}]$ *is obtained by replacing the or-demultiplexers by multiplexers and by interchanging the fan-out connections and the or-gates;*

- *a transpose-dual synthesis of (q×p) matrix of Boolean functions* $[f_{ij}]$ *is obtained by replacing the or-demultiplexers by multiplexers, the or-gates by fanout connections and the fanout-connections by and-gates.*

If the initial synthesis and its dual evaluate simultaneously all the Boolean functions of any row of the (p×q) matrices $[f_{ij}]$ *and* $[\bar{f}_{ij}]$ *, the different rows being available in a programmable way, then the dual syntheses evaluate simultaneously all the Boolean functions of any column of the matrices* $[f_{ij}]$ *and* $[\bar{f}_{ij}]$ *, the different columns being available in a programmable way.*

This hardware interpretation of the synthesis procedure is illustrated in figure 20 ; examples illustrating the various network configurations of figure 20 are given in section 7.2.

Laws	(or)-interpreted matrix-instruction Synthesis : theorem 4.1		Transpose (or)-interpreted matrix-instruction Synthesis : theorem 4.1 + transposition	
	Elementary instruction	Logical gate	Elementary instruction	Logical gate
t_i	if then else (or)	or-demultiplexer	then if	multiplexer
Im	join-or	or-gate	fork	fanout
U	fork	fanout	join-or	or-gate

Laws	(and)-interpreted matrix-instruction Synthesis : theorem 4.1 + duality		Transpose (and)-interpreted matrix-instruction Synthesis : theorem 4.1 + transposition+duality	
	Elementary instruction	Logical gate	Elementary instruction	Logical gate
t_i	if then else (and)	and-demultiplexer	then if	multiplexer
Im	join-and	and-gate	fork	fanout
U	fork	fanout	join-and	and-gate

disjoint columns

dualization

transposition

Figure 19. The synthesis of matrix-instructions : duality and transposition principles

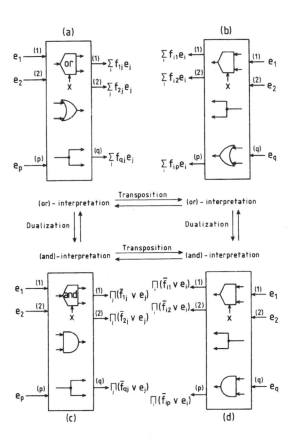

Figure 20 : Hardware implementation of
matrix instructions

7.2. Example 2 (continued)

In order to illustrate the P-function technique for the synthesis of
any type of matrix-instruction, we somewhat generalize the data of example 2.

Observe that the instructions (111a, 111b) are a particular case
of the problem of transmitting messages having a priority k ($1 \leqslant k \leqslant p$) through
a node connected to q adjacent nodes ; this problem is formulated by the program
(119) made-up of two matrix instructions :

$$
\begin{array}{cc}
N_1 & \tau_1 \\
\vdots & \vdots \\
N_p & \tau_p \\
\end{array}
\left|
\begin{array}{ccc}
f_{11} & \cdots & f_{1q} \\
\vdots & & \vdots \\
f_{p1} & \cdots & f_{pq} \\
\sigma_1 & \cdots & \sigma_q \\
M_1 & \cdots & M_q \\
\end{array}
\right|
\tag{119a}
$$

$$
\begin{array}{cc}
M_1 & \tau'_1 \\
\vdots & \vdots \\
M_q & \tau'_1
\end{array}
\begin{bmatrix}
f_{11} & \cdots & f_{p1} \\
\vdots & & \vdots \\
f_{1q} & \cdots & f_{pq}
\end{bmatrix}
\qquad (119b)
$$

$$
\begin{array}{ccc}
\sigma'_1 & \cdots & \sigma'_p \\
N'_1 & \cdots & N'_p
\end{array}
$$

Assume that the packet switched message arriving at node N may be routed along four routes ; moreover the message has the choice between two priorities. The routing algorithm to be synthesized is described by the program (120). The interpretation of the predicates and commands is summarized below :

- τ_i is the signal which indicates that the node is ready to handle a message with priority i, $1 \leqslant i \leqslant 2$; we assume that $\tau_1 \, \tau_2 = \phi$ so that the matrix (120a) is (or)-interpreted.

- σ_j is the command which executes the opening of the route j ; $1 \leqslant j \leqslant 4$.

- τ'_j is the signal which indicates that the message sending along route j is terminated.

- σ'_i is the command for accepting a message with priority i entering at node N ; the matrix (120b) is (and)-interpreted.

$$
\begin{array}{cc}
N_1 & \tau_1 \\
N_2 & \tau_2
\end{array}
\begin{bmatrix}
f_{11} & f_{12} & f_{13} & f_{14} \\
f_{21} & f_{22} & f_{23} & f_{24}
\end{bmatrix}
\qquad (120a)
$$

$$
\begin{array}{cccc}
\sigma_1 & \sigma_2 & \sigma_3 & \sigma_4 \\
M_1 & M_2 & M_3 & M_4
\end{array}
$$

$$
\begin{array}{cc}
M_1 & \tau'_1 \\
M_2 & \tau'_2 \\
M_3 & \tau'_3 \\
M_4 & \tau'_4
\end{array}
\begin{bmatrix}
f_{11} & f_{21} \\
f_{12} & f_{22} \\
f_{13} & f_{23} \\
f_{14} & f_{24}
\end{bmatrix}
\qquad (120b)
$$

$$
\begin{array}{cc}
\sigma'_1 & \sigma'_2 \\
N'_1 & N'_2
\end{array}
$$

The synthesis problem reduces to the realization of the (or)-interpreted matrix-instruction $[f_{ij}]$ and of its (and)-interpreted transpose $[f_{ji}]$.

The values of the functions f_{ij}, $1 \leqslant i \leqslant 2$, $1 \leqslant j \leqslant 4$ are deduced from the previous treatment of the routing problem in section 6.3. We assume that a message with priority 1 may never be sent through route 4 and that a message with priority 2 may never be sent through route 1 ; this allows us to write the expressions of the Boolean functions f_{ij} :

$$f_{11} = (x_{(1,2)} \vee \bar{x}_{(2,1)})(x_{(1,3)} \vee \bar{x}_{(3,1)})$$

$$f_{12} = (\bar{x}_{(1,2)} \vee x_{(2,1)})(x_{(2,3)} \vee \bar{x}_{(3,2)})$$

$$f_{13} = (\bar{x}_{(1,2)} \vee x_{(2,1)})(\bar{x}_{(2,3)} \vee x_{(3,2)}) \vee (x_{(1,2)} \vee \bar{x}_{(2,1)})(\bar{x}_{(1,3)} \vee x_{(3,1)})$$

$$f_{14} = 0 \tag{121}$$

$$f_{21} = 0$$

$$f_{22} = (\bar{x}_{(4,2)} \vee x_{(2,4)})(x_{(2,3)} \vee \bar{x}_{(3,2)})$$

$$f_{23} = (\bar{x}_{(4,2)} \vee x_{(2,4)})(\bar{x}_{(2,3)} \vee x_{(3,2)}) \vee (x_{(4,2)} \vee \bar{x}_{(2,4)})(\bar{x}_{(4,3)} \vee x_{(3,4)})$$

$$f_{24} = (x_{(4,2)} \vee \bar{x}_{(2,4)})(x_{(4,3)} \vee \bar{x}_{(3,4)})$$

The transformation between the systems of P-functions is written below ; for sake of conciseness, we have written "ij" for "$x_{(i,j)}$",

$$A_1 = \langle f_{11}, f_{21} ; \sigma_1 \rangle$$

$$A_2 = \langle f_{12}, f_{22} ; \sigma_2 \rangle$$

$$A_3 = \langle f_{13}, f_{23} ; \sigma_3 \rangle \tag{122a}$$

$$A_4 = \langle f_{14}, f_{24} ; \sigma_4 \rangle$$

$$B_1 = A_3 \, t^r_{13} \, A_1 = \langle 12 \vee \overline{21}, - ; 13 \, \sigma_1 + \overline{13} \, \sigma_3 \rangle$$

$$B_2 = A_1 \, t^r_{31} \, A_3 = \langle 12 \vee \overline{21}, - ; \overline{31} \, \sigma_1 + 31 \, \sigma_3 \rangle$$

$$B_3 = A_3 \, t^r_{23} \, A_2 = \langle \overline{12} \vee 21, \overline{42} \vee 24 ; \overline{23} \, \sigma_3 + 23 \, \sigma_2 \rangle$$

$$B_4 = A_2 \, t^r_{32} \, A_3 = \langle \overline{12} \vee 21, \overline{42} \vee 24 ; \overline{32} \, \sigma_2 + 32 \, \sigma_3 \rangle$$

$$B_5 = A_4 \, t^r_{34} \, A_3 = \langle - , 42 \vee \overline{24} ; \overline{34} \, \sigma_4 + 34 \, \sigma_3 \rangle$$

$$B_6 = A_3 \, t^r_{43} \, A_4 = \langle - , 42 \vee \overline{24} ; \overline{43} \, \sigma_3 + 43 \, \sigma_4 \rangle$$

$$B_{12} = B_1 \cup B_2 = \langle 12 \vee \overline{21}, - ; (13 \vee \overline{31}) \, \sigma_1 + (\overline{13} \vee 31) \, \sigma_3 \rangle$$

$$B_{34} = B_3 \cup B_4 = \langle \overline{12} \vee 21, \overline{42} \vee 24 ; (\overline{23} \vee 32) \, \sigma_3 + (\overline{32} \vee 23) \, \sigma_2 \rangle$$

$$B_{56} = B_5 \cup B_6 = \langle - , 42 \vee \overline{24} ; (\overline{43} \vee 34) \, \sigma_3 + (\overline{34} \vee 43) \, \sigma_4 \rangle$$

$$C_1 = B_{34} \, t^r_{12} \, B_{12} = \langle 1, - ; 12(13 \vee \overline{31})\sigma_1 + \overline{12}(\overline{32} \vee 23)\sigma_2 + [12(\overline{13} \vee 31) \vee \overline{12}(\overline{23} \vee 32)] \, \sigma_3 \rangle$$

$$C_2 = B_{12} \, t^r_{21} \, B_{34} = \langle 1, - ; \overline{21}(13 \vee \overline{31})\sigma_1 + 21(\overline{32} \vee 23)\sigma_2 + [\overline{21}(\overline{13} \vee 31) \vee 21(\overline{23} \vee 32)] \, \sigma_3 \rangle$$

$$C_3 = B_{56} \, t^r_{24} \, B_{34} = \langle -, 1 ; 24(\overline{32} \vee 23)\sigma_2 + \overline{24}(\overline{34} \vee 43)\sigma_4 + [24(\overline{23} \vee 32) \vee \overline{24}(\overline{43} \vee 34)] \, \sigma_3 \rangle$$

$$C_4 = B_{34} \ t_{42}^r \ B_{56} = <-, \ 1 \ ; \ \overline{42}(\overline{32}\text{v}23) \ \sigma_2 + 42(\overline{34}\text{v}43) \ \sigma_4 + [\overline{42}(32\text{v}\overline{23})\text{v}42(\overline{43}\text{v}34)] \ \sigma_3>$$

$$C_{12} = C_1 \text{U} C_2 = <1, \ - \ ; \ f_{11} \ \sigma_1 + f_{12} \ \sigma_2 + f_{13} \ \sigma_3 + f_{14} \ \sigma_4>$$

$$C_{34} = C_3 \text{U} C_4 = <-, \ 1 \ ; \ f_{21} \ \sigma_1 + f_{22} \ \sigma_2 + f_{23} \ \sigma_3 + f_{24} \ \sigma_4>$$

$$(122b)$$

A realization of the (or)-interpreted matrix-instruction $[f_{ij}]$ based on the transformation from system (122a) to system (122b) is depicted in figure 21. The realization of the (and)-interpreted matrix-instruction $[f_{ji}]$ may be deduced from figure 21. In view of the synthesis procedure of section 7.1. we have to replace *demultiplexers* by *multiplexers*, fanout connections by and-gates, and or-gates by fanout connections respectively. It could evidently also be possible to use the theorem of section 6.2. with the laws $\perp_i$ and $\cap$.

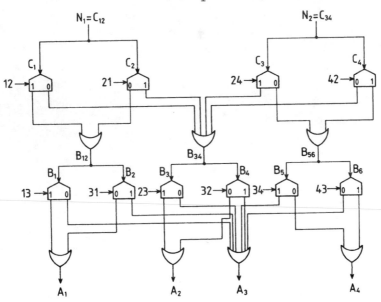

Figure 21 Implementation of the choice of routes with two possible priorities

The realization of figure 21 provides us with the materialization of the matrix of Boolean functions (120a) in terms of demultiplexers-(or), or-gates and fan-out connections. This realization corresponds to the general implementation scheme of figure 20a. From figure 21 we could deduce realizations for transpose instructions, dual instructions and transpose-dual instructions according to the implementation schemes of figures 20b, 20c and 20d respectively.

7.3. Conclusions of part I

The purpose of part I of this text was the introduction of a formalism and of a computation method for implementing algorithms in synchronous as well as in asynchronous structures.

We have shown that well known instructions such as *if then else, fork, join, while do* might be represented as *row-matrices* or as *column matrices*. We defined an *(or)-interpreted matrix instruction* which encompassed and generalized the above instructions. This instruction provided us with a compact tool for describing algorithms and for synthesizing them in a synchronous structure : the *Glushkov model of computation*. We showed that the synthesis of a program be means of elementary instructions reduced to the *factorization* of a matrix as a product of elementary matrices.

While *(or)-interpreted matrix-instructions* were able to represent and to implement an algorithm in a synchronous structure, we needed a supplementary instruction namely the *(and)-interpreted matrix-instruction* to represent and to implement an algorithm in an asynchronous structure : the *parallel program schema* (or *Karp and Miller model of computation*).

We have associated to the matrix formalism a computation method for deriving optimal implementations of algorithms in synchronously as well as in asynchronously organized structures. This computation method was based on the concept of *P-function*. The algebra associated to the P-function concept allowed us to build in a mathematical way optimal implementations for algorithms.

Part II : Implementation of algorithms

Chapter 8 : <u>Representation of instructions by means of parallel flowcharts or of
Petri nets</u>.

        Parallel flowcharts and *Petri nets* are well known tools for the ana-
lysis and synthesis of algorithms. A short introduction to parallel flowcharts is
given in section 8.1 ; in particular we show how parallel flowcharts may be *interpreted* for describing instructions and programs. The representation of low-level
and of high-level instructions by means of parallel flowcharts is given in section
8.2. The fundamental step in the development of computation and decision procedures
regarding parallel flowcharts is the introduction of a *vector addition* system which
encodes the parallel flowchart. We introduce the vector addition system in section
8.3. and we show how the dynamic description of the parallel flowchart, i.e. the
description of how the initiations and the terminations of its operations evolve
during a period of time, is described by the reachability set of the vector addition system. A comparison between the fields of application of parallel flowcharts
and of the P-function technique is made in section 8.4. We show that the parallel
flowchart and its associated vector addition system is a powerful tool for describing the *connection between instructions* while the algebra of P-functions is mainly a synthesis tool for implementing high-level instructions in terms of low-level
instructions. Parallel flowcharts and P-functions are thus design tools whose respective domains of application are complementary.

8.1. <u>Representation of instructions and of algorithms</u>

        Over the last decade the *Petri net* , which is equivalent (Peterson
and Bredt [1974]) to the *parallel flowchart* defined in section 1.5, has gained increased usage and acceptance as a basic model of systems of asynchronous concurrent computation. Petri nets are issued from the thesis of Petri [1962] ; they
have considerably been developed by numerous researchers (Holt and Commonor [1970],
Hack [1975], Moalla [1976] , Moalla, Pulou and Sifakis [1978] , Ramchandani [1973]
Sifakis [1977a, 1977b, 1978] , Gosh [1977]); review papers and books have also been
devoted to Petri net theory (Peterson [1977, 1982]).

        The parallel flowchart is issued from the work of Karp and Miller
[1969] and Keller [1973] . It seems that at present time the formalism of Petri nets
is more widely used than the formalism of parallel flowchart. However, since the
parallel graph schema was one of our starting points for the description of algorithms and since the parallel flowchart is issued from the parallel graph schema
we shall, mainly for a reason of coherence, adopt in this text the notations and
the formalism of the parallel flowchart. Note that this choice is of little impor-

tance at our level : parallel flowcharts will only be used for some illustrative purposes in our text. A comparison of the notations and conventions for parallel flowcharts and Petri nets is given in Figure 22.

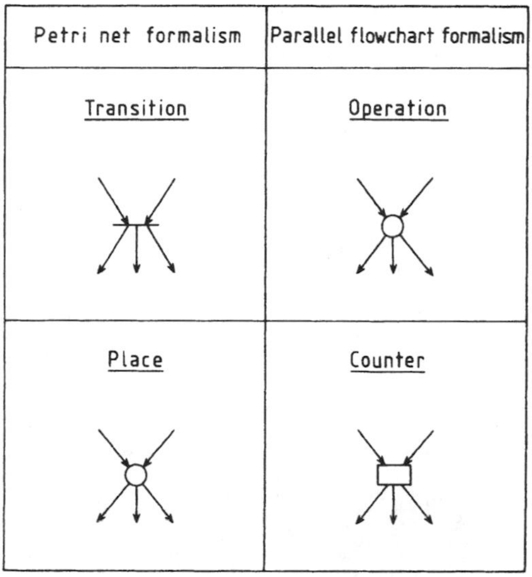

Figure 22 : A comparison between the Petri net and the parallel
flowchart formalisms

We have seen in section 1.5 that a parallel flowchart could be represented by a directed graph using two types of nodes. Figure 23 represents a parallel flowchart. The pictorial representation of a parallel flowchart as a graph used in this illustration is of common practice. The graph contains two types of nodes : rectangles called *counters* (or *places*) and circles called *operations* (or *transitions*). These nodes, counters and operations, are connected by directed arcs (which are eventually marked with predicates) from counters to operations and from operations to counters . If an arc is directed from a counter to an operation, the counter is an *input counter* for that operation iff the predicate which marks the arc is 1. If an arc is directed from an operation to a counter, the counter is an *output counter* for that operation iff the predicate which marks the arc is 1. Predicates identically equal to 1 are dropped from the arcs.

The execution of a parallel flowchart is controlled by the contents of its counters. An operation is *enabled* when all its input counters have a content equal to "1". The operation *fires* by removing a "1" from their input counters and by placing the "1" in the output counters of the operation. The above rules are quite sufficient for the restricted use that we do of parallel flowcharts in this text. For a more detailed and sophisticated definition of parallel flowcharts and of Petri-nets see e.g. Peterson [1977, 1982].

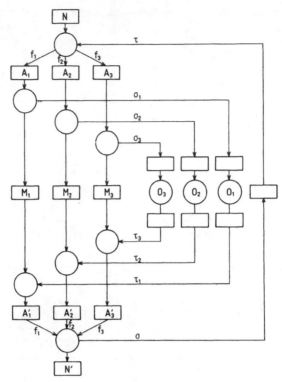

Figure 23 : A parallel flowchart representation of the program (123)

In order to represent algorithms and instructions we shall interpret the parallel flowcharts as follows (see also figures 23, 24)

- The *input counters* and the *output counters* of an operation represent the *input labels* and the *output labels* of the instruction respectively ;
- The *firing* of the operation corresponds to the *execution* of the instruction.

The program (111a, 111b) of section 6.3 is represented in the left part (or control part) of figure 23.

The interpretations of *counters* as *instruction labels* and of *firing of operation as execution of instruction* naturally leads to a separation of an instruction into a decision part and an execution part. The program (111a, 111b) is equivalent to :

$$N \quad \tau[\ f_1 \qquad f_2 \qquad f_3\ ] \tag{123a}$$
$$A_1 \qquad A_2 \qquad A_3$$

$$A_i \qquad \sigma_i \qquad M_i \qquad (1 \leqslant i \leqslant 3) \tag{123b}$$

$$M_i \qquad \tau_i \qquad A'_i \qquad (1 \leqslant i \leqslant 3) \tag{123c}$$

$$
\begin{array}{cc}
A'_1 & \left[\begin{array}{c} f_1 \\ f_2 \\ f_3 \end{array}\right] \\
A'_2 & \\
A'_3 & \\
\end{array}
\qquad\qquad (123\mathrm{d})
$$

$$\sigma$$

$$N$$

(123a) is a decision instruction of the type *row* ;

(123b) and (123c) are execution instructions of the types *do* and *has been done* respectively ;

(123d) is a decision instruction of the type *column* .

      We have represented the execution of the operations O_i in the operational flowchart of the control part by arcs to which are associated the commands σ_i and the termination signals τ_i.

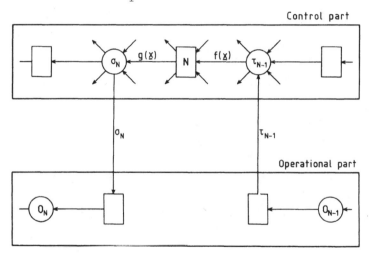

Figure 24. A parallel flowchart representation for the cooperation between control and operation automata

      We finally verify that the interpretations of the counters and of the operations lead us to adopt the scheme of figure 24 for representing the cooperation between the control and the operational parts.

8.2. Representation of low-level and of high-level instructions

      A representation of row and of column-instructions by means of parallel flowcharts is given in figure 25. Consider first the (and)-instructions; we easily recognize that if (as assumed in section 8.1.) :

104

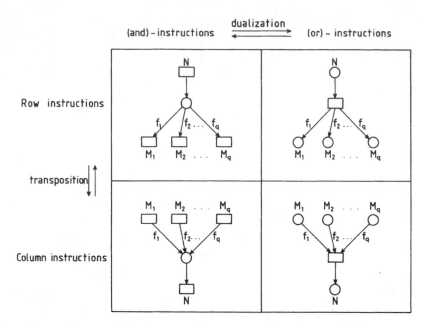

Figure 25: The parallel flowchart representation of the
duality and of the transposition principles

- the input and output counters of an operation represent the input and output
  labels of the instruction respectively ;

- the firing of the operation corresponds to the execution of the instruction,
  then the (and)-interpreted row and column instructions are represented in the
  left part of figure 25 ;

      The (or)-instructions are represented in the right part of figure 25.
We observe that the representation of the (or)-instructions are obtained from the
representation of the (and)-instructions by :

- interchanging the counters with the operations ;
- giving a dual interpretation to the counters and to the operations, i.e. :

    - the input and output operations of a counter represent the input and output
  labels of the instruction respectively ;
    - the presence of a "1" in a counter corresponds to the execution of the
  instruction.

      From the parallel flowcharts of figure 25 we deduce the two following
propositions.

Proposition 1 : Duality principle

*From the representation of an instruction by means of a parallel flowchart we de-
duce the representation of a dual instruction (i.e. an instruction interpreted
in a dual way) by interchanging the counters with the operations and by giving a*

dual interpretation for the counters and the operations.

Proposition 2 : Transposition principle

From the representation of an instruction by means of a parallel flowchart we deduce the representation of a tranpose instruction by changing the direction of the arrows on the arcs.

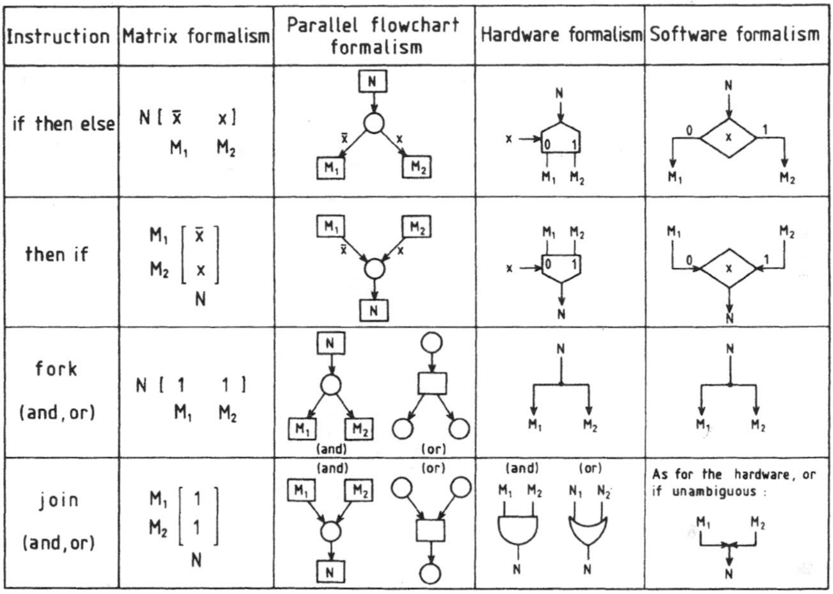

Instruction	Matrix formalism	Parallel flowchart formalism	Hardware formalism	Software formalism
if then else	$N[\ \bar{x}\quad x\ ]$ $\quad M_1\quad M_2$	N / $\bar{x}$, x / M_1, M_2	$x \to [0\ 1]$ / $M_1\ M_2$	N / x / M_1, M_2
then if	$\begin{matrix} M_1 \\ M_2 \end{matrix}\begin{bmatrix} \bar{x} \\ x \end{bmatrix}$ N	M_1, M_2 / $\bar{x}$, x / N	$M_1\ M_2$ / $x \to [0\ 1]$ / N	M_1, M_2 / x / N
fork (and,or)	$N[\ 1\quad 1\ ]$ $\quad M_1\quad M_2$	(and) M_1 M_2 ; (or)	N / M_1, M_2	N / M_1, M_2
join (and,or)	$\begin{matrix} M_1 \\ M_2 \end{matrix}\begin{bmatrix} 1 \\ 1 \end{bmatrix}$ N	(and) M_1 M_2 ; (or)	(and) $M_1\ M_2$; (or) $N_1\ N_2$ / N	As for the hardware, or if unambiguous : M_1 M_2 / N

Figure 26: Matrix formalism, parallel flowchart formalism and hardware formalism for representing low-level instructions.

Figure 26 gives us, for the elementary instructions and for their transpose, the correspondence between matrix formalism, parallel flowchart formalism and hardware formalism.

From anyone of the parallel flowcharts of figure 25 we deduce parallel flowcharts for representing any kind of interpreted matrix-instructions. Consider e.g. the parallel flowchart of figure 25 representing an (and)-interpreted row-instruction. From this parallel flowchart we deduce by induction the parallel flowcharts of figure 27 representing (or;and) and (and;and)-interpreted matrix instructions. From the (or;and)- and (and;and) representations we in turn derive by using the transposition principle the (and;or)- and the (or;or)-interpretations respectively. The four parallel flowcharts corresponding to the four interpretations of matrix instructions are given in figure 27.

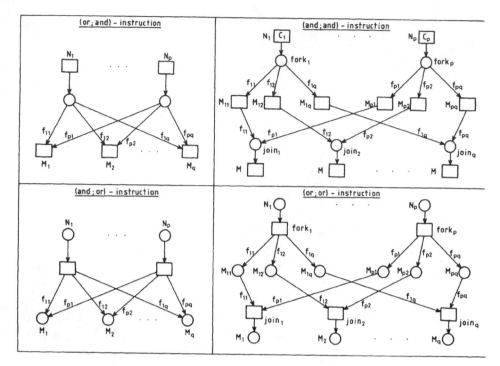

Figure 27 : A parallel flowchart representation of matrix-instructions.

Finally a parallel-flowchart description of the (or;and)-interpreted matrix instruction :

$$
\begin{array}{l}
\begin{matrix} N_1 \\ \vdots \\ N_p \end{matrix}
\begin{matrix} \tau_1 \\ \vdots \\ \tau_p \end{matrix}
\begin{bmatrix} f_{11} & \cdots & f_{1q} \\ \vdots & & \vdots \\ f_{p1} & \cdots & f_{pq} \end{bmatrix}
\begin{matrix} \\ \\ \\ \sigma_1 & \cdots & \sigma_q \\ M_1 & & M_q \end{matrix}
=
\begin{matrix} N_1 \\ \vdots \\ N_p \end{matrix}
\begin{bmatrix} \tau_1 & & 0 \\ & \ddots & \\ 0 & & \tau_p \end{bmatrix}
\begin{bmatrix} f_{11} & \cdots & f_{1q} \\ \vdots & & \vdots \\ f_{p1} & \cdots & f_{pq} \end{bmatrix}
\begin{bmatrix} \sigma_1 & & 0 \\ & \ddots & \\ 0 & & \sigma_q \end{bmatrix} \\
\qquad\qquad\qquad\qquad\qquad N'_1 \cdots N'_p \quad M'_1 \cdots M'_q \quad M_1 \cdots M_q
\end{array}
$$

$$(124)$$

is given in figure 28.

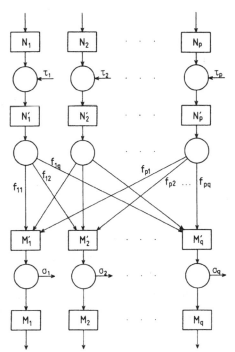

Figure 28: A parallel flowchart description of the (or;and)-interpreted matrix-instruction

8.3. Vector addition systems

As stated in section 1.5, the fundamental step in the development of computation and decision procedures regarding parallel flowcharts is the introduction of a simple geometric structure, namely the *vector addition system*, and the proof that certain questions about vector addition systems are computable and decidable (Karp and Miller [1969]).

Let us introduce a simplified vector addition system (with respect to the more general vector addition systems defined by Karp and Miller [1969] and Keller [1973] ; see also Thayse [1979]); it will be quite sufficient for describing the instructions and the information flow in programs.

Given a parallel flowchart with k counters representing instruction labels, let N_0 be a k-dimensional vector whose components represent the initial contents of the counters. The possible evolution of the parallel flowchart, and of the instruction or the program represented by it, can be described with the help of a k-dimensional vector addition system $(\underline{d}, W)$ defined as follows :

1. $\underline{d} = \{d_i\} = \{N_0(i)\}$ for i=1,2,...,k.

2. W contains as many vectors as operations, i.e. as instructions ; denoting by $\underline{w}(h)$ the h-th component of a vector $\underline{w} \in W$ which corresponds to the execution of

the instruction $\underline{w}$, k components are given by :

$.\underline{w}(h) = -1$ for all the components h corresponding to the counters decreased by the execution of $\underline{w}$ (the input counters of $\underline{w}$) ;

$.\underline{w}(h) = 1$ for all the components h corresponding to the counters increased by the execution of $\underline{w}$ (the output counters of $\underline{w}$) ;

$.\underline{w}(h) = -f_i$ for all the components h corresponding to the counters decreased by the execution of $\underline{w}$ iff $f_i=1$ (the input counters of $\underline{w}$ if $f_i=1$) ;

$.\underline{w}(h) = f_i$ for all the components h corresponding to the counters increased by the execution of $\underline{w}$ iff $f_i=1$ (the output counters of $\underline{w}$ if $f_i=1$) ;

$\underline{w}(h) = 0$ for all other components.

The vector $\underline{d}$ is the initial state of the program or of the parallel flowchart, and the vectors of $\underline{w}$ show how the counters and the operations of the parallel flowchart are connected. Thus $(\underline{d},W)$ constitutes a steady state description of the parallel flowchart, i.e. a description showing the system interconnection only (and not the evolution of the system during a given period of time).

The vector addition system associated with the parallel flowchart of figure 28 is shown in figure 29 ; d_i $(1 \leqslant i \leqslant p)$ are the initial states corresponding to the activations of $N_i (1 \leqslant i \leqslant p)$ respectively.

The vector addition systems associated to the (and;and)- and to the (or;or)-instructions of figure 27 are shown in figure 30a and 30b respectively.

We verify that the transpose operation on an instruction (or on its associated flowchart) results in a sign change of the vector addition system: indeed the input counters are changed into output counters and inversely.

We also verify that the dualization of an instruction results in a sign change and in a transposition of the vector addition system ; this is illustrated by figures 30a and 30b which are obtained from each other by a sign change and a transposition.

The dynamic description of the parallel flowchart, i.e. the description of how the initiations and the terminations of the different operations of a parallel flowchart evolve during a period of time, is described by the *reachability set* R of the vector addition system.

The *reachability set* R of a vector addition system $(\underline{d};W)$ is the set of vectors of the form $\underline{d} + \underline{w}_1 + \underline{w}_2 + \ldots + \underline{w}_s$, with $\underline{w}_i \in W$, such that $\underline{d} + \underline{w}_1 + \ldots + \underline{w}_i \geqslant 0$ for i=1,2,...,s. One knows indeed that the contents of the counters must always be the nonnegative integers 0 or 1. The vector $\underline{d}$ is then the initial state of control of the program, and the vectors of the reachability set R are the different states through which the control automaton of the program evolves in consequence of the initiation and of the termination of the program operations.

	N_1	N_2	N_p	N'_1	N'_2	N'_p	M'_1	M'_2	M'_q	M_1	M_2	M_q
has been done τ_1	-1	0	0	1	0	0	0	0	0	0	0	0
has been done τ_2	0	-1	0	0	1	0	0	0	0	0	0	0
has been done τ_p	0	0	-1	0	0	1	0	0	0	0	0	0
fork$_1$	0	0	0	-1	0	0	f_{11}	f_{12}	f_{1q}	0	0	0
fork$_2$	0	0	0	0	-1	0	f_{21}	f_{22}	f_{2q}	0	0	0
fork$_p$	0	0	0	0	0	-1	f_{p1}	f_{p2}	f_{pq}	0	0	0
do σ_1	0	0	0	0	0	0	-1	0	0	1	0	0
do σ_2	0	0	0	0	0	0	0	-1	0	0	1	0
do σ_q	0	0	0	0	0	0	0	0	-1	0	0	1

	N_1	N_2	N_p	N'_1	N'_2	N'_p	M'_1	M'_2	M'_q	M_1	M_2	M_q
d_1 = *begin* N_1	1	0	0	0	0	0	0	0	0	0	0	0
d_2 = *begin* N_2	0	1	0	0	0	0	0	0	0	0	0	0
d_p = *begin* N_q	0	0	1	0	0	0	0	0	0	0	0	0

Figure 29 : Vector addition system associated with the parallel flowchart of figure 28.

	N_1	N_p	M_{11}	M_{12}	M_{1q}	M_{p1}	M_{p2}	M_{pq}	M_1	M_2	M_q
$fork_1$	-1		f_{11}	f_{12}	f_{1q}						
$fork_p$		-1				f_{p1}	f_{p2}	f_{pq}			
$join_1$			$-f_{11}$			$-f_{p1}$			1		
$join_2$				$-f_{12}$			$-f_{p2}$			1	
$join_q$					$-f_{1q}$			$-f_{pq}$			1

(a)

	$fork_1$	$fork_p$	$join_1$	$join_2$	$join_q$
N_1	1	0	0	0	0
N_p	0	1	0	0	0
M_{11}	$-f_{11}$	0	f_{11}	0	0
M_{12}	$-f_{12}$	0	0	f_{12}	0
M_{1q}	$-f_{1q}$	0	0	0	f_{1q}
M_{p1}	0	$-f_{p1}$	f_{p1}	0	0
M_{p2}	0	$-f_{p2}$	0	f_{p2}	0
M_{pq}	0	$-f_{pq}$	0	0	f_{pq}
M_1	0	0	-1	0	0
M_2	0	0	0	-1	0
M_q	0	0	0	0	-1

(b)

Figure 30a : The vector addition system representation of the duality principle

Figure 30b : The vector addition system representation of the transposition principle

States	N_1	N_2	N_p	N'_1	N'_2	N'_p	M'_1	M'_2	M'_q	M_1	M_2	M_q	Next states
begin $N_1=S_1$	1	0	0	0	0	0	0	0	0	0	0	0	$(S_2 \; ; \; \tau_1)$
S_2	0	0	0	1	0	0	0	0	0	0	0	0	$(S_3 \; ; \; fork_1)$
S_3	0	0	0	0	0	0	1	1	1	0	0	0	$(S_4 ; \sigma_1)(S_5 ; \sigma_2)(S_6 ; \sigma_q)$
S_4	0	0	0	0	0	0	0	1	1	1	0	0	$(S_7 ; \sigma_2)(S_8 ; \sigma_q)$
S_5	0	0	0	0	0	0	1	0	1	0	1	0	$(S_7 ; \sigma_1)(S_9 ; \sigma_q)$
S_6	0	0	0	0	0	0	1	1	0	0	0	1	$(S_8 ; \sigma_1)(S_9 ; \sigma_2)$
S_7	0	0	0	0	0	0	0	0	1	1	1	0	$(S_{10} ; \sigma_q)$
S_8	0	0	0	0	0	0	0	1	0	1	0	1	$(S_{10} ; \sigma_2)$
S_9	0	0	0	0	0	0	1	0	0	0	1	1	$(S_{10} ; \sigma_1)$
S_{10}	0	0	0	0	0	0	0	0	0	1	1	1	(go to M_1, M_2 and M_q)

Figure 31. Reachability set of the vector addition system of figure 29.

The reachability set R of the vector addition system of figure 29 is shown in figure 31 for the value $(f_1 \ f_2 \ f_3) = (1 \ 1 \ 1)$ of the Boolean functions f_i. Each state S_j is followed by an instruction of the type $(S_k ; \psi_\ell)$ if the next state reached is S_k after execution of the instruction ψ_ℓ.

At every time the reached state S_j of R represents the contents of the counters and the instruction presently in execution.

The reachability set R may also be depicted by the transition graph shown in figure 32. A transition graph consists of a set of nodes with various arrow drawn between them. In the transition graph associated with a reachability set R, an arrow labeled ψ_ℓ is directed from the node N_i to the node N_j if the execution of the instruction ψ_ℓ produces a transition from the state N_i to the state N_j.

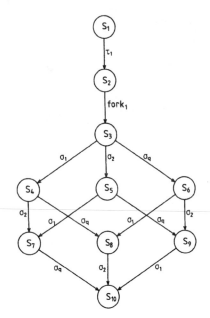

Figure 32 : The transition graph representation for the reachability set of figure 31.

Let us finally note that the reachability set of figure 31 can best be interpreted as a program in the following way :

S_1 : initial state ; when instruction τ_1 is executed, go to S_2.

S_2 : when instruction $fork_1$ is executed, go to S_3.

S_3 : if instruction σ_1 is executed go to S_4,

     if instruction σ_2 is executed go to S_5,

     if instruction σ_q is executed go to S_6.

S_4 : ... etc.

8.4. A comparison between the fields of application of parallel flowcharts and of the P-function technique.

The algebra of P-functions has been used in part I for the (optimal) synthesis of matrix instructions. We have seen in this chapter that the parallel flowchart and its associated geometric structure i.e. the vector addition system is used for describing the connection between matrix instructions. The algebra of P-functions is thus mainly a synthesis tool for implementing the realization of matrix-instructions in terms of low-level instructions while the vector addition system is an analysis tool for verifying the interaction between connected matrix-instructions. It follows that P-functions and vector addition systems may be considered as complementary mathematical tools.

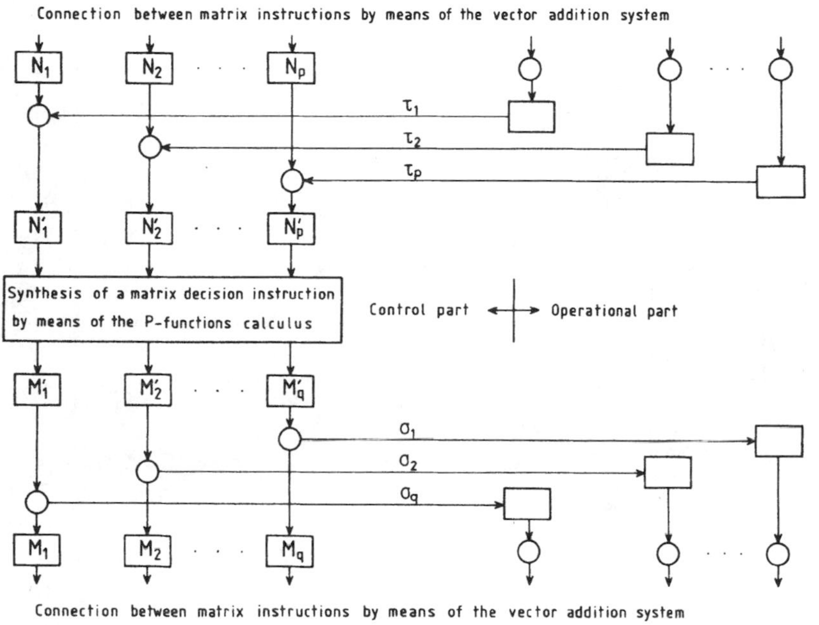

Connection between matrix instructions by means of the vector addition system

Figure 33: A comparison between the application fields of the parallel flowchart representation and of the P-function technique

The respective fields of application of P-functions and of vector addition systems are depicted schematically in figure 33.

The respective computation techniques used in the P-functions calculus and in the vector addition systems are compared in figure 34. The vector addition system analyzes the result of the execution of the various instructions in terms of contents of counters associated to instruction labels. The P-function calculus generates systems of P-functions associated to instruction labels by means

Laws acting on P-functions   Instruction labels   Vector addition system

Counters and their associated P-functions	t_{τ_1}	t_{τ_2}	t_{τ_p}	Laws$\{t_i\}$,U	t_{σ_1}	t_{σ_2}	t_{σ_q}	done τ_1	done τ_2	done τ_p	fork$_1$	fork$_2$	fork$_p$	do σ_1	do σ_2	do σ_q
$M_1: \langle \tau_1 f_{11}\sigma_1, \tau_2 f_{21}\sigma_1, \tau_p f_{p1}\sigma_1 ; 1\rangle$											f_{11}	f_{21}	f_{p1}	1		
$M_2: \langle \tau_1 f_{12}\sigma_2, \tau_2 f_{22}\sigma_2, \tau_p f_{p2}\sigma_2 ; 1\rangle$											f_{12}	f_{22}	f_{p2}		1	
$M_q: \langle \tau_1 f_{1q}\sigma_q, \tau_2 f_{2q}\sigma_q, \tau_p f_{pq}\sigma_q ; 1\rangle$											f_{1q}	f_{2q}	f_{pq}			1
$M_1': \langle \tau_1 f_{11}, \tau_2 f_{21}, \tau_p f_{p1} ; \sigma_1\rangle$				Transforma‑ tions on P‑functions	M_1'									-1		
$M_2': \langle \tau_1 f_{12}, \tau_2 f_{22}, \tau_p f_{p2} ; \sigma_2\rangle$						M_2'									-1	
$M_q': \langle \tau_1 f_{1q}, \tau_2 f_{2q}, \tau_p f_{pq} ; \sigma_q\rangle$							M_q'									-1
$N_1': \langle \tau_1, -, - ; \sum_j f_{1j}\sigma_j\rangle$								1			-1					
$N_2': \langle -, \tau_2, - ; \sum_j f_{2j}\sigma_j\rangle$									1			-1				
$N_p': \langle -, -, \tau_p ; \sum_j f_{pj}\sigma_j\rangle$										1			-1			
$N_1: \langle 1, -, - ; \tau_1(\sum_j f_{1j}\sigma_j)\rangle$	N_1							-1								
$N_2: \langle -, 1, - ; \tau_2(\sum_j f_{2j}\sigma_j)\rangle$		N_2							-1							
$N_p: \langle -, -, 1 ; \tau_p(\sum_j f_{pj}\sigma_j)\rangle$			N_p							-1						

Figure 34. A comparison between the computation techniques of the vector addition system and of the tabular P-function technique.

of transformations acting on P-functions and on an initial system of P-functions. It follows that instruction labels which are represented by counters in the vector addition system and by P-functions in the P-calculus are the common concept that we shall use for our comparison. The instruction labels of the matrix instruction (124 are written in the control column of figure 34. These instruction labels correspond to the counters of the vector addition system which is written in the left part of figure 34. This vector addition system corresponds to the parallel flowchart of figure 28 and hence is nothing but a rewriting of the vector addition system of figure 29. The same instruction labels are associated to P-functions the transformations of which are schematically depicted in the right part of figure 34.

Chapter 9 : Synchronous and asynchronous implementation of instructions

We show in section 9.1 how the synchronous Glushkov model of computation must be modified in order to accept an asynchronous treatment of data . The transition from a synchronous to an asynchronous model of computation requires in addition :

- the implementation of (and)-interpreted matrix instructions in the control part ;
- the generation of termination signals τ in the operational part.

In an asynchronous realization of an algorithm it may be requested that the program must be able to accept new data as soon as it has terminated the handling of the preceding data so that several data may be concurrently treated at different levels of the algorithm realization. The additional instructions which are needed when several data are allowed to be *concurrently in progress* in the algorithm implementation are described in section 9.2. We introduce the concept of *feedback-instruction* which plays with respect to programs the same role as the feedback connection with respect to circuits.

A general scheme for asynchronous implementation of matrix instructions is presented in section 9.3. In particular we prove that the feedback-instruction associated to a matrix-instruction is its transpose-dual matrix-instruction.

An example is developed in section 9.4.

9.1. The use of (and)-interpreted instructions in asynchronous design

As it has been seen in chapter 1, to describe systems performing computations, Glushkov [1965] has proposed a model of cooperation between two synchronous subsystems called *control automaton* and *operational automaton* respectively. The separation between command part and operational part allowed us to concentrate upon the command part the essential of the synthesis problem and this independently of the particular materialization of the computations in the operational part.

An adequate model for representing algorithms must maintain the separation between the two parts and illustrate their cooperation. According to these objectives Glushkov [1977] adopted the row-instruction (125) which was originally proposed by Mishchenko [1973] :

$$N \quad [\ f_1(\underline{x}) \ , \ f_2(\underline{x}) \ , \ \dots \ , \ f_q(\underline{x}) \ ]$$

$$\sigma_1 \qquad \sigma_2 \qquad \qquad \sigma_q \qquad\qquad (125)$$

$$M \qquad\quad M \qquad\qquad M$$

Remember that this row instruction is interpreted as follows :

1) While starting the execution of N, one first computes the values of all the
   Boolean functions $f_j(\underline{x})$. This is the *evaluation phase* (the Boolean variables
   $\underline{x}$ are the elementary predicates of the problem).

2) We perform the commands σ_j corresponding to the functions f_j equal to 1 ; these
   commands activate operations O_j in the operational part. This is the *execution*
   phase.

3) We go to the next instruction M.

      In a synchronous system the next instruction M is reached at the next
clock pulse regardless of the particular durations of the operations O_j. In an asynchronous system the next instruction M may be reached as soon as all the activated
operations O_j are finished. The asynchronous operation mode leads us to replace
the instruction (125) by the pair of instructions (126a, 126b) :

$$
N \begin{bmatrix} f_1(\underline{x}) , & f_2(\underline{x}) , & \cdots , & f_q(\underline{x}) \end{bmatrix}
$$

$$
\begin{array}{cccc}
\sigma_1 & \sigma_2 & \cdots & \sigma_q \\
M_1 & M_2 & \cdots & M_q
\end{array}
\qquad (126a)
$$

$$
\begin{array}{cc}
M_1 & \tau_1 \\
M_2 & \tau_2 \\
\vdots & \vdots \\
M_q & \tau_q
\end{array}
\begin{bmatrix}
f_1(\underline{x}) \\
f_2(\underline{x}) \\
\vdots \\
f_q(\underline{x})
\end{bmatrix}
\qquad (126b)
$$

$$
M
$$

Instruction (126a) is a row-instruction which is interpreted as (125) : the only
difference lies in the fact that there are multiple next addresses. Instruction
(126b) is an (and)-interpreted column-instruction which is the transpose of instruction (126a). Remember that this column instruction is interpreted as follows :

1) While starting the execution of (126b) we first compute the values of all the
   Boolean functions $f_j(\underline{x})$.

2) We go to the next instruction M as soon as all the termination signals τ_j have
   been received (from the operational part) corresponding to the functions $f_j(\underline{x})$
   equal to 1.

      According to instructions (126), the Glushkov model of computation
whose schematic configuration is remembered in figure 35a must be modified so as
to become that of figure 35b. The operational part receives orders σ from the con-

trol part : these orders initiate operations. The termination of these operations generates signals τ which are directed toward the control part. The contents of the memories of the operational part determines the value of the binary variables which select the sequence of the instructions in the control part. The scheme of figure 35b corresponds to the parallel program schema which has been introduced by Karp and Miller [1969].

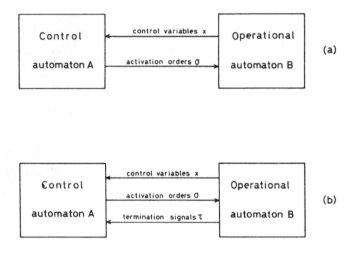

Figure 35   (a) : Glushkov model of computation or algorithmic
                   state machine

            (b) : Karp and Miller model of computation or parallel
                  program schema.

If we now suppress in (125) the constraint of having a unique next address M, i.e. if instruction (125) is replaced by the following :

$$
N \begin{bmatrix} f_{11} & f_{12} & \cdots & f_{1r_1} & \cdots & f_{q1} & f_{q2} & \cdots & f_{qr_q} \\ \sigma_{11} & \sigma_{12} & \cdots & \sigma_{1r_1} & \cdots & \sigma_{q1} & \sigma_{q2} & \cdots & \sigma_{qr_q} \\ M_1 & M_1 & \cdots & M_1 & \cdots & M_q & M_q & \cdots & M_q \end{bmatrix} \quad (127)
$$

an asynchronous realization of (127) requires the transformation of this instruction into the equivalent program :

$$
N \begin{bmatrix} f_{11} & f_{12} & \cdots & f_{1r_1} & \cdots & f_{q1} & f_{q2} & \cdots & f_{qr_q} \\ \sigma_{11} & \sigma_{12} & \cdots & \sigma_{1r_1} & \cdots & \sigma_{q1} & \sigma_{q2} & \cdots & \sigma_{qr_q} \\ M_{11} & M_{12} & \cdots & M_{1r_1} & \cdots & M_{q1} & M_{q2} & \cdots & M_{qr_q} \end{bmatrix} \qquad (128a)
$$

$$
\begin{matrix}
M_{i1} & \tau_{i1} \\
M_{i2} & \tau_{i2} \\
\vdots & \vdots \\
M_{ir_i} & \tau_{ir_i}
\end{matrix}
\begin{bmatrix}
f_{i1} \\
f_{i2} \\
\vdots \\
f_{ir_i}
\end{bmatrix}
\qquad (1 \leqslant i \leqslant q) \qquad (128b)
$$

$$M_i$$

      The above instructions allow us to see that the transition from a synchronous to an asynchronous model of computation requires in addition :

- the implementation of (and)-interpreted instructions of the type (126b) or (128b) in the control part ;

- the generation of termination signals τ in the operational part.

      Some possible additional requirements of the asynchronous implementation will be studied in next section.

9.2. The use of feedback-instructions in concurrent processing of datas

      We may require that for an asynchronous realization of an algorithm, no new data are put into the system before the previous data were completely treated and the corresponding results were obtained. This leads to the simplest organization for the control unit. It may also be required that an instruction must be able to accept new datas as soon as it has terminated the execution of its own operations so that several data can be simultaneously treated at different levels of the algorithm realization. This kind of organization clearly optimizes the ratio of occupation of the system ; in counterpart it increases the number of instructions of the algorithm and hence the cost of the implementation. This will be illustrated in this section.

      Consider the (or)-interpreted matrix-instruction (129) :

$$
\begin{matrix}
N_1 & \tau_1 \\
\vdots & \vdots \\
N_p & \tau_p
\end{matrix}
\begin{bmatrix}
f_{11} & \cdots & f_{1q} \\
\vdots & & \vdots \\
f_{p1} & \cdots & f_{pq} \\
\sigma_1 & \cdots & \sigma_q \\
M_1 & \cdots & M_q
\end{bmatrix}
\qquad (129)
$$

Assume that instruction (129) is working, i.e. is in the state of being executed. It is clear that this instruction can not be activated again before it has completed its execution. This constraint requires the materialization of a new instruction which will inhibate any new activation of the inputs $(N_1, N_2, \ldots, N_p)$ before the operations that have been enabled by the commands $(\sigma_1, \sigma_2, \ldots, \sigma_q)$ have terminated their execution. Assume that the end-execution signals associated to these operations are denoted $(\tau_1^+, \tau_2^+, \ldots, \tau_q^+)$. The (or)-interpreted matrix-instruction (129) must be associated with a *feedback-instruction* (130) whose role is to prevent any new activation of the instruction (129) before its precedent execution. The feedback-instruction which is written

$$
\begin{array}{cc}
M_1 & \tau_1^+ \\
\vdots & \vdots \\
M_q & \tau_q^+
\end{array}
\left[
\begin{array}{ccc}
f_{11} & \cdots & f_{p1} \\
\vdots & & \vdots \\
f_{1q} & \cdots & f_{pq}
\end{array}
\right]
\qquad (130)
$$
$$
 N_1 \quad \cdots \quad N_p
$$

is nothing but the (and)-interpreted transpose of the matrix-instruction (129). The interconnections between the (or)-interpreted matrix-instruction (129) and its feedback-instruction (130) is depicted by the program (131) and by the parallel flow chart representation of figure 36.

$$
\begin{array}{c}
P_i \\
N_i^f
\end{array}
\left[
\begin{array}{c}
1 \\
1
\end{array}
\right]
\qquad (1 \leqslant i \leqslant p) \qquad\qquad (131a)
$$
$$
 N_i
$$

$$
\begin{array}{cc}
N_1 & \tau_1 \\
\vdots & \vdots \\
N_p & \tau_p
\end{array}
\left[
\begin{array}{ccc}
f_{11} & \cdots & f_{1q} \\
\vdots & & \vdots \\
f_{p1} & \cdots & f_{pq}
\end{array}
\right]
\qquad (131b)
$$
$$
\begin{array}{ccc}
\sigma_1 & \cdots & \sigma_q \\
M_1 & \cdots & M_q
\end{array}
$$

$$
M_j \quad \tau_j^+
\left[
\begin{array}{cc}
1 & 1
\end{array}
\right]
\qquad (1 \leqslant j \leqslant q) \qquad\qquad (131c)
$$
$$
 M_j^f \quad Q_j
$$

$$
\begin{array}{c}
M_1^f \\
\vdots \\
M_q^f
\end{array}
\left[
\begin{array}{ccc}
f_{11} & \cdots & f_{p1} \\
\vdots & & \vdots \\
f_{1q} & \cdots & f_{pq}
\end{array}
\right]
\qquad (131d)
$$
$$
 N_1^f \quad \cdots \quad N_p^f
$$

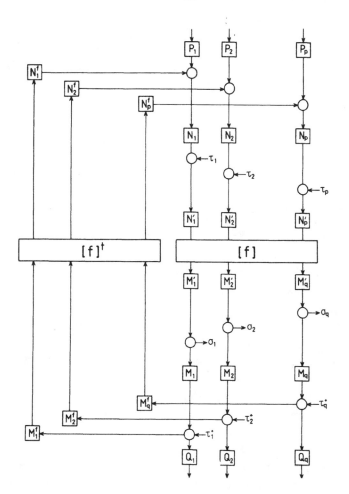

Figure 36 : Connection between a matrix-instruction and
its feedback instruction

The program (131) is made   of the initial matrix-instruction (131b), of the
feedback-instruction (131d) and of p+q row and column instructions (131a, 131c)
which connect the matrix-instruction with the feedback-instruction.

The program (131) and its parallel flowchart representation of figure
36 work as follows :

- The program starts with all the counters N_i^f at the value 1 and all the other
  counters at the value 0.
- Since the matrix is (or)-interpreted, only one of the input labels P_i $(1 \leqslant i \leqslant p)$
  can be reached for a fixed value of the predicates $\underline{x}$; when the input label P_i is
  reached the instruction $[f_{ij}]$ is activated through its input label N_i and the
  counters associated to P_i and N_i^f are decreased by 1 and thus put at the value 0.

- If the instruction label P_i is reached again before the matrix-instruction $[f_{ij}]$ has terminated its preceding execution, the value 0 of the counter N_i^f of the feed-back-instruction $[f_{ji}]$ prevents any new execution of the matrix-instruction $[f_{ij}]$.

Remember that the above analysis is always based on the hypothesis that the predicates $\underline{x}$ can not change during the execution of an instruction in the control part. The end-of-execution signals $\underline{\tau}$ are predicates which can change of value during the execution of a computation. It is this difference of behavior between the predicates $\underline{\tau}$ and $\underline{x}$ which led us to introduce two distinct kinds of predicates.

9.3. A general scheme for asynchronous implementation of matrix-instructions

We have seen in section 9.1 that the transition from a synchronous to an asynchronous model of computation requests in addition to the implementation of (or)-interpreted matrix-instructions, the implementation of (and)-interpreted matrix-instructions which are associated to the presence of multiple next addresses in the (or)-instructions.

We have seen in section 9.2 that the requirement that instructions must be able to accept new data as soon as they have terminated the execution of their own operation (so that several data may be simultaneously treated at different levels of the algorithm realization) requires in addition the implementation of feedback-instructions.

The purpose of this section is to summarize the combined results of sections 9.1 and 9.2. in order to derive a general implementation scheme for matrix-instructions with concurrent acceptation of datas.

In order to simplify the parallel flowchart representation we first assume that the (or)-interpreted matrix-instructions to be implemented have disjoint (or orthogonal) rows ; this means that :

$$(\bigvee_j f_{ij}) (\bigvee_j f_{kj}) \equiv 0 \qquad \forall i \neq k .$$

This is generally not a too restrictive assumption as long as the matrix-instruction is considered. Indeed, since the matrix is (or)-interpreted, the end-of-execution signals must be disjoint, i.e. :

$$\tau_i \tau_k \neq \phi \qquad \forall i \neq k .$$

It is then always possible to associate to each τ_i $(1 \leqslant i \leqslant p)$ a minterm $m_i(\underline{y})$ in the Boolean variables $\underline{y}$ such that :

$$(\text{occurrence of } \tau_i) \Rightarrow m_i(\underline{y}) = 1, \ m_k(\underline{y}) = 0 \quad \forall k \neq i .$$

We then verify that the two matrix instructions (132a) and (132b) are equivalent
and that moreover (132b) has disjoint rows :

$$
\begin{array}{cc}
N_1 & \tau_1 \\
N_2 & \tau_2 \\
\vdots & \vdots \\
N_p & \tau_p
\end{array}
\begin{bmatrix}
f_{11} & f_{12} & \cdots & f_{1q} \\
f_{21} & f_{22} & \cdots & f_{2q} \\
\vdots & & & \\
f_{p1} & f_{p2} & \cdots & f_{pq}
\end{bmatrix}
\begin{array}{c}
\\ \\ \\ \\
\sigma_1 \quad \sigma_2 \quad \cdots \quad \sigma_q \\
M_1 \quad M_2 \quad \cdots \quad M_q
\end{array}
\;\equiv\;
\begin{array}{cc}
N_1 & \tau_1 \\
N_2 & \tau_2 \\
\vdots & \vdots \\
N_p & \tau_p
\end{array}
\begin{bmatrix}
m_1 f_{11} & m_1 f_{12} & \cdots & m_1 f_{1q} \\
m_2 f_{21} & m_2 f_{22} & \cdots & m_2 f_{2q} \\
\vdots & & & \\
m_p f_{p1} & m_p f_{p2} & \cdots & m_p f_{pq}
\end{bmatrix}
\begin{array}{c}
\\ \\ \\ \\
\sigma_1 \quad \sigma_2 \quad \cdots \quad \sigma_q \\
M_1 \quad M_2 \quad \cdots \quad M_q
\end{array}
$$

$$(132a) \hspace{5cm} (132b)$$

The transpose of a matrix-instruction with disjoint rows is a matrix-instruction
with disjoint columns.

        The following theorem holds for matrix instructions with disjoint
rows.

Theorem

The feedback-instruction associated to a matrix-instruction is its transpose-dual-matrix instruction.

Proof (see also section 9.2)

Consider the (or)-interpreted matrix-instruction with disjoint-rows :

$$
\begin{array}{cc}
N_1 & \tau_1 \\
\vdots & \vdots \\
N_p & \tau_p
\end{array}
\begin{bmatrix}
m_1 f_{11} & \cdots & m_1 f_{1q} \\
\vdots & & \vdots \\
m_p f_{p1} & \cdots & m_p f_{pq}
\end{bmatrix}
\begin{array}{c}
\\ \\
\sigma_1 \quad \cdots \quad \sigma_q \\
M_1 \quad \cdots \quad M_q
\end{array}
$$

Since this matrix-instruction can not be activated (or reached) again before the
operations that were enabled by a preceding execution of the matrix-instruction
have terminated their execution, the feedback-instruction is clearly of the type

$$
\begin{array}{cc}
M_1 & \tau_1^f \\
\vdots & \vdots \\
M_q & \tau_q^f
\end{array}
\begin{bmatrix}
m_1 f_{11} & \cdots & m_p f_{p1} \\
\vdots & & \vdots \\
m_1 f_{1q} & \cdots & m_p f_{pq}
\end{bmatrix}
\begin{array}{c}
\\ \\
\sigma_1^f \quad \cdots \quad \sigma_p^f \\
N_1 \quad \cdots \quad N_p
\end{array}
$$

where τ_j^f ($1 \leqslant j \leqslant q$) is the signal which indicates the end-of-execution of the operation that was enabled by σ_j (i.e. $\tau_j^f = \tau_j^+$) and where σ_i^f ($1 \leqslant i \leqslant p$) is the signal which allows a new activation of N_i. A dual type of proof shows that the feedback-instruction associated to an (and)-interpreted matrix-instruction with disjoint columns is an (or)-interpreted matrix-instruction with disjoint rows. □

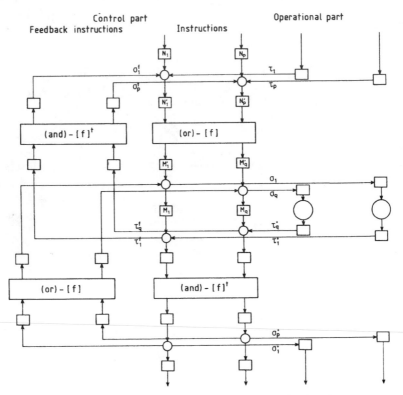

Figure 37 : Architecture for the materialization of programs accepting a concurrent treatment of data

The architecture suggested by the theorem is depicted in figure 37. The additional materialization which is requires firstly by an asynchronous organization of the control unit and secondly by the requirement of concurrent treatment of datas clearly appears in this figure. The instruction (or)-[f] realizes the synchronous implementation. The instruction (and)-[f]^t is the additional instruction requested by an asynchronous implementation. A second materialization of both the instructions (or)-[f] and (and)-[f]^t is required by a concurrent treatment of input data .

The scheme of figure 37 allows us also to give a complete hardware description of a matrix instruction. We indeed know that the counters of a parallel flowchart may e.g. be realized by RS-flip flops. (see e.g. Dadda [1976], Blanchard and Gillon [1977]).

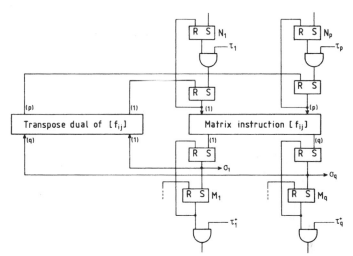

Figure 38 : Materialization of a matrix-instruction
by means of RS flip-flops.

Figure 38 proposes a schematic implementation of the input and output logic of
an (or)-interpreted matrix-instruction which is connected to its (and)-interpreted
feedback-instruction. Since (or)-interpreted matrix-instructions and their transpose (and)-interpreted matrix-instructions can be materialized by means of demultiplexers, or-gates and fanout connections and by means of multiplexers, and-gates
and fanout connections respectively (see chapters 5,6,7) the scheme of figure 38
provides us with a hardware materialization of matrix-instructions.

9.4. Example 2 (continued)

We continue the example 2 with the constraints which were introduced
in section 7.2, i.e. : the choice between four routes for messages having two possible priorities. Assume that to the first priority we associate the value 0 of a
Boolean variable y while to the second priority we associate the value 1 of the
Boolean variable y. The synchronous materialization of the algorithm requires the
implementation of the instruction (133)

$$
\begin{array}{c}
N_1 \\
N_2 \\
\\
\\
\end{array}
\left[
\begin{array}{cccc}
\bar{y}\, f_{11} & \bar{y}\, f_{12} & \bar{y}\, f_{13} & \bar{y}\, f_{14} \\
y\, f_{21} & y\, f_{22} & y\, f_{23} & y\, f_{24} \\
\sigma_1 & \sigma_2 & \sigma_3 & \sigma_4 \\
M & M & M & M
\end{array}
\right]
\qquad (133)
$$

where the Boolean functions f_{ij} are given by (121). The asynchronous materialization of the algorithm requires the implementation of the program (134) :

$$
\begin{array}{cc}
N_1 & \tau_1 \\
N_2 & \tau_2 \\
\end{array}
\left[
\begin{array}{cccc}
\bar{y}\, f_{11} & \bar{y}\, f_{12} & \bar{y}\, f_{13} & \bar{y}\, f_{14} \\
y\, f_{21} & y\, f_{22} & y\, f_{23} & y\, f_{24} \\
\end{array}
\right]
$$

$$
\begin{array}{cccc}
\sigma_1 & \sigma_2 & \sigma_3 & \sigma_4 \\
M_1 & M_2 & M_3 & M_4 \\
\end{array}
$$

$$
\begin{array}{cc}
M_1 & \tau_1^+ \\
M_2 & \tau_2^+ \\
M_3 & \tau_3^+ \\
M_4 & \tau_4^+ \\
\end{array}
\left[
\begin{array}{cc}
\bar{y}_1\, f_{11} & y\, f_{21} \\
\bar{y}\, f_{12} & y\, f_{22} \\
\bar{y}\, f_{13} & y\, f_{23} \\
\bar{y}\, f_{14} & y\, f_{24} \\
\end{array}
\right]
\qquad (134)
$$

$$
\begin{array}{cc}
\sigma_1^+ & \sigma_2^+ \\
Q_1 & Q_2 \\
\end{array}
$$

$$
\begin{array}{cc}
Q_1 \\
Q_2 \\
\end{array}
\left[
\begin{array}{c}
\bar{y} \\
y \\
\end{array}
\right]
$$

$$
M
$$

Finally if the system must be able to work under the hypothesis of concurrent data., the architecture of the program (134) with its feedback-instructions is depicted in figure 39. The materialization of the parallel flowchart of figure 39 then derives from figure 21.

A detailed hardware materialization of the routing program (123) is proposed in figure 40.

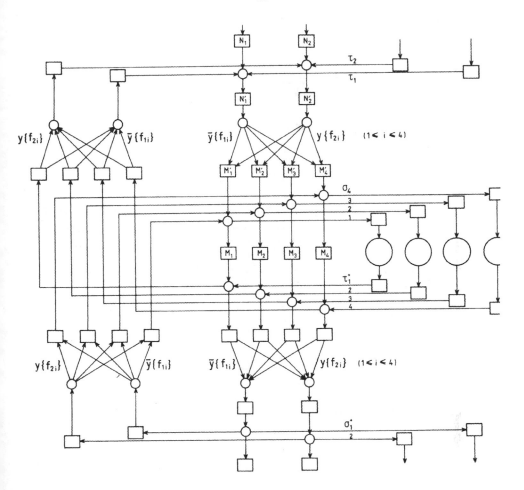

Figure 39 : Architecture for a routing algorithm

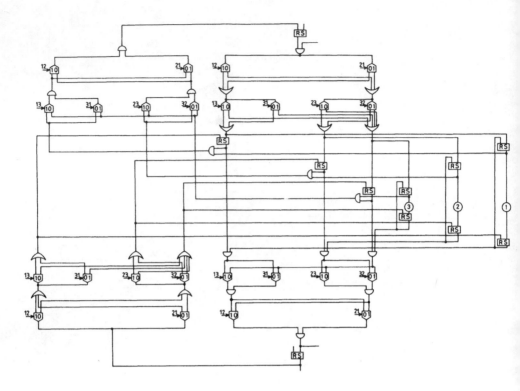

Figure 40 : Hardware realization for a routing algorithm

Chapter 10 : Programmed implementation of instructions

This chapter constitutes the basic chapter of part II of this text.
First remember that one of the main purposes of part I was the introduction of a
formalism and of a computation method which allowed us to transform any high-level
instruction in terms of low-level instructions. We showed that this transformation
immediately led to an hardware implementation of algorithms in terms of multiplexers
demultiplexers, or-gates, and-gates and fanout connections. To this hardware implementation was associated a hardware description language or software description
of the logic network. This hardware description language may never be confused
with a programming language or with a programmed implementation of the algorithm.
We indeed show in section 10.1 that, except for the case of realization of (or)-in-
terpreted matrix-instructions with disjoint columns, the hardware description language leads to non-safe programmed implementations of algorithms. Otherwise stated,
the hardware description language which is the result of the transformation process
developed in part I, leads to a safe programmed implementation if and only if the
transformation process is applied to an (or)-interpreted matrix-instruction with
disjoint columns. When applied to (or)-interpreted matrix-instructions with non-disjoint columns or to (and)-interpreted matrix-instructions, the transformation process produces a hardware description language which may result in a non-safe programmed implementation. Safe programs are characterized in section 10.1. In particular we show that a software realization of an (or)-interpretation matrix-instruction
is safe if and only if all its join-or instructions are degenerate instructions ;
similarly a software realization of an (and)-interpreted matrix-instruction is safe
if and only if it does not contain fork instructions.

Section 10.2 is devoted to the realization of safe programs. We show
how the program transformation technique developed in part I of this text must be
modified in order to produce only safe programs.

The computation of safe programs by means of P-functions is developed in section 10.3.

Safe programs for the routing problem are evaluated in section
10.4.

Finally a general type of architecture for safe program implementation is presented in section 10.5. Note that since safe programs are obtained from
the hardware description language by imposing additional constraints the cost of
a safe program (in terms of number of instructions) is generally higher than the
cost of a hardware implementation (in terms of number of gates). The requirement
of the safe character of a program decreases its degree of parallelism and increases its complexity.

10.1. Characterization of safe programs

As it has been seen in chapter 8, high-level and low-level instructions may both be represented by means of parallel flowcharts. It turns thus out
that the synthesis of a high-level instruction (or matrix-instruction) by means of
low-level instructions may be stated in terms of parallel flowcharts. The subject
of this section is the synthesis of a high-level instruction as a safe interconnection of low-level instructions ; the term *safe* is defined below.

First remember that two algorithms are said to be *equivalent* if and
only if for every input data they perform the same computation and produce the same
result. Accordingly two parallel flowcharts are said to be equivalent if and only
if they represent equivalent algorithms ; the following proposition holds.

Proposition 1

*The synthesis of a matrix-instruction reduces to the transformation of a parallel
flowchart whose arcs are marked with Boolean functions into an equivalent parallel
flowchart whose arcs are marked with Boolean variables.*

A parallel flowchart is said to be *safe* if and only if its counters
cannot take values larger than 1. A *software realization* of an algorithm, or *program*, is said to be *safe* if and only if it may be represented by means of a safe
parallel flowchart.

First we shall show that the synthesis of an (or)-interpreted matrix-
instruction with non-disjoint columns, as it has been developed in chapter 5, may
produce non-safe parallel flowcharts (and hence non safe programs). Then we show
that the hardware materialization of a non-safe parallel flowchart as it has been
developed in chapter 5 works correctly. In counterpart, the software realization of
a non-safe parallel flowchart may produce an undesired *repetitive execution* of an
instruction. The substitution of a *unique execution* by a *multiple execution* is generally prohibited in a program. Finally we show how the synthesis method of chapter 5 must be restricted in order to produce only safe programs.

Consider the example of section 5.3. and its materialization of
figure 18 ; this materialization is partly rewritten in figure 41. We have written
in figures 41a and 41c the flowchart representation and the hardware implementation
of a part of program (94). The parallel flowchart of figure 41a is not safe : if
$C_{12}=1$ at time t_1, then $C_1=C_2=1$ at time t_2 for $x_{(1,2)} = \bar{x}_{(2,1)} = 1$ and $B_{12} = 2$ at
time t_3. Two successive occurrences of a 1 in the counter B_{12} produce two executions
of the next instruction and this is generally prohibited. The hardware materialization of figure 41c contains a critical race : a single pulse at the network input
may produce two pulses at the network output. However these two pulses cannot occur
for a realistic assumption on the network delays. Indeed the reset at the network
input is produced by the set signal at the network output which is directed to the

input through a feedback connection. The second pulse may only occur if the delay from input to output through the path $(\overline{21})$ is longer than the delay from input to output through the path (12) plus the delay from output to input through the feedback network. This assumption on the delays is unrealistic ; an incorrect transient behaviour of the logic network may in any way be avoided by adding an appropriate delay in the network feedback connections.

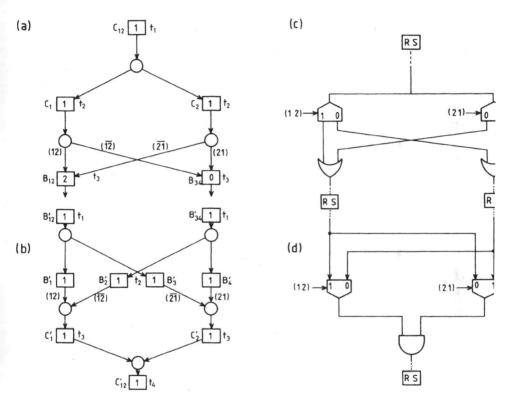

Figure 41 : A comparison between software and hardware implementations .

The figures 41b and 41d represent the transpose-dual representation of the figures 41a and 41c respectively. These architectures appear in the (and)-interpreted matrix-instruction which is the transpose of the (or)-interpreted matrix-instruction with disjoint columns. Again the parallel flowchart of figure 41b presents a fault which could alter the execution of a software implementation based on it. If the counters B'_{12} and B'_{34} contain a 1 at time t_1, then the counters B'_1, B'_2, B'_3 and B'_4 contain a 1 at time t_2 and the counters C'_1 and C'_2 contain a 1 at time t_3. The program is thus executed correctly ; however, for any value of the predicates $x_{(1,2)}$ and $x_{(2,1)}$, two of the counters B'_1, B'_2, B'_3, B'_4 remain at the value 1. The remaining 1's may produce an incorrect behaviour of the next program execution since the system does not start with correct initial conditions (all the counters at the value zero). Similar arguments as those developed above in this section allow us to verify that the hardware realization of figure 41c works correctly.

In any case we see that the faults which occur in the software materialization of algorithms are produced by the presence of *join-or instructions* in the synthesis of (or)-interpreted matrix-instructions. We indeed verify that only the join-or instruction may generate values greater than 1 in the counters. Moreover the undesired remaining "1's" in the transpose-dual architectures are produced by *fork instructions* which are the transpose-dual of join-or instructions.

We have seen in chapter 4 that the join-or instructions that appear in the synthesis of (or)-interpreted matrix-instructions with disjoint columns are *degenerate instructions*. Degenerate join-or instructions cannot produce non-safe programs ; indeed, the main characteristic of (or)-interpreted matrix-instructions with disjoint columns is that there exists for any combination of the predicates x_i, one and only one activated path between any network input and network output. A single activated path cannot produce multiple "1's" in the parallel flowchart representing the network. The following proposition holds.

Proposition 2

A software realization of an (or)-interpreted matrix-instruction is safe if and only if all its join-or instructions are degenerate instructions.

The fork instructions that occur in the synthesis of (and)-interpreted matrix-instructions generate *remaining* 1's in the counters, i.e. 1's that do not leave the counters at the instruction execution. These remaining 1's produce a non-safe behaviour of the instruction during its next execution. Indeed the new 1's which are produced by the next execution of an instruction together with its remaining 1's produce values greater than 1 in the counters. The following proposition holds.

Proposition 3

A software realization of an (and)-interpreted matrix-instruction is safe if and only if it does not contain fork instructions.

Summarizing the above results, we see that faults in non-safe programs are basically due to the fact that the software realization of an instruction contains internal memory devices : the counters associated with the elementary instructions. Those internal counters memorize the undesired transient behaviour of the system. The hardware realization of an instruction contains memory elements only at its inputs and outputs. Accordingly the internal faulty transient behaviour is not memorized.

The next section will be devoted to the realization of safe programs.

10.2. Realization of safe programs

First consider the realization of the row-instruction :

$$N \quad [f_1 \qquad f_2 \quad \cdots \quad f_q]$$
$$\sigma_1 \qquad \sigma_2 \quad \cdots \quad \sigma_q$$
$$M_1 \qquad M_2 \quad \cdots \quad M_q$$

by means of a safe program.

For sake of clearness we first propose a safe realization for q=2 and q=3. An elementary induction will then provide us with the general solution for any q.

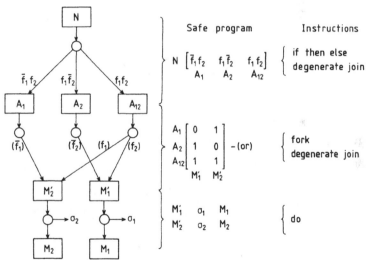

Figure 42 : Realization of a safe program equivalent to a matrix-instruction

Consider the parallel flowchart of figure 42 ; the upper part of this parallel flowchart (i.e. between the counters N and A_1, A_2, A_3) realizes the instruction :

$$N \quad [\bar{f}_1 f_2 \qquad f_1 \bar{f}_2 \qquad f_1 f_2]$$
$$A_1 \qquad A_2 \qquad A_{12}$$

As usual it is assumed that $\bar{f}_1 \bar{f}_2 \equiv 0$; otherwise an additional output label A_0 could be added. This instruction is a row-instruction with disjoint columns and may be realized by means of *if then else* and *degenerate join* instructions. The medium part of the parallel flowchart, i.e. between the counters A_1, A_2, A_{12} and M'_1, M'_2 realizes the matrix-instruction :

$$
\begin{array}{c}
A_1 \\
A_2 \\
A_{12}
\end{array}
\left[
\begin{array}{cc}
0 & 1 \\
1 & 0 \\
1 & 1
\end{array}
\right]
$$
$$
\quad M'_1 \qquad M'_2
$$

Since only one of the input labels A_j may be reached, this matrix-instruction is (or)-interpreted and its join-instructions are degenerate. It is thus made-up with *fork* and *degenerate join* instructions. The lower part of the parallel flowchart of figure 42 realizes execution instructions.

 The medium part between the counters A_1, A_2, A_3 and M'_1, M'_2 could also be represented by the following matrix instruction :

$$
\begin{array}{c}
A_1 \\
A_2 \\
A_{12}
\end{array}
\left[
\begin{array}{cc}
0 & \bar{f}_1 \\
\bar{f}_2 & 0 \\
f_2 & f_1
\end{array}
\right]
$$
$$
\quad M'_1 \qquad M'_2
$$

This matrix instruction corresponds to the between parentheses predicates associated to the arrows of figure 42. The realization of this matrix instruction is more complex than the formely proposed solution since it makes use of *then if* instructions instead of *degenerate* instructions; it will not be retained for implementations. This matrix instruction presents however some interesting theoretical properties ; this will appear later on in this section.

 In summary the parallel flowchart of figure 42 being realized by means of *if then else*, *fork* and *degenerate join* instructions is *safe*. Since

$$
\left[\begin{array}{ccc} \bar{f}_1 f_2 & f_1 \bar{f}_2 & f_1 f_2 \end{array} \right]
\left[
\begin{array}{cc}
0 & 1 \\
1 & 0 \\
1 & 1
\end{array}
\right]
=
\left[\begin{array}{cc} f_1 & f_2 \end{array} \right]
$$

the program realizes the requested row instruction. A similar matrix factorization provides us e.g. for q=3 with the following safe program :

$$N \left[\bar{f}_1\bar{f}_2 f_3 \quad \bar{f}_1 f_2 \bar{f}_3 \quad \bar{f}_1 f_2 f_3 \quad f_1 \bar{f}_2 \bar{f}_3 \quad f_1 \bar{f}_2 f_3 \quad f_1 f_2 \bar{f}_3 \quad f_1 f_2 f_3 \right]$$

$$A_{001} \qquad A_{010} \qquad A_{011} \qquad A_{100} \qquad A_{101} \qquad A_{110} \qquad A_{111}$$

$$
\begin{array}{c}
A_{001} \\
A_{010} \\
A_{011} \\
A_{100} \\
A_{101} \\
A_{110} \\
A_{111}
\end{array}
\begin{bmatrix}
0 & 0 & 1 \\
0 & 1 & 0 \\
0 & 1 & 1 \\
1 & 0 & 0 \\
1 & 0 & 1 \\
1 & 1 & 0 \\
1 & 1 & 1
\end{bmatrix}
$$

$$\sigma_1 \qquad \sigma_2 \qquad \sigma_3$$

$$M_1 \qquad M_2 \qquad M_3$$

For an iteration purpose that will appear further on, we have written the indexes of the labels A_j in their binary representation.

The above type of program transformation is of general nature ; the treatment of the general case is formally simplified by introducing some exponential notations which are classical in Boolean algebra (see e.g. Rudeanu [1974] or Davio, Deschamps and Thayse [1978]).

Let f be a Boolean function; the *lattice exponentiation* is defined as follows :

$$f^{(e)} = f \quad \text{iff} \quad e = 1 \; ,$$
$$= \bar{f} \quad \text{iff} \quad e = 0 \; .$$

The product of Boolean functions in direct or in complemented form is written :

$$\bigwedge_{i=1,q} f_i^{(e_i)} = \underline{f}^{(\underline{e})} \; , \qquad e_i \in \{0,1\} \quad \forall i \quad .$$

The vector of (2^q-1) minterms of $\underline{f}=(f_1,f_2,\ldots,f_q)$ sorted in lexicographical order :

$$[\; \bar{f}_1 \ldots \bar{f}_{q-1} f_q, \; \bar{f}_1 \ldots f_{q-1}\bar{f}_q, \; f_1 \ldots f_{q-1}f_q, \; \ldots , \; f_1 \ldots f_{q-1} \, f_q \;]$$

is written

$$[\; \underline{f}^{(\underline{e})} \;] \; , \qquad 0 < \underline{e} = (e_1, e_2, \ldots, e_q) \leqslant 2^q - 1 \; .$$

The $(2^q-1) \times q$ binary matrix whose k-th row is the integer k represented in its binary form is written either

$$[\ e_1, \ e_2 \ , \ \dots, \ e_q \ ] \ , \quad 0 \leqslant e_i \leqslant 1 \ , \quad 0 < \underline{e} \ ,$$

or $[\underline{e}]$, if no ambiguity occurs.

The following theorem allows us to implement any row-instruction or any (or)-interpreted matrix-instruction by means of a safe program. The proof of this theorem immediately derives from a perfect induction applied on the parallel program schema of figure 42.

Theorem 1.

The program represented by the matrix product :

$$N \quad \begin{bmatrix} \underline{f}^{(e)} \\ A_{\underline{e}} \end{bmatrix} \begin{bmatrix} e_1 & e_2 & \cdots & e_q \\ M_1 & M_2 & \cdots & M_q \end{bmatrix}$$

constitutes a safe realization of the row instruction :

$$N \quad \begin{bmatrix} f_1 & f_2 & \cdots & f_q \\ M_1 & M_2 & \cdots & M_q \end{bmatrix}$$

Consider now the safe realization of (or)-interpreted matrix-instructions. Let us represent the vector of (2^q-1) minterms of $\underline{f}_i = (f_{i1}, f_{i2}, \dots, f_{iq})$ sorted in lexicographical order by $[\underline{f}_i{}^{(\underline{e})}]$, $0 < \underline{e} = (e_1, \dots, e_q) \leqslant 2^q-1$.

Corollary 1.

The program represented by the matrix product :

$$\begin{matrix} N_1 \\ N_2 \\ \vdots \\ N_p \end{matrix} \begin{bmatrix} [\underline{f}_1{}^{(\underline{e})}] \\ [\underline{f}_2{}^{(\underline{e})}] \\ \\ [\underline{f}_p{}^{(\underline{e})}] \\ A_{\underline{e}} \end{bmatrix} \begin{bmatrix} e_1 & e_2 & \cdots & e_q \\ M_1 & M_2 & \cdots & M_q \end{bmatrix}$$

constitutes a safe realization of the (or)-interpreted matrix-instruction :

$$\begin{matrix} N_1 \\ N_2 \\ \vdots \\ N_p \end{matrix} \begin{bmatrix} f_{11} & f_{12} & \cdots & f_{1q} \\ f_{21} & f_{22} & \cdots & f_{2q} \\ \vdots & \vdots & & \vdots \\ f_{p1} & f_{p2} & \cdots & f_{pq} \end{bmatrix}$$
$$\begin{matrix} M_1 & M_2 & \cdots & M_q \end{matrix}$$

Consider afterwards the realization of the (and)-interpreted column·
instruction:

$$
\begin{array}{cc}
N_1 & \tau_1 \\
N_2 & \tau_2 \\
\vdots & \vdots \\
N_q & \tau_q
\end{array}
\left[
\begin{array}{c}
f_1 \\
f_2 \\
\vdots \\
f_q
\end{array}
\right]
$$
$$M$$

by means of a safe program. Assume moreover that this column-instruction belongs to
the following program :

$$
N
\begin{bmatrix}
f_1 & f_2 & \cdots & f_q
\end{bmatrix}
$$
$$
\begin{array}{cccc}
\sigma_1 & \sigma_2 & \cdots & \sigma_q \\
M_1 & M_2 & \cdots & M_q
\end{array}
$$

(135)

$$
\begin{array}{cc}
M_1 & \tau_1 \\
M_2 & \tau_2 \\
\vdots & \vdots \\
M_q & \tau_q
\end{array}
\left[
\begin{array}{c}
f_1 \\
f_2 \\
\vdots \\
f_q
\end{array}
\right]
$$
$$N'$$

(The cooperation of a row-instruction with an (and)-interpreted column-instruction
constitutes the most usual use for column-instructions).

For sake of clearness we again propose a safe realization of the
program (135) for q=2 and q=3; an elementary induction will then provide us with
the general solution for any q.

Consider the parallel flowchart of figure 43 ; the upper part of
this parallel flowchart, i.e. between the counters N and M_1, M_2 realizes a row-
instruction (for q=2) while the lower part of this parallel flowchart, i.e. between
the counters M_1, M_2 and N' realizes the corresponding (and)-interpreted column-instruction. The program realized by this parallel flowchart is written down in (136)
The (and)-interpreted column-instruction is realized by means of an (and)-interpre-
ted matrix-instruction the two rows of which (N_1 and N_2) are composed of disjoint
columns. The row-instructions N_1 and N_2 may thus be realized by means of *if then
else* and *degenerate join* instructions. Since the matrix-instruction is (and)-inter-
preted the non-zero elements of the two rows N_1 and N_2 are related by means of join·
and instructions. Finally the labels B_1, B_2 and B_{12} are connected by means of a joi
-or instruction : since one and only one of the labels B_1,B_2 and B_{12} may be reached

this join-or instruction is a degenerate instruction.

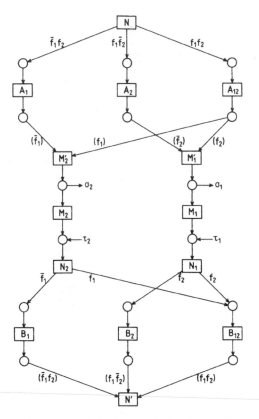

Figure 43 : Parallel flowchart for the safe realization
of the program (135)

In summary, the column instruction being realized by means of *if then else*, *join-and* and *degenerate join* instructions is *safe*. Again the degenerate join-or instruction which appears in the realization of the column instruction could be replaced by the following column instruction :

$$
\begin{array}{c}
B_1 \\
B_2 \\
B_{12}
\end{array}
\left[
\begin{array}{c}
\bar{f}_1 f_2 \\
f_1 \bar{f}_2 \\
f_1 f_2
\end{array}
\right]
$$

$$N'$$

This column instruction corresponds to the between parantheses predicates of the lower part of figure 43. The realization of this matrix instruction is more complex than the formely proposed solution : it is indeed implemented by means of *then if*

$$
\begin{array}{l}
\begin{array}{cc}
N & \left[\begin{array}{ccc} \bar{f}_1 f_2 & f_1 \bar{f}_2 & f_1 f_2 \end{array}\right] \\
 & \begin{array}{ccc} A_1 & \;\;A_2 & \;\;A_{12} \end{array}
\end{array}
\\[2ex]
\begin{array}{c}A_1\\A_2\\A_{12}\end{array}
\left[\begin{array}{cc} 0 & 1 \\ 1 & 0 \\ 1 & 1 \end{array}\right]
\text{ instruction equivalent to : }
\begin{array}{c}A_1\\A_2\\A_{12}\end{array}
\left[\begin{array}{cc} 0 & \bar{f}_1 \\ \bar{f}_2 & 0 \\ f_2 & f_1 \end{array}\right]
\\
\quad\;\; M'_1 \;\; M'_2 \qquad\qquad\qquad\qquad\qquad\qquad\qquad\;\; M'_1 \;\; M'_2
\\[2ex]
M'_1 \quad \sigma_1 \quad M_1 \\
M'_2 \quad \sigma_2 \quad M_2
\end{array}
\left.\vphantom{\begin{array}{c}1\\1\\1\\1\\1\\1\\1\\1\\1\\1\end{array}}\right\}\text{row instruction realization}
\qquad (136)
$$

$$
\begin{array}{l}
M_1 \quad \tau_1 \quad N_1 \\
M_2 \quad \tau_2 \quad N_2
\end{array}
$$

$$
\begin{array}{l}
\begin{array}{c}N_1\\N_2\end{array}
\left[\begin{array}{ccc} 0 & \bar{f}_2 & f_2 \\ \bar{f}_1 & 0 & f_1 \end{array}\right]
\\
\quad\;\; B_1 \;\;\; B_2 \;\;\; B_{12}
\\[2ex]
\begin{array}{c}B_1\\B_2\\B_{12}\end{array}
\left[\begin{array}{c} 1 \\ 1 \\ 1 \end{array}\right]
\text{ instruction equivalent to : }
\begin{array}{c}B_1\\B_2\\B_{12}\end{array}
\left[\begin{array}{c} \bar{f}_1 f_2 \\ f_1 \bar{f}_2 \\ f_1 f_2 \end{array}\right]
\\
\quad\;\; N' \qquad\qquad\qquad\qquad\qquad\qquad\qquad\qquad\;\; N'
\end{array}
\left.\vphantom{\begin{array}{c}1\\1\\1\\1\\1\\1\\1\\1\end{array}}\right\}\text{column instruction realization}
$$

instructions while the *degenerate join-or* instructions do not request any physical materialization. The representation by means of *then-if* instructions presents however some interesting theoretical properties that will appear later on in this section. We indeed observe that the parallel flowchart of figure 43 has an upper part between the counters N and M_1, M_2 which exactly corresponds to the lower part between the counters M_1, M_2 and N' : *this parallel flowchart is symmetric with respect to the counters M_1, M_2 if and only if the arrows are marked with the between parentheses predicates*. This symmetry disappears if the between parentheses predicates are removed ; we shall see that to the symmetric parallel flowchart will correspond a program with symmetric behaviour properties. A similar parallel flowchart provides us for q=3 with the safe program (137).

$$N \begin{bmatrix} \bar{f}_1\bar{f}_2 f_3 & \bar{f}_1 f_2 \bar{f}_3 & \bar{f}_1 f_2 f_3 & f_1 \bar{f}_2 \bar{f}_3 & f_1 \bar{f}_2 f_3 & f_1 f_2 \bar{f}_3 & f_1 f_2 f_3 \end{bmatrix}$$
$$\qquad\;\; A_{001} \qquad\; A_{010} \qquad\; A_{011} \qquad\; A_{100} \qquad\; A_{101} \qquad\; A_{110} \qquad\; A_{111}$$

$$
\begin{array}{c}
A_{001} \\ A_{010} \\ A_{011} \\ A_{100} \\ A_{101} \\ A_{110} \\ A_{111}
\end{array}
\begin{bmatrix}
0 & 0 & 1 \\
0 & 1 & 0 \\
0 & 1 & 1 \\
1 & 0 & 0 \\
1 & 0 & 1 \\
1 & 1 & 0 \\
1 & 1 & 1
\end{bmatrix}
\begin{array}{ccc}
\sigma_1 & \sigma_2 & \sigma_3 \\[4pt]
M_1 & M_2 & M_3
\end{array}
\qquad \text{or equivalently :} \qquad
\begin{array}{c}
A_{001} \\ A_{010} \\ A_{011} \\ A_{100} \\ A_{101} \\ A_{110} \\ A_{111}
\end{array}
\begin{bmatrix}
0 & 0 & \bar{f}_1\bar{f}_2 \\
0 & \bar{f}_1\bar{f}_3 & 0 \\
0 & \bar{f}_1 f_3 & \bar{f}_1 f_2 \\
\bar{f}_2\bar{f}_3 & 0 & 0 \\
\bar{f}_2 f_3 & 0 & f_1 \bar{f}_2 \\
f_2 \bar{f}_3 & f_1 \bar{f}_3 & 0 \\
f_2 f_3 & f_1 f_3 & f_1 f_2
\end{bmatrix}
\begin{array}{ccc}
\sigma_1 & \sigma_2 & \sigma_3 \\[4pt]
M_1 & M_2 & M_3
\end{array}
$$

$$(137)$$

$$
\begin{array}{cc}
M_1 & \tau_1 \\ M_2 & \tau_2 \\ M_3 & \tau_3
\end{array}
\begin{bmatrix}
0 & 0 & 0 & \bar{f}_2\bar{f}_3 & \bar{f}_2 f_3 & f_2 \bar{f}_3 & f_2 f_3 \\
0 & \bar{f}_1\bar{f}_3 & \bar{f}_1 f_3 & 0 & 0 & f_1 \bar{f}_3 & f_1 f_3 \\
\bar{f}_1\bar{f}_2 & 0 & \bar{f}_1 f_2 & 0 & f_1 \bar{f}_2 & 0 & f_1 f_2
\end{bmatrix}
$$
$$\qquad\quad B_{001} \quad\; B_{010} \quad\; B_{011} \quad\; B_{100} \quad\; B_{101} \quad\; B_{110} \quad\; B_{111}$$

$$
\begin{array}{c}
B_{001} \\ B_{010} \\ B_{011} \\ B_{100} \\ B_{101} \\ B_{110} \\ B_{111}
\end{array}
\begin{bmatrix}
1 \\ 1 \\ 1 \\ 1 \\ 1 \\ 1 \\ 1
\end{bmatrix}
\begin{array}{c} \\ N' \end{array}
\qquad \text{or equivalently :} \qquad
\begin{array}{c}
B_{001} \\ B_{010} \\ B_{011} \\ B_{100} \\ B_{101} \\ B_{110} \\ B_{111}
\end{array}
\begin{bmatrix}
\bar{f}_1\bar{f}_2 f_3 \\
\bar{f}_1 f_2 \bar{f}_3 \\
\bar{f}_1 f_2 f_3 \\
f_1 \bar{f}_2 \bar{f}_3 \\
f_1 \bar{f}_2 f_3 \\
f_1 f_2 \bar{f}_3 \\
f_1 f_2 f_3
\end{bmatrix}
\begin{array}{c} \\ N' \end{array}
$$

Let us denote by $\left[\underline{f}^{(\underline{e})}\right]_{f_i=1}$ the vector of (2^q-1) minterms of $\underline{f}=(f_1,f_2,\ldots,f_q)$ sorted in lexicographical order where f_i has been replaced by 1 and $\bar{f}_i$ by 0.

The following theorem allows us to implement any row instruction and any subsequent (and)-interpreted column instruction by means of a safe program. The proof of this theorem immediately derives from a perfect induction applied on the parallel program schema of figure 43 ; it encompasses theorem 1 of this section.

<u>Theorem 2</u>

The program represented by the matrix product

$$
N \begin{bmatrix} \underline{f}^{(\underline{e})} \\ A_{\underline{e}} \end{bmatrix} \begin{bmatrix} e_1 & e_2 & \cdots & e_q \\ M_1 & M_2 & \cdots & M_q \end{bmatrix}
$$

constitutes a safe realization of the row instruction ;

$$
N \begin{bmatrix} f_1 & f_2 & \cdots & f_q \\ \sigma_1 & \sigma_2 & \cdots & \sigma_q \\ M_1 & M_2 & \cdots & M_q \end{bmatrix} ;
$$

the program represented by the matrix product :

$$
\begin{bmatrix} M_1 & \tau_1 \\ M_2 & \tau_2 \\ \vdots & \\ M_q & \tau_q \end{bmatrix} \begin{bmatrix} \left[\underline{f}^{(\underline{e})}\right]_{f_1=1} \\ \left[\underline{f}^{(\underline{e})}\right]_{f_2=1} \\ \vdots \\ \left[\underline{f}^{(\underline{e})}\right]_{f_q=1} \end{bmatrix} \begin{bmatrix} 1 \\ 1 \\ \vdots \\ 1 \end{bmatrix}
$$

$$
B_{\underline{e}} \qquad \qquad N'
$$

constitutes a safe realization of the (and)-interpreted column instruction

$$
\begin{bmatrix} M_1 & \tau_1 \\ M_2 & \tau_2 \\ \vdots & \vdots \\ M_q & \tau_q \end{bmatrix} \begin{bmatrix} f_1 \\ f_2 \\ \vdots \\ f_q \end{bmatrix}
$$

$$
N'
$$

As stated above the use of *then if* instructions instead of *degenerate or* instructions in the safe realization of row- and of column-instructions allows a symmetric treatment of these instructions. The following theorem is obtained from a perfect induction process on the parallel flowchart of figure 43 or on the program (137).

Theorem 3

1) *From the matrix factorization*

$$\begin{bmatrix} f_1 & f_2 & \cdots & f_q \end{bmatrix} = \begin{bmatrix} \underline{f}^{(\underline{e})} \end{bmatrix} \; \begin{bmatrix} \begin{bmatrix} \underline{f}^{(\underline{e})} \end{bmatrix}^t_{f_1=1} & \cdots & \begin{bmatrix} \underline{f}^{(\underline{e})} \end{bmatrix}^t_{f_q=1} \end{bmatrix}$$

we deduce a safe realization for a row instruction in terms of if then else, fork and then if instructions.
From the transposed matrix factorization

$$\begin{bmatrix} f_1 \\ \vdots \\ f_q \end{bmatrix} = \begin{bmatrix} \begin{bmatrix} \underline{f}^{(\underline{e})} \end{bmatrix}_{f_1=1} \\ \vdots \\ \begin{bmatrix} \underline{f}^{(\underline{e})} \end{bmatrix}_{f_q=1} \end{bmatrix} \; \begin{bmatrix} \underline{f}^{(\underline{e})} \end{bmatrix}$$

we deduce a safe realization for a column instruction in terms of if then else, join-and, then if instructions.

2) *The two safe realizations are deduced from each other by performing the following substitutions :*

$$\text{row realization} \begin{cases} \text{if then else} \longleftrightarrow \text{then if} \\ \text{then if} \longleftrightarrow \text{if then else} \\ \text{fork} \longleftrightarrow \text{join-and} \end{cases} \text{column realization}$$

3) *The safe realizations proposed by theorem 2 are deduced from the safe realizations proposed on point 1) by replacing the then if instructions by degenerate join-or instructions.*

Let us illustrate the above theorem 3 by means of a short example, consider the problem of the choice of routes between two possible routes (see section 5.3). The problem reduces to a safe realization of the program :

$$N \begin{bmatrix} f_1 & f_2 \\ \sigma_1 & \sigma_2 \\ M_1 & M_2 \end{bmatrix}$$

$$
\begin{array}{cc}
M_1 & \tau_1 \\
M_2 & \tau_2
\end{array}
\left[
\begin{array}{c}
f_1 \\
f_2
\end{array}
\right]
$$

N'

with :

$$f_1 = x_{(1,2)} \lor \bar{x}_{(2,1)}$$
$$f_2 = x_{(2,1)} \lor \bar{x}_{(1,2)}$$

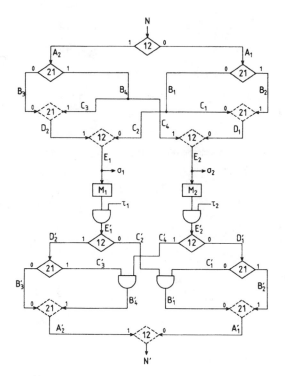

Figure 44 : Symmetric realization of a safe program

A realization grounded on the statement of theorem 3 is depicted in figure 44. In this realization the dotted *then if* instructions may be replaced by *degenerate join-or* instructions.

Using the notations (67) and (71) which were introduced in section 4.4. the program of figure 44 is written as follows :

$$\begin{array}{ll}
N\ (\overline{12}\ A_1\ ,\ 12\ A_2) & *\ (\overline{12}\ A_1'\ ,\ 12\ A_2')\ N' \\
A_1(\overline{21}\ B_1\ ,\ 21\ B_2) & *\ (\overline{21}\ B_1'\ ,\ 21\ B_2')\ A_1' \\
A_2(\overline{21}\ B_3\ ,\ 21\ B_4) & *\ (\overline{21}\ B_3'\ ,\ 21\ B_4')\ A_2' \\
B_1\ (C_1\ ,\ C_2) & (C_1'\ ,\ C_2'\ )\ B_1' \\
B_4\ (C_3\ ,\ C_4) & (C_3'\ ,\ C_4'\ )\ B_4' \\
(\overline{21}\ B_3\ ,\ 21\ C_3)\ D_2\ * & D_2'\ (\overline{21}\ B_3'\ ,\ 21\ C_3'\ ) \\
(\overline{21}\ C_1\ ,\ 21\ B_2)\ D_1\ * & D_1'\ (\overline{21}\ C_1'\ ,\ 21\ B_2'\ ) \\
(\overline{12}\ D_1\ ,\ 12\ C_4)\ E_2\ * & E_2'\ (\overline{12}\ D_1'\ ,\ 12\ C_4'\ ) \\
(\overline{12}\ C_2\ ,\ 12\ D_2)\ E_1\ * & E_1'\ (\overline{12}\ C_2'\ ,\ 12\ D_2'\ ) \\
E_1\ \sigma_1\ M_1 & M_1\ \tau_1\ E_1' \\
E_2\ \sigma_2\ M_2 & M_2\ \tau_2\ E_2'
\end{array}$$

(138a)

The instructions which are marked with an asterix are those which may be replaced by a degenerate join-or instruction and may thus be dropped. This substitution transforms the program (138a) into the equivalent program (138b) :

$$\begin{array}{ll}
 & (C_1'\ ,\ C_2')\ N' \\
N\ (\overline{12}\ A_1\ ,\ 12\ A_2) & (C_3'\ ,\ C_4')\ N' \\
A_1(\overline{21}\ B_1\ ,\ 21\ E_2) & D_1'\ (\ \overline{21}\ C_1'\ ,\ 21\ N') \\
A_2(\overline{21}\ E_1\ ,\ 21\ B_4) & D_2'\ (\ \overline{21}\ N'\ ,\ 21\ C_3') \\
B_1(E_1\ ,\ E_2) & E_1'\ (\ \overline{12}\ C_2'\ ,\ 12\ D_2') \\
B_4(E_1\ ,\ E_2) & E_2'\ (\ \overline{12}\ D_1'\ ,\ 12\ C_4') \\
E_1\ \sigma_1\ M_1 & M_1\ \tau_1\ E_1' \\
E_2\ \sigma_2\ M_2 & M_2\ \tau_2\ E_2'
\end{array}$$

(138b)

10.3. Computation of safe programs by means of P-functions

Theorem 1 of section 10.2 and the transformation formalism of section 3.2 (see the transformations (28),(33),(34)) allow us to state that the matrix product :

$$N\begin{bmatrix} \underline{f}^{(\underline{e})} \\ A_{\underline{e}} \end{bmatrix} \begin{bmatrix} e_1 & e_2 & \cdots & e_q \\ \sigma_1 & \sigma_2 & \cdots & \sigma_q \\ M_1 & M_2 & \cdots & M_q \end{bmatrix}$$

which generates a safe realization for the row-instruction

$$N \begin{bmatrix} f_1 & f_2 & \cdots & f_q \\ \sigma_1 & \sigma_2 & \cdots & \sigma_q \\ M_1 & M_2 & \cdots & M_q \end{bmatrix}$$

is obtained by performing the following transformation between P-functions :

$$N : <1 ; \sum_{\underline{e}} \underline{f}^{(\underline{e})} \ \sigma_{\underline{e}} > \xleftarrow{\{t_i\}} \{<\underline{f}^{(\underline{e})} ; \sigma_{\underline{e}}> : A_{\underline{e}}\} \quad 0 < \underline{e} \leqslant 2^q-1 \tag{139}$$

with $\sigma_{\underline{e}} = \sum_i e_i \ \sigma_i$.

The transformation (139) synthesizes a program made up of *if then else* and of *degenerate join* instructions which realizes the first factor of the matrix product, i.e. :

$$N \begin{bmatrix} \underline{f}^{(\underline{e})} \\ A_{\underline{e}} \end{bmatrix}$$

The second factor of the matrix product, i.e. :

$$A_{\underline{e}} \begin{bmatrix} e_1 & e_2 & \cdots & e_q \\ \sigma_1 & \sigma_2 & \cdots & \sigma_q \\ M_1 & M_2 & \cdots & M_q \end{bmatrix}$$

is realized in a self-evident way by means of *fork* and of *degenerate join* instructions.

For example the synthesis of the routing problem considered in section 10.2 is obtained by performing the following transformation between P-functions:

$$\left.\begin{array}{l} A_1 : <\bar{f}_1 f_2 = \bar{x}_{(1,2)} \ x_{(2,1)} \ ;\sigma_2> \\[2mm] A_2 : <f_1 \bar{f}_2 = x_{(1,2)} \ \bar{x}_{(2,1)} \ ;\sigma_1> \\[2mm] A_{12}: <f_1 f_2 = x_{(1,2)} \ x_{(2,1)} \ \vee \\[1mm] \qquad \bar{x}_{(1,2)}\bar{x}_{(2,1)} \ ;\sigma_1 + \sigma_2> \end{array}\right\} \xrightarrow{t_{12}, t_{21}} \begin{array}{l} <1 ; f_1\bar{f}_2\sigma_1 + \bar{f}_1 f_2\sigma_2 + \\[2mm] \qquad f_1 f_2(\sigma_1 + \sigma_2)> = \\[2mm] <1 ; f_1\sigma_1 + f_2\sigma_2> \end{array}$$

This transformation produces the program depicted in the upper part of figure 45.

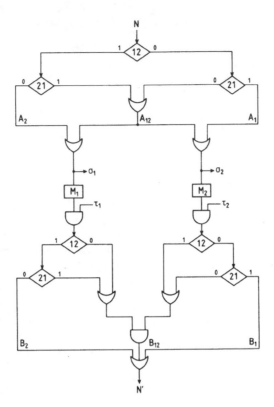

<u>Figure 45</u>: Realization of a safe program

Theorem 2 of section 10.2 allows us to state that the synthesis of an (and)-interpreted column-instruction reduces to the synthesis of q row-instructions :

$$ M_i \quad \tau_i \quad \left[\underline{\frac{f^{(e)}}{}} \right]_{f_i=1} $$
$$ B_{\underline{e}} $$

which are connected by means of *join-and* instructions ; each of these row-instructions may be synthesized by performing a transformation of the form (139).

Continuing the example of section 10.2, we perform the following transformations for the synthesis of the column-instruction :

$$ \left. \begin{array}{l} B_2 : \langle \bar{f}_2 \; ; \lambda \rangle \\ B_{12} : \langle f_2 \; ; \tau_2 \rangle \end{array} \right\} \xrightarrow{t_{12}, t_{21}} \langle 1 \; ; \lambda \, \bar{f}_2 + \tau_2 f_2 \rangle $$

$$ \left. \begin{array}{l} B_1 : \langle \bar{f}_1 \; ; \lambda \rangle \\ B_{12} : \langle f_1 \; ; \tau_1 \rangle \end{array} \right\} \xrightarrow{t_{12}, t_{21}} \langle 1 \; ; \lambda \, \bar{f}_1 + \tau_1 f_1 \rangle $$

These two transformations produce the program depicted in the lower part of figure 45 (compare the realizations of figures 44 and 45).

The corollary 1 of section 10.2 and the transformation formalism of section 3.2 (see the transformations (28), (33), (34), (45)) allow us to state that a safe realization of an (or)-interpreted matrix-instruction is obtained by pe forming the following transformation between systems of P-functions :

$$
\left.\begin{array}{l}
N_1 : <1,\ldots,\ldots ; \sum_{\underline{e}} f_1^{(\underline{e})}\ \sigma_{\underline{e}}> \\[2mm]
N_2 : <.,1,\ldots,.; \sum_{\underline{e}} f_2^{(\underline{e})}\ \sigma_{\underline{e}}> \\[2mm]
\vdots \\[2mm]
N_q : <.,.,\ldots,1; \sum_{\underline{e}} f_p^{(\underline{e})}\ \sigma_{\underline{e}}>
\end{array}\right\} \{t_i\}^p
\left\{
\begin{array}{l}
<\underline{f}_1^{(\underline{e})},\ \underline{f}_2^{(\underline{e})},\ldots,\ f_p^{(\underline{e})};\ \sigma_{\underline{e}}>: A_{\underline{e}} \qquad (140) \\[2mm]
0 < \underline{e}=(e_1,e_2,\ldots,e_q) \leqslant 2^q-1
\end{array}\right.
$$

The transformations (139, 140) may be performed in cooperation with the optimizatic process described in section 4.3. in order to obtain an optimal safe program (e.g. a safe program containing the smallest number of *if then else* instructions). Finally a straightforward adaptation of the above transformations allows us to synt size safe programs for the implementation of (and)-interpreted matrix-instructions with disjoint columns (see section 9.4.). The writing of the formal transformation left to the reader.

Let us now briefly consider the architecture proposed by theorem 3 and illustrated in figure 44 for the routing example. The synthesis of a row-instru tion by means of this architecture is characterized by a design made up of *if then else*, *fork* and *then if* instructions. The *then if* instructions are in place of the *degenerate join* instructions of the formerly studied architectures.

The architecture of theorem 3 can be obtained by performing the following steps.

1. Obtain a *decision tree* which evaluates the row-instruction (by decision tree we mean a decision program without reconvergent instruction, i.e. free of *join-or* and *degenerate join-or* instructions; in figure 44, the program between the labels N and B_1, B_2, B_3, B_4 is a decision tree) ;

2. The leaves of the tree (which may be *fork* instruction labels such as B_1 and B_4 in figure 44) are connected together by means of *then if* instructions in place of the *degenerate join* instructions : since two leaves have one and only one predecessor which represents an *if then else* instruction, a reconvergence of the two leaves is obtained through the transpose of the instruction associated with their predecessor. (e.g. in figure 44, B_3 and B_4 have A_2 as predecessor : to A_2 is associated an *if then else* instruction with decision variable 21 ; B_3 and B_4 may thus reconverge through a *then if* instruction having the same decision variable 21)

The synthesis problem reduces to the obtention of a decision tree which evaluates a row-instruction.

Let $\{p_j(\underline{f}^{(\underline{e})})\}$ be the set of all the prime implicants of $\underline{f}^{(\underline{e})}$. The decision tree is obtained by performing the following transformation between P-functions :

$$N : \langle 1; \sum_{\underline{e}} \underline{f}^{(\underline{e})} \; \sigma_{\underline{e}} \rangle \xleftarrow{\{t_i\}} \{\langle p_j(\underline{f}^{(\underline{e})}); \sigma_{\underline{e}} \rangle : A_{\underline{e}j}\} \tag{141}$$

This immediately derives from the two following items.

1. Since $\displaystyle \mathop{v}_{\underline{e}} \mathop{v}_{j} p_j(\underline{f}^{(\underline{e})}) = \mathop{v}_{\underline{e}} \underline{f}^{(\underline{e})} = 1$,

   an iterative application of the composition laws $\{t_i\}$ on the domain functions $\{p_j(f^{(\underline{e})})\}$ produces a domain function equal to 1 ; to this 1-domain function is associated the codomain function :

   $$\sum_{\underline{e}} (\mathop{v}_{j} p_j (\underline{f}^{(\underline{e})})) \; \sigma_{\underline{e}} = \sum_{\underline{e}} \underline{f}^{(\underline{e})} \; \sigma_{\underline{e}}$$

   so that the decision program associated to the transformation (141) realizes the requested row instruction.

2. The initial domain functions $p_j(\underline{f}^{(\underline{e})})$ are cubes ; the compositions of cubes by means of the laws t_i produce new domain functions which are also cubes. A decision program is a decision tree if and only if all its instructions have associated P-functions whose domain are cubes (see section 13.1).

The decision program derived from the transformation (141) realizes thus the requested row-instruction and is moreover a decision tree.

For example the decision tree of the upper part of figure 44 (i.e. the decision program between the labels N and B_1, B_2, B_3, B_4) is obtained by performing the following transformation between P-functions :

$$\left.\begin{array}{l} B_1 : \langle \bar{x}_{(1,2)} \; \bar{x}_{(2,1)} \; ; \; \sigma_1 + \sigma_2 \rangle \\[6pt] B_2 : \langle \bar{x}_{(1,2)} \; x_{(2,1)} \; ; \; \sigma_2 \rangle \\[6pt] B_3 : \langle x_{(1,2)} \; \bar{x}_{(2,1)} \; ; \; \sigma_1 \rangle \\[6pt] B_4 : \langle x_{(1,2)} \; x_{(2,1)} \; ; \; \sigma_1 + \sigma_2 \rangle \end{array}\right\} \xrightarrow{t_{12}, t_{21}} \langle 1; f_1\sigma_1 + f_2\sigma_2 \rangle$$

10.4. Example 2 (continued)

Let us now consider the more elaborate example which was introduced in sections 5.2 and 6.3. The routing functions are (see also (89) and figure 14) :

$$f_1 = (12 \vee \overline{21})(13 \vee \overline{31})$$

$$f_2 = (\overline{12} \vee 21)(23 \vee \overline{32})$$

$$f_3 = (12 \vee \overline{21})(\overline{13} \vee 31) \vee (\overline{12} \vee 21)(\overline{23} \vee 32) .$$

For sake of conciseness the variables $x_{(i,j)}$ are written ij. The synthesis of the row instruction (91) or (111a) :

$$N \quad \tau \begin{bmatrix} f_1 & f_2 & f_3 \\ \sigma_1 & \sigma_2 & \sigma_3 \\ M_1 & M_2 & M_3 \end{bmatrix}$$

requires the evaluation of the orthogonal set of Boolean functions $\underline{f}^{(e)}$, $0 < e \leqslant 7$:

$$f^{(001)} = \overline{f}_1\overline{f}_2 f_3 \; ; \; f^{(010)} = \overline{f}_1 f_2\overline{f}_3 \; ; \; f^{(011)} = \overline{f}_1 f_2 f_3 \; ; \; f^{(100)} = f_1\overline{f}_2\overline{f}_3 \; ;$$
$$f^{(101)} = f_1\overline{f}_2 f_3 \; ; \; f^{(110)} = f_1 f_2\overline{f}_3 \; ; \; f^{(111)} = f_1 f_2 f_3.$$

The synthesis of the column instruction (111b) :

$$\begin{matrix} M_1 & \tau_1 \\ M_2 & \tau_2 \\ M_3 & \tau_3 \end{matrix} \begin{bmatrix} f_1 \\ f_2 \\ f_3 \end{bmatrix}$$

$$\sigma$$

$$N'$$

requires the evaluation of the orthogonal sets of Boolean functions
$[\underline{f}^{(e)}]_{f_i=1}$, $0 \leqslant \underline{e} \leqslant 7$, $1 \leqslant i \leqslant 3$; let us note $g_i^{(\underline{e})}$ for $[\underline{f}^{(\underline{e})}]_{f_i=1}$

We have :

$$g_1^{(00)} = \overline{f}_2\overline{f}_3 \; , \; g_1^{(01)} = \overline{f}_2 f_3 \; , \; g_1^{(10)} = f_2\overline{f}_3 \; , \; g_1^{(11)} = f_2 f_3 \; ;$$

$$g_2^{(00)} = \overline{f}_1\overline{f}_3 \; , \; g_2^{(01)} = \overline{f}_1 f_3 \; , \; g_2^{(10)} = f_1\overline{f}_3 \; , \; g_2^{(11)} = f_1 f_3 \; ;$$

$$g_3^{(00)} = \overline{f}_1\overline{f}_2 \; , \; g_3^{(01)} = \overline{f}_1 f_2 \; , \; g_3^{(10)} = f_1\overline{f}_2 \; , \; g_3^{(11)} = f_1 f_2$$

A safe realization of the program (111) i.e. :

$$N \quad \tau \begin{bmatrix} f_1 & f_2 & f_3 \\ \sigma_1 & \sigma_2 & \sigma_3 \\ M_1 & M_2 & M_3 \end{bmatrix}$$

$$\begin{array}{cc} M_1 & \tau_1 \\ M_2 & \tau_2 \\ M_3 & \tau_3 \end{array} \begin{bmatrix} f_1 \\ f_2 \\ f_3 \end{bmatrix}$$

$$\sigma$$
$$N'$$

derives from the materialization of the matrix-instructions of the program (142).

$$N \quad \tau \begin{bmatrix} f^{(001)} & f^{(010)} & f^{(011)} & f^{(100)} & f^{(101)} & f^{(110)} & f^{(111)} \end{bmatrix}$$

$$A_{001} \quad A_{010} \quad A_{011} \quad A_{100} \quad A_{101} \quad A_{110} \quad A_{111}$$

$$\begin{array}{c} A_{001} \\ A_{010} \\ A_{011} \\ A_{100} \\ A_{101} \\ A_{110} \\ A_{111} \end{array} \begin{bmatrix} 0 & 0 & 1 \\ 0 & 1 & 0 \\ 0 & 1 & 1 \\ 1 & 0 & 0 \\ 1 & 0 & 1 \\ 1 & 1 & 0 \\ 1 & 1 & 1 \end{bmatrix}$$

$$\sigma_1 \quad \sigma_2 \quad \sigma_3$$
$$M_1 \quad M_2 \quad M_3$$

$$\begin{array}{c} M_1 \, \tau_1 \\ M_2 \, \tau_2 \\ M_3 \, \tau_3 \end{array} \begin{bmatrix} 0 & 0 & 0 & g_1^{(00)} & g_1^{(01)} & g_1^{(10)} & g_1^{(11)} \\ 0 & g_2^{(00)} & g_2^{(01)} & 0 & 0 & g_2^{(10)} & g_2^{(11)} \\ g_3^{(00)} & 0 & g_3^{(01)} & 0 & g_3^{(01)} & 0 & g_3^{(11)} \end{bmatrix}$$

$$B_{001} \quad B_{010} \quad B_{011} \quad B_{100} \quad B_{101} \quad B_{110} \quad B_{111}$$

$$\begin{array}{c} B_{001} \\ B_{010} \\ B_{011} \\ B_{100} \\ B_{101} \\ B_{110} \\ B_{111} \end{array} \begin{bmatrix} 1 \\ 1 \\ 1 \\ 1 \\ 1 \\ 1 \\ 1 \end{bmatrix}$$

$$\sigma$$
$$N'$$

(142)

The synthesis of the row-instruction of (141) i.e. : $N \ \tau \ [f^{(\underline{e})}]$ is obtained by performing the following transformation between systems of P-functions :

$$\{<f^{(e_1e_2e_3)} \ ; \ \sigma_{e_1e_2e_3} >\} \xrightarrow{t_{ij}} <1 \ ; \ \sum_{e_1e_2e_3} f^{(e_1e_2e_3)} \ \sigma_{e_1e_2e_3} >$$

$$0 < (e_1, e_2, e_3) \leqslant 7$$

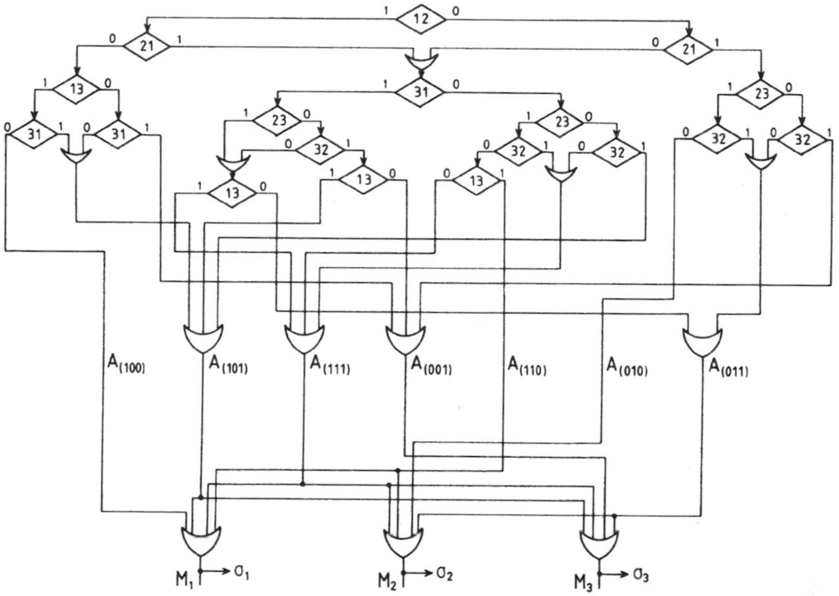

Figure 46 : Safe realization of the row-instruction (111a)

The resulting program is depicted in figure 46. The synthesis of the (and)-interpreted matrix-instruction of (141), is obtained by performing the three following transformations between systems of P-functions :

$$\{<g_k^{(e_1e_2)} \ ; \ \sigma_{e_1e_2} >\} \xrightarrow{t_{ij}} <1 \ ; \ \sum_{e_1e_2} g_k^{(e_1e_2)} \ \sigma_{e_1e_2} > \ , \ 1 \leqslant k \leqslant 3$$

$$0 \leqslant (e_1, e_2) \leqslant 3$$

and by connecting the resulting programs by means of *join-and* instructions. The computation of the above transformation and of the resulting program is left to the reader. Note that in these transformations the notation σ_e has no particular physical meaning : it is used only for marking pseudo-Boolean expressions. The connection of the various matrix instructions of program (142) is illustrated by means of figure 47.

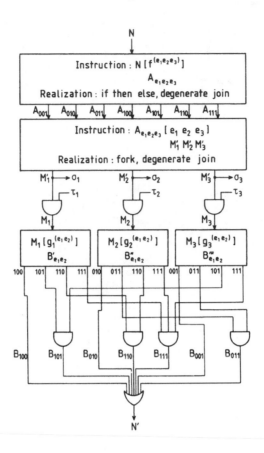

Figure 47 : Safe realization of the program (111a, 111b)

10.5. A general type of architecture for safe program implementation.

The architecture for safe program implementation proposed in sections 10.2 and 10.3 is schematically represented in figure 48a. For row instructions with a unique output label, i.e. instructions of the form :

$$N \begin{bmatrix} f_1 & f_2 & \cdots & f_q \\ \sigma_1 & \sigma_2 & \cdots & \sigma_q \\ M & M & \cdots & M \end{bmatrix}$$

another safe program architecture may be investigated ; an asynchronous implementation of this row instruction is obtained from the following safe program (143) which is equivalent to the row-instruction (λ means as usual the empty execution) :

$$N \begin{bmatrix} \bar{f}_1 & f_1 & \bar{f}_2 & f_2 & \cdots & \bar{f}_q & f_q \\ \lambda & \sigma_1 & \lambda & \sigma_2 & \cdots & \lambda & \sigma_q \\ M_1 & M_1' & M_2 & M_2' & \cdots & M_q & M_q' \end{bmatrix}$$

$$M_i' \quad \tau_i \quad M_i \qquad\qquad 1 \leqslant i \leqslant q \tag{143}$$

$$\begin{matrix} M_1 \\ M_2 \\ \vdots \\ M_q \end{matrix} \begin{bmatrix} 1 \\ 1 \\ \vdots \\ 1 \end{bmatrix}$$

$$M$$

A graphical representation of program (143) is given in figure 48b. Clearly the architectures 48a and 48b are two extremal implementations and any intermediate architecture can lead to an interesting safe program design. It is beyond the scope of the present text to give an exhaustive study of safe program architecture. We only mention an architecture which immediately derives from the safe programs studied in section 10.2 and which is schematized in figure 48a.

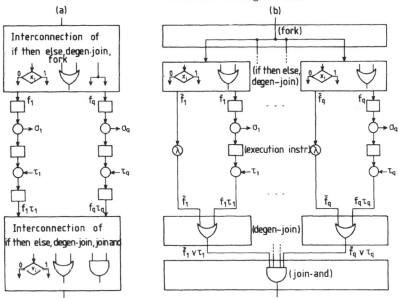

Figure 48 : Architectures for safe programs

      Figure 48a is composed of an upper part which realizes a row-instruction and of a lower part which realizes a column-instruction. *Any program formed by a tree-interconnection of upper parts of figure 48a is also a safe realization for a row-instruction. Any program formed by a tree-interconnection of lower parts of figure 48b is also a safe realization for a column-instruction.*

These tree-like architectures are illustrated by means of figure 49 which realizes the program (144) : this program may be interpreted as a routing program with four routes.

$$N \begin{bmatrix} f_1 & f_2 & f_3' & f_3'' \\ \sigma_1 & \sigma_2 & \sigma_3' & \sigma_3'' \\ M_1 & M_2 & M_3' & M_3'' \end{bmatrix}$$

$$\tag{144}$$

$$\begin{matrix} M_1 & \tau_1 \\ M_2 & \tau_2 \\ M_3' & \tau_3' \\ M_3'' & \tau_3'' \end{matrix} \begin{bmatrix} f_1 \\ f_2 \\ f_3' \\ f_3'' \end{bmatrix}$$
$$N'$$

$$f_1 = (12 \vee \overline{21})(13 \vee \overline{31})$$
$$f_2 = (\overline{12} \vee 21)(23 \vee \overline{32})$$
$$f_3' = (12 \vee \overline{21})(\overline{13} \vee 31)$$
$$f_3'' = (\overline{12} \vee 21)(\overline{23} \vee 32)$$

The synthesis of these programs may easily be expressed in terms of P-functions.

The synthesis of the program (143) is obtained by performing the q following transformations on systems of P-functions :

$$\left. \begin{matrix} <\overline{f}_j ; \lambda > \\ \\ <f_j ; \sigma_j> \end{matrix} \right\} \xrightarrow{\{t_k\}} <1 ; \overline{f}_j \lambda + f_j \sigma_j> , \quad 1 \leqslant j \leqslant q \tag{145}$$

Similarly, tree-like programs of the type of figure 49 are obtained by restricting the union law on P-functions :

$$<g ; h_1> \ \cup \ <g ; h_2> = <g ; h_1 + h_2>$$

in the following way :
the union law U may act on two P-functions with identical domain g if and only if the products of the coefficients of a given symbol σ_k in h_1 and h_2 is equal to zero.

It is finally interesting to note that when external constraints (such e.g. the requirement of the safe character) decreases the parallelism of a program, its complexity increases. This can be illustrated by comparing the figures 16, 46 and 49.

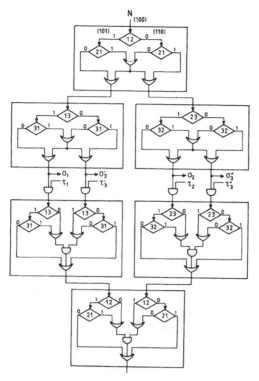

Figure 49 : Safe realization of the program (144)

Chapter 11 : <u>Microprogrammed implementation of instructions</u>

By microprogrammed implementation we mean materialization by means
of large scale integrated components.

Section 11.1 is first devoted to a short introduction to microprogrammed implementation. We then show how row instructions with disjoint column may be
realized by means of a *conditional program*. This conditional program is in turn implemented by means of a sequentialized structure. In a sequentialized structure we
perform one after the other two otherwise unrelated instructions.

Section 11.2 is devoted to a short introduction to microprogrammed
implementation of safe programs.

The present chapter gives only a concise summary to microprogrammed
materializations. More about these modern architectures may be found in Davio,
Deschamps and Thayse [1983a, 1983b] , Mange, Sanchez and Stauffer [1982] , Mano
[1979].

11.1. <u>Introduction to microprogrammed implementation</u>

By *microprogrammed implementation* of instructions and of programs we
essentially mean the materialization of the safe programs studied in chapter 10 by
means of *large scale integrated components* such as *Read-Only-Memories* (ROM's) and
Programmable-Logic-Arrays (PLA's).

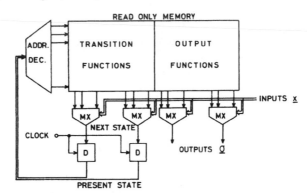

Figure 50 : Direct implementation of a matrix-instruction

We usually distinguish two types of microprogrammed implementations
which are illustrated in figures 50 and 51 respectively. In a first type of implementation (see figure 50), the elementary predicates or condition variables x of
a matrix-instruction are examined simultaneously. Roughly speaking, we can say
that a matrix-instruction or a program made up of matrix-instructions defines a
synchronous sequential machine whose input variables are x, output variables are

subsets of $\underline{\sigma}$ and internal variables encode the set $\{\underline{N},\underline{M}\}$ of the input and output labels. All operations included in a given matrix-instruction (test of the condition variables value, execution of the orders $\underline{\sigma}$ and transition to the next state) are performed in one clock period. The next step consists in implementing the sequential machine so defined in an integrated component. This step is schematically described in figure 50 which uses an address-decoder connected to a read-only-memory as integrated component. The memory words (or rows) are organized into two fields the next-state (or next-address) field and the output field. The architecture of figure 50 is the simplest architecture for an integrated implementation of algorithms. For a reason of cost (Davio, Deschamps and Thayse [1983a, 1983b])this architecture is never used in practice; it will thus not be considered further on. The interested reader may find a systematic study of algorithm implementation by means of the architecture of figure 50 in Clare [1973], Leung, Michel and Lebeux [1977], Sholl [1974, 1975], Davio, Deschamps and Thayse [1983a, 1983b] .

In the architecture of figure 50, the condition variables are examined simultaneously. We shall now investigate the possibility of examining these variables one at a time and we shall show how this sequential examination of the condition variables is reflected in the architecture of figure 51.

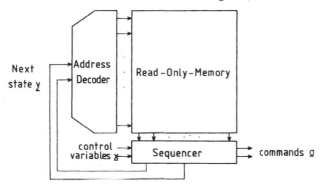

Figure 51 : Sequential implementation of a conditional program

A *conditional program* is a program all of whose instructions (except the last one) belong to either one of the following two types :

$$N \ [\ \bar{x}_i \qquad x_i \ ] \qquad (\textit{if then else instruction}) \qquad (146a)$$
$$ M_1 \qquad M_2$$

$$N \qquad \sigma \qquad M \qquad (\textit{execution instruction}) \qquad (146b)$$

It is not difficult to reflect the characteristic of a conditional program in the architecture of figure 51. The striking feature of a conditional program is that it contains instructions with two information items : N_1 and N_2 in the decision instruc tion and σ and M in the execution instruction. In such a situation, the control ROM word would be divided in four fields (see figure 51) :

1. A field containing k ($2^k \geqslant n$) columns indicates the index of the condition variable under test ;

2. A 1 column field defines the type of instruction : 0 represents a decision instruction while 1 represents an execution instruction.

3. The third field gives one of the next instruction numbers M_1 or M.

4. The last field gives the other next instruction number M_2 or the command σ.

A series of multiplexers realizes the information transfers under the control of the condition variable x_i selected by the field 1. During the execution of a decision instruction that information is used by an input identification circuit to select the variable x_i among the set of the condition variables. The value of the latter is in turn to select the appropriate next step address M_1 or M_2. Finally the next address is introduced into the ROM through an address decoder which selects the word labelled M_1 or M_2. Execution instructions are handled in a similar way.

Under that form the control automaton has all the main features of the model proposed by Wilkes [1951] for microprogrammed structures. The implementation structure of figure 51 is essentially the structure proposed by Mange [1978] for binary decision programs (see also Mange, Sanchez and Stauffer [1982]).

The implementation of a matrix instruction by the microprogrammed structure of figure 51 requires that it should be transformed into a conditional program, i.e. a program made up of instructions (146a, 146b). We have seen (see chapter 4) that the transformation algorithms based on the concept of P-function allowed to transform any (or)-interpreted matrix-instruction with disjoint columns into a conditional program. Consequently, the transformation (47) allows us also to translate this matrix-instruction into a microprogrammed structure.

A microprogrammed realization of the conditional program of figure 9 is given in figure 52. In view of their implementation the decision instructions of figure 9 are coded (000),...,(101), while the condition variables are coded :

$$x_1 : (00) , x_2(01) , x_3 : (10) .$$

The conditional program of figure 9 allows us to introduce the following simplifications with respect to the general microprogrammed structure of figure 51. The condition variable of any ultimate decision instruction being x_2 and the next instruction of any execution instruction being always coded (000), we may merge the branching instructions having x_2 as condition variables with their next execution instruction. Hence, the fields of the microprogrammed structure are as depicted in figure 53.

159

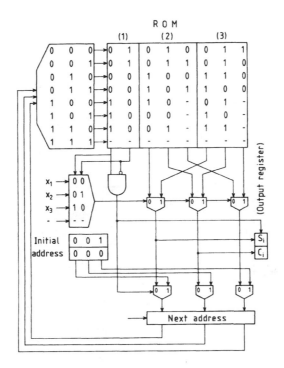

Figure 52 : Microprogrammed implementation of the
conditional program of figure 9.

	Variable identification field (1)	0-address field (2)	1-address field (3)
Next address	0 0 1 0	M_1	M_2
Next execution	0 1	σ_1	σ_2

Figure 53 : Configuration of the instruction fields for the
implementation of figures 52 and 54

Observe also that fields (1) and (2) of figure 51 are mergeable. Indeed, codings
(00) and (10) in field (1) mean decision instructions with condition variables x_1
and x_3 respectively, while the coding (01) means a decision instruction with condition variable x_2 merged with an execution instruction. Finally the initial instruction (000) is obtained from a second set of multiplexers (see figure 52).

A microprogrammed realization of the program of figure 5 is depicted
in figure 54. The coding of the instructions is given in figure 5 ; in particular
we assume in figure 54 that the initial addresses (000) and (001), which correspond

to the instruction labels D_1 and D_2 respectively, are available externally.

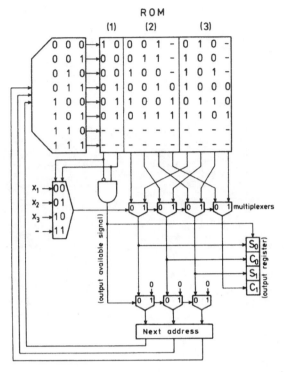

Figure 54 : Microprogrammed implementation of the conditional
program of figure 5.

The purpose of the present section was to introduce microprogrammed
implementation of instructions and to derive a microprogrammed structure for the
realization of an (or)-interpreted matrix-instruction with disjoint columns. Much
advanced research on microprogrammed implementation of programs has been published
by Cerny, Davio, Deschamps, Mange, Sanchez, Stauffer and Thayse : Cerny, Mange
and Sanchez [1979], Mange [1979, 1980, 1981], Stauffer [1980], Mange, Sanchez and
Stauffer [1982], Davio, Deschamps and Thayse [1983a, 1983b], Thayse [1980, 1981a,
1981b, 1981c, 1982]. We shall present in next section an introduction to microprogrammed implementation of (or)-interpreted and of (and)-interpreted matrix-instructions.

11.2. Microprogrammed implementation of safe programs

We have seen in section 10.5 that any program formed by a tree interconnection of upper parts of figure 48a is a safe realization for a row-instruction.
Moreover any program formed by a tree-interconnection of lower parts of figure 48a
is a safe realization for a column-instruction. It turns out that microprogrammed

implementations of a row- and of a column-instruction are deduced from the microprogrammed implémentations of the upper and of the lower parts of figure 48a respectively. These microprogrammed implementations are deduced in a straightforward
way from the realization proposed in section 11.1. Consider e.g. the coding of
figure 53; it is clear that the next executions σ_1 and σ_2 may be replaced by multi-
ple next executions $\underline{\sigma}_1 = (\sigma_{11} \ldots \sigma_{1r})$ and $\underline{\sigma}_2 = (\sigma_{21} \ldots \sigma_{2r})$ respectively. The
fork instructions which may appear in the safe realization of row-instructions (see
the upper part of figure 47) are implicitly contained in the multiple next executi‹
instructions. This can best be illustrated by continuing the example of figure 49.
A microprogrammed implementation of the row-instruction part (i.e. between N and
σ_1, σ_3', σ_2, σ_3'') of figure 49 is proposed in figure 55. This microprogrammed implementation works as follows.

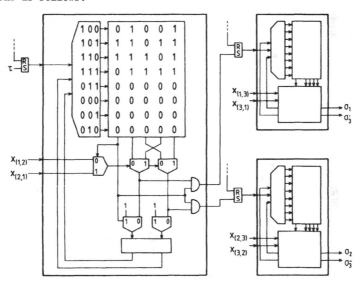

Figure 55 : Microprogrammed implementation of the safe program
of figure 49.

- The initial state is coded : 000 ;
- As soon as the instruction is enabled (τ=1) the state becomes : 100 ;
- According to the value of the variable 12 (coded : 0), the program goes to the
  next instructions coded : 101 or 110 ;
- Assume that 12=0 ; the next state is 110 and the variable to be tested is 21
  (coded : 1) : this is also the ultimate decision instruction of the program.
- Assume that 21=1 ; the two next decision programs containing the condition variables 13, 31 and 23, 32 respectively are both enabled and the next instruction in
  the microprogrammed structure is coded 111. As long as τ remains equal to 1 the
  program remains in the state : 111.

Similar microprogrammed structures are used for the implementation of decision programs in terms of the condition variables 13, 31 and 23, 32 respectively. This completes the microprogrammed materialization of the row-instruction part of figure 49. Since the column-instruction part of figure 49 is essentially made-up of row-instructions connected together by means of join-and instructions, its microprogrammed implementation is derived from the design structure proposed in section 11.1. The obtention of the microprogrammed implementation structure for the lower part of figure 49 is left to the reader.

The contents of this chapter 11 constitutes only a short introduction to implementation of programs by means of microprogrammed structures. More about microprogrammed materialization may be found in the books by Davio, Deschamps and Thayse [1983a, 1983b] and Mange, Sanchez and Stauffer [1982].

Chapter 12 : <u>A summary and the conclusions of part II</u>

We have introduced in part I of this text a formalism and a calculus which allowed us to transform any high-level instruction in terms of low-level instructions. This transformation immediately leads to an hardware implementation of algorithms. To this hardware implementation is associated a hardware description language. The purpose of part II was to derive the additional rules that were needed to transform that *hardware description language* into a *safe programming language*. These additional rules have been expressed in terms of parallel flowcharts.

Representation of instructions and of programs in terms of parallel flowcharts is described in chapter 8. We interpret the duality and the transposition principles with respect to the parallel flowchart representation. A first conclusion is that the algebra of P-functions is mainly a synthesis tool for implementing the realization of matrix-instructions in terms of low-level instructions while the parallel flowchart formalism is an analysis tool for verifying the safe connection of matrix-instructions. It follows that P-functions and vector addition systems may be considered as complementary mathematical tools.

The concept of safe program is studied in chapter 10. We show that the hardware description language (of part I of this text) must satisfy the property of *safe program* in order to become a programming language. This programming language will in turn lead to programmed and microprogrammed implementations of algorithms.

We show in particular that a programmed realization of an (or)-interpreted marix-instruction is safe if and only if all its *join-or* instructions are degenerate instructions. A programmed realization of an (and)-interpreted matrix-instruction is safe if and only if it does not contain *fork* instructions.

Program transformation rules are presented for the synthesis of safe programs.

In summary part II of this text has been devoted to the study of the additional properties that must satisfy a hardware description language in order to become a safe programming language. Particular types of implementations of a programming language such as e.g. the microprogrammed implementation are presented. The results of this part are more implementation-dependent than those of part I. They are also merely preliminary research results which have to be tested and developed in the future. The problem of optimizing algorithm implementation is a typical example of a non-classical discrete optimization problem. It shares with these problems of high algorithmic complexity. Further investigations could be devoted to improve the presently available class of implementation architectures, to obtain efficient heuristics or to study the consequence on the architecture of some functional properties of Boolean functions such as the degeneracy or the decomposability, the discovery of which has an impact on the computation method and on its implementation.

The problem of implementing algorithms in programmed and microprogrammed structures is very attractive, since it is a core problem that can be extended in various directions :

1) implementation of incompletely specified functions, simultaneous synthesis of a number of functions ;

2) use of multivalued integrated devices ;

3) general transformations of arbitrary programs into conditional programs.

Several extensions relative to programmed and microprogrammed implementations of algorithms may be found in Moalla, Sifakis and Silva [1980], Davio, Deschamps and Thayse [1983a, 1983b], Mange, Sanchez and Stauffer [1982].

Part III : <u>The algebra of P-functions</u>

Chapter 13 : <u>Laws acting on P-functions</u>

        The P-functions were introduced in chapter 13 with respect to a for-
mulation for the synthesis of algorithms. The purpose of chapter 13 is the study
of the P-function as a mathematical tool associated with the concept of Boolean
function. The results of the present chapter are twofold : some propositions whose
proofs were presented in a rather informal way will rigorously be stated and some
laws acting on P-functions will be extended. A number of new definitions and theorems will also be introduced.

        The concept of *P-function associated to a Boolean function* f is in-
troduced in section 12.1 and *composition laws* acting on pairs of P-functions are
presented. A composition law t_x and a reduced composition law t_x^r acting on pairs
of P-functions have been introduced in sections 3.3 and 4.2. respectively. The composition law t_x^k introduced in section 12.1 encompasses and generalizes the laws
t_x and t_x^r. Theorems relative to these composition laws are stated. The concept of
prime P-function is introduced : we show that the instructions of an optimal program
are characterized by the fact that their associated P-functions are prime P-functions. Several particular types of P-functions such as e.g. the *P-cubes* are defined
and their use in the synthesis of programs is given : a P-cube is a P-function whose
domain function is a cube ; it is used in the synthesis of (optimal) binary trees.

        The theorem which connects the properties of the P-functions and of
their composition laws to the characteristics of conditional programs is stated in
section 12.2. In particular we show that the composition laws t_x and t_x^r are used
in the synthesis of optimal conditional programs and of optimal simple conditional
programs respectively. The result of the synthesis procedure (obtention of an
(optimal) program, simple program or tree) is given in terms of the initial system
of P-functions (prime P-cubes , prime P-functions) and of the chosen composition law
$(t_x$ or $t_x^r)$.

        A new law, namely the *decomposition law* acting on a P-function, is in-
troduced in section 12.3. The properties of this law are stated and their use in
conditional program synthesis is presented. The decomposition law may be considered
as the inverse of the composition law. While a composition law generates a *leaves-
to-root synthesis procedure* for programs, the decomposition law generates a *root-
to-leaves synthesis procedure*.

        Sections 12.4, 12.5 and 12.6 are short sections devoted to the in-
terpretations of *lattices of P-functions* with respect to logical design, to *pseudo-
Boolean notations* for P-functions and to P-functions associated to *incompletely
specified Boolean functions* respectively.

13.1. P-functions associated with Boolean functions ; composition laws

Let $f(\underline{x})$ be a Boolean function of n variables $\underline{x} = (x_1, x_2, \ldots, x_n)$.
P-functions are ordered pairs of Boolean functions associated with f.

Definition 1. (P-function)

The pair of functions $<g;h>$ is a P-function of f (one will write $<g;h>\nabla f$) if and only if :

$$fg = hg \qquad\qquad (147)$$

The first component g of the P-function will be called the *domain-function of P(f)*,
while the second component will be called the *codomain function*. The relation (147)
means indeed that the function f evaluated in the domain D characterized by the
equation $g(\underline{x})=1$ reduces to the function $h(\underline{x})$: the condition g=1 defines a domain
where f=h.

Let us prove some elementary properties of the algebra of P-functions.

Lemma

(1) $<g;h>\nabla f$ *and* $g' \leqslant g \Rightarrow <g';h> \nabla f.$

(2) $<g_1;h>\nabla f$ *and* $<g_2;h> \nabla f \Rightarrow <g_1 g_2;h> \nabla f$ *and* $<g_1 \vee g_2;h> \nabla f.$

Proof

(1) $<g;h> \nabla f$ and $g' \leqslant g \Rightarrow fg = hg$ and $gg' = g' \Rightarrow$

   $fgg' = hgg'$ and $fg' = hg' \Rightarrow <g';h> \nabla f.$

(2) $<g_1;h> \nabla f$ and $<g_2;h> \nabla f \Rightarrow fg_1 = hg_1$ and $fg_2 = hg_2 \Rightarrow$

   $fg_1 g_2 = hg_1 g_2$ and $f(g_1 \vee g_2) = h(g_1 \vee g_2) \Rightarrow <g_1 g_2;h> \nabla f$ and $<g_1 \vee g_2;h> \nabla f.$ □

From the preceding lemma we deduce that the set

$$\{g_i \mid <g_i;h> \nabla f\}$$

is closed for the operations of conjunction and of disjunction. It constitutes thus
a sublattice of the lattice of Boolean functions and has consequently a maximum
element denoted $[f,h]$.
The relation

$$[f,h] = 1$$

is thus satisfied on each vertex where f=h and on these vertices only. Let us denote
by $(f \oplus h)$ a Boolean function equal to 0 on the vertices where f=h and equal to 1
otherwise. One has thus :

$$[f,h] = \overline{f \oplus h} \qquad\qquad (148)$$

Definition 2. (Prime P-functions)

A prime P-function is a P-function $\langle g;h\rangle$ whose domain g is maximal (for the codomain h).

    In view of (148) a prime P-function is thus necessarily of the form :

$$\langle \overline{f \oplus h} \; ; \; h\rangle$$

We defined the composition law t_x acting on pairs of P-functions in section 3.3 (see relation (36)).

Theorem 1. (Theorem on the composition law t_x)

 $\langle g_1;h_1\rangle \; \nabla f$ *and* $\langle g_2;h_2\rangle \; \nabla f$ $\Rightarrow$

 $\langle g_1;h_1\rangle \; t_x \; \langle g_2;h_2\rangle = \langle g_2\bar{x} \vee g_2 x \; ; \; h_1\bar{x} \vee h_2 x\rangle \; \nabla f$

Moreover $g_1 = [f,h_1]$ *and* $g_2 = [f,h_2]$ $\Rightarrow$

 $g_1\bar{x} \vee g_2 x = [f, \; h_1\bar{x} \vee h_2 x]$

Proof.

One has immediately :

 $f(\bar{x}g_1 \vee x g_2) = \bar{x}fg_1 \vee xfg_2$

 $(\bar{x}h_1 \vee xh_2)(\bar{x}g_1 \vee xg_2) = \bar{x}h_1 g_1 \vee xh_2 g_2$.

The first part of the proposition follows then from the relations

 $fg_1 = h_1 g_1$ and $fg_2 = h_2 g_2$

Let us now prove the preservation of the maximality property of the domain function $\bar{x}g_1 \vee xg_2$. On has successively :

$$\overline{f \oplus (\bar{x}h_1 \vee xh_2)} = \bar{f} \oplus (\bar{x}h_1 \oplus xh_2)$$
$$= (\bar{x}\bar{f} \oplus x\bar{f}) \oplus (\bar{x}h_1 \oplus xh_2)$$
$$= \bar{x}(\bar{f} \oplus h_1) \oplus x(f \oplus h_2) = \bar{x}g_1 \vee xg_2 \quad . \qquad \square$$

    We defined the reduced composition law t_x^r acting on pairs of P-functions in section 4.2 (see relation (51)).

Theorem 2. (Theorem on the reduced composition law t_x^r)

 $\langle g_1;h_1\rangle \; \nabla f$ *and* $\langle g_2;h_2\rangle \; \nabla f$ $\Rightarrow$

 $\langle g_1;h_1\rangle \; t_x^r \; \langle g_2;h_2\rangle = \langle g_1 \; (x=0) \; g_2(x=1) \; ; \; h_1\bar{x} \vee h_2 x\rangle \; \nabla f$

Moreover if $g_1 = [f, h_1]$ *and* $g_2 = [f, h_2]$, *then* $g_1(x=0)\, g_2(x=1)$ *is the greatest function independent of x and contained in* $[f, (\bar{x}h_1 \vee xh_2)]$.

Proof

Taking into account the fact that

$$\bar{x}g_1(x) \vee xg_2(x) = \bar{x}g_1(0) \vee xg_2(1)$$

and applying theorem 1, one obtains :

$$\langle \bar{x}g_1(0) \vee xg_1(1) \; ; \; \bar{x}h_1 \vee xh_2 \rangle \, \nabla f.$$

The property then results from the fact that :

$$g_1(x=0)\, g_2(x=1) \leqslant \bar{x}g_1(x=0) \vee xg_2(x=1) \tag{149}$$

and from the application of part (1) of the lemma. Moreover one knows that if g_1 and g_2 are maximal domain functions, $\bar{x}g_1 \vee xg_2$ is also a maximal domain function. Since $g_1(x=0)\, g_2(x=1)$ is the *meet difference* (see Thayse [1978]) of this last function, it is the greatest function independent of x and satisfying (149). ☐

The reduced law t_x^r suggests us also the possibility of defining the concept of prime P-function with respect to a given composition law. If $\langle \bar{f}; 0 \rangle$ and $\langle f; 1 \rangle$ are the initial P-functions of f then :

- A *prime P-function* is a P-function $\langle g; h \rangle$ obtained from an iterated application of the composition laws t_x on $\{\langle \bar{f}; 0 \rangle , \langle f; 1 \rangle\}$ and whose domain g is maximal (for a given domain h).

- A *reduced prime P-function* is a P-function $\langle g; h \rangle$ obtained from an iterated application of the composition laws t_x^r on $\{\langle \bar{f}; 0 \rangle , \langle f; 1 \rangle\}$ and whose domain g is larger than any domain g' of a P-function $\langle g'; h \rangle$ obtained by application of the same law t_x^r on the same P-functions $\{\langle \bar{f}; 0 \rangle , \langle f; 1 \rangle)\}$.

Clearly if $\langle g; h \rangle$ is a prime P-function and if $\langle g_r; h \rangle$ is a reduced prime P-function, then :

$$g_r \leqslant g.$$

The interest of theorems 1 and 2 derives from the fact that they prove that the sets of prime P-functions and of reduced prime P-functions are *closed* for the composition laws t_x and t_x^r respectively. Otherwise stated, prime P-functions and reduced prime P-functions are obtained by composition of prime P-functions and of reduced prime P-functions respectively : non prime P-functions may be dropped at each step of the iterative obtention of prime P-functions. We shall see (section 13.2) that the instructions of an optimal program are associated to prime P-function and to reduced prime P-functions.

The composition law t_x and the reduced composition law t_x^r are particular cases of a composition law t_x^k defined as follows.

<u>Definition 3.</u> (Composition law)

A composition law t_x^k is a law acting on pairs of P-functions and satisfying the two following conditions :

(1) $\langle g_1;h_1 \rangle \; \forall f$ *and* $\langle g_2;h_2 \rangle \; \forall f \Rightarrow$

$$\langle g_1;h_1 \rangle \; t_x^k \; \langle g_2;h_2 \rangle = \langle g_k(g_1,g_2,x) \; ; \; h_1\bar{x} \vee h_2 x \rangle$$

$$= \langle g_k \; ; \; h_1\bar{x} \vee h_2 x \rangle \; \forall f \; ;$$

(2) *An iterated use of the laws t_x^k, $\forall x \in \underline{x}$, acting on $\{\langle g_j;h_j \rangle \mid \underset{j}{\vee} g_j \equiv 1\}$ produces in at least one way a P-function having a 1 as domain function.*

<u>Theorem 3</u> (Theorem on composition law t_x^k)

A composition law t_x^k associates to a pair of P-functions :

$\langle g_1;h_1 \rangle \; \forall f$ *and* $\langle g_2;h_2 \rangle \; \forall f$ *a P-function*
$\langle g_k;h \rangle \; \forall f$ *with :*

$$\langle g_k;h \rangle = \langle g_1(x=0) \; g_2(x=1) \leqslant g_k \leqslant \bar{x}g_1 \vee xg_2 \; ; \; \bar{x}h_1 \vee xh_2 \rangle \; .$$

<u>Proof</u>

The domain function g_k must be smaller than its maximal element, i.e. $\bar{x}g_1 \vee xg_2$ (see theorem 1) ; moreover, any composition law should be able to produce a domain function equal to 1. The law t_x^k must be such that :

$$\langle \bar{x}\alpha_1 \vee x\beta_1 \vee \gamma_1;h_1 \rangle \; t_x^k \; \langle \bar{x}\alpha_2 \vee x\beta_2 \vee \gamma_2;h_2 \rangle = \langle 1; \; \bar{x}h_1 \vee xh_2 \rangle$$

if and only if $\alpha_1\beta_2 = 1$. One verifies that the smallest composition law acting on x and which actually produces the term $\alpha_1\beta_2$ is t_x^r . □

<u>Definition 4</u> (P-cubes)

A P-cube is a P-function whose domain function is a cube : a prime P-cube is a P-cube $\langle g;h \rangle$ whose domain q is maximal (for the codomain h).

We easily verify that $\langle f;1 \rangle$, $\langle \bar{f};0 \rangle$ and $\langle 1;f \rangle$ are prime P-functions of f. Let $\{p_i\}$ and $\{\bar{q}_j\}$ be the prime implicants of f and of $\bar{f}$ respectively (remember that the prime implicants of $\bar{f}$ are the complements of the prime implicates of f); $\langle p_i;1 \rangle$ and $\langle \bar{q}_j;0 \rangle$ are prime cubes of f.

Definition 5 (Total description of f)

The set of P-functions

$$\{<g_i;h_i> \mid <g_i;h_i> \nabla f , \; i \in I\}$$

constitutes a total description of f if and only if the solutions of :

$$\bigvee_{i \in I} g_i(\underline{x}) = 1 \quad .$$

*characterize the domain where f is defined; in particular if f is a completely de-
fined function the domain functions g_i must satisfy the condition :*

$$\bigvee_{i \in I} g_i(\underline{x}) \equiv 1 \; .$$

We verify that the sets of P-functions $\{<\bar{f};0> , <f;1>\}$,
$\{\{<p_i;1>\} , \{<\bar{q}_j;0>\}\}$ and $<1;f>$ are total descriptions of f.

The P-function $<g;h>\nabla f$ constitutes a *partial description* of f in the
domain characterized by g=1.

Theorem 4 (Theorem on total descriptions of f)

*Starting with a total description of f : $\{<g_i;h_i> \mid \bigvee_i g_i \equiv 1\}$, the iterative
generation of P-functions by means of composition laws produces in at least one way
the total description $<1;f>$ of f.*

Proof

The proof immediately derives from the definition 3 of composition law and from the
definition 5 of total description of f : if $\nabla g_i \equiv 1$, an iterative use of laws $t_{x_i}^k$
necessarily produces a P-function whose domain is 1, i.e. the total description
$<1;f>$ of f. □

Examples

Consider first the Boolean function described by the Karnaugh map of figure 56.

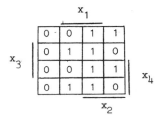

Figure 56 : Karnaugh map

Total description of f by means of the two prime P-functions :

$$A_1 = \langle x_4 x_3 x_2 \lor x_4 \bar{x}_3 x_1 \lor \bar{x}_4 \bar{x}_3 x_2 \lor \bar{x}_4 x_3 x_1 \; ; \; 1 \rangle = \langle f; 1 \rangle$$

$$A_2 = \langle x_4 x_3 \bar{x}_2 \lor x_4 \bar{x}_3 \bar{x}_1 \lor \bar{x}_4 \bar{x}_3 \bar{x}_2 \lor \bar{x}_4 x_3 \bar{x}_1 \; ; \; 0 \rangle = \langle \bar{f}; 0 \rangle$$

Generation of reduced prime P-functions by means of the composition law t_x^r (Theorem 2) :

$$B_1 = A_2 t_1^r A_1 = \langle x_4 \bar{x}_3 \lor \bar{x}_4 x_3 \; ; \; x_1 \rangle$$

$$B_2 = A_2 t_2^r A_1 = \langle x_4 x_3 \lor \bar{x}_4 \bar{x}_3 \; ; \; x_2 \rangle$$

$$B_3 = A_1 t_3^r A_2 = \langle \bar{x}_4 x_2 \bar{x}_1 \lor x_4 \bar{x}_2 x_1 \; ; \; \bar{x}_3 \rangle$$

$$B_4 = A_2 t_3^r A_1 = \langle x_4 x_2 \bar{x}_1 \lor \bar{x}_4 \bar{x}_2 x_1 \; ; \; x_3 \rangle$$

$$B_5 = A_1 t_4^r A_2 = \langle x_3 \bar{x}_2 x_1 \lor \bar{x}_3 x_2 \bar{x}_1 \; ; \; \bar{x}_4 \rangle$$

$$B_6 = A_2 t_4^r A_1 = \langle x_3 x_2 \bar{x}_1 \lor \bar{x}_3 \bar{x}_2 x_1 \; ; \; x_4 \rangle$$

$$C_1 = B_1 t_3^r B_2 = \langle x_4 \; ; \; \bar{x}_3 x_1 \lor x_3 x_2 \rangle$$

$$C_2 = B_2 t_3^r B_1 = \langle \bar{x}_4 \; ; \; \bar{x}_3 x_2 \lor x_3 x_1 \rangle$$

$$C_3 = B_1 t_4^r B_2 = \langle x_3 \; ; \; \bar{x}_4 x_1 \lor x_4 x_2 \rangle$$

$$C_4 = B_2 t_4^r B_1 = \langle \bar{x}_3 \; ; \; \bar{x}_4 x_2 \lor x_4 x_1 \rangle$$

$$C_5 = B_3 t_4^r B_4 = B_5 t_3^r B_6 = \langle x_2 \bar{x}_1 ; \; \bar{x}_4 \bar{x}_3 \lor x_4 x_3 \rangle$$

$$C_6 = B_4 t_4^r B_3 = B_6 t_3^r B_5 = \langle \bar{x}_2 x_1 \; ; \; \bar{x}_4 x_3 \lor x_4 \bar{x}_3 \rangle$$

$$D = C_2 t_4^r C_1 = C_4 t_4^r C_3 = \langle 1; f \rangle$$

Total description of f by means of prime P-cubes :

$$A_1 = \langle x_4 x_3 x_2 \; ; \; 1 \rangle \; , \; A_2 = \langle x_4 \bar{x}_3 x_1 \; ; \; 1 \rangle \; , \; A_3 = \langle \bar{x}_4 \bar{x}_3 x_2 \; ; \; 1 \rangle$$

$$A_4 = \langle \bar{x}_4 x_3 x_1 \; ; \; 1 \rangle \; ; \; A_5 = \langle x_2 x_1 \; ; \; 1 \rangle \; , \; A_6 = \langle x_4 x_3 \bar{x}_2 ; 0 \rangle$$

$$A_7 = \langle x_4 \bar{x}_3 \bar{x}_1 \; ; \; 0 \rangle \; ; \; A_8 = \langle \bar{x}_4 \bar{x}_3 \bar{x}_2 \; ; \; 0 \rangle \; , \; A_9 = \langle \bar{x}_4 x_3 \bar{x}_1 \; ; \; 0 \rangle$$

$$A_{10} = \langle \bar{x}_2 \bar{x}_1 \; ; \; 0 \rangle$$

Generation of prime P-cubes by means of the composition law t_x^r (Theorem 2) :

$$B_1 = A_7 t_1^r A_2 = \langle x_4 \bar{x}_3 \; ; \; x_1 \rangle \; , \; B_2 = A_9 t_1^r A_4 = \langle \bar{x}_4 x_3 \; ; \; x_1 \rangle \; ,$$

$$B_3 = A_6 t_2^r A_1 = \langle x_4 x_3 \; ; \; x_2 \rangle \; , \; B_4 = A_8 t_2^r A_3 = \langle \bar{x}_4 \bar{x}_3 \; ; \; x_2 \rangle \; .$$

$$C_1 = B_1 t_3^r B_3 = \langle x_4 \; ; \; \bar{x}_3 x_1 \lor x_3 x_2 \rangle$$

$$C_2 = B_4 t_3^r B_2 = \langle \bar{x}_4 \; ; \; x_3 x_1 \lor \bar{x}_3 x_2 \rangle$$

$$D = C_2 t_4^r C_1 = \langle 1; f \rangle$$

Consider now the Boolean function defined by the Karnaugh map of figure 57.

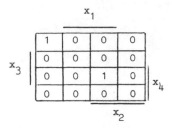

Figure 57 : Karnaugh map

Total description of f by means of prime P-functions :

$$A_1 = <x_4 x_3 x_2 x_1 \lor \bar{x}_4 \bar{x}_3 \bar{x}_2 \bar{x}_1 \; ; \; 1> = <f;1>$$
$$A_2 = <\bar{x}_1 x_2 \lor x_1 \bar{x}_2 \lor \bar{x}_3 x_4 \lor x_4 \bar{x}_3 \lor \bar{x}_3 x_2 \lor \bar{x}_1 x_3 \; ; \; 0> = <\bar{f};0>$$

Generation of prime P-functions by means of the composition law t_x (Theorem 1) :

$$B_1 = A_1 t_3 A_2 = <\bar{x}_4 \bar{x}_3 \bar{x}_2 \bar{x}_1 \lor x_3 \bar{x}_4 \lor x_3 \bar{x}_1 \lor x_3 \bar{x}_2 \; ; \; \bar{x}_3>$$
$$B_2 = A_2 t_2 A_1 = <x_1 \bar{x}_2 \lor \bar{x}_2 x_3 \lor \bar{x}_2 x_4 \lor x_4 x_3 x_2 x_1 \; ; \; x_2>$$

$$C = B_1 t_4 B_2 = <\bar{x}_4 x_3 \lor \bar{x}_2 \bar{x}_1 \lor x_4 \bar{x}_2 \lor x_3 \bar{x}_1 \; ; \; \bar{x}_4 x_3 \lor x_4 x_2>$$
$$D_1 = C \; t_2 A_2 = <\bar{x}_1 \lor \bar{x}_2 x_4 \lor \bar{x}_2 x_3 \lor x_2 \bar{x}_4 \lor x_2 \bar{x}_3 \; ; \; \bar{x}_4 \bar{x}_3 \bar{x}_2>$$
$$D_2 = A_2 t_3 C = \; <x_1 \lor x_3 \bar{x}_4 \lor \bar{x}_3 x_4 \lor x_3 \bar{x}_1 \lor \bar{x}_3 x_2 \; ; \; x_4 x_3 x_2>$$

$$E = D_1 t_1 D_2 = <1;f>$$

13.2. Synthesis of binary instructions by means of P-functions and of composition laws.

By *binary instruction*, we mean a row-instruction of the form :

$$N \begin{bmatrix} \bar{f}(\underline{x}) & , & f(\underline{x}) \\ \sigma_1 & & \sigma_2 \\ M_1 & & M_2 \end{bmatrix}$$

We shall consider the synthesis of this binary instruction by means of a *conditional program*, i.e. a program made of *if then else* instructions with $x_i \in \underline{x}$ as condition variables and of *execution instructions* with σ_1, σ_2 as orders.

The conditional programs will be divided into the following classes of decreasing degree of generality :

1) A *(non-simple) conditional program* is a program where a condition variable may be tested several times during a computation.

2) A *simple conditional program* is a program where a condition variable may be tested at most once during a computation.

3) A *conditional tree* is a program free of reconvergent decision instructions (i.e. free of degenerate join-or instructions in the decision program).

The optimality criteria that are generally considered in the design of conditional programs are the following :

1) The maximal duration of computation (*time criterion*) ;

2) The number of instructions (*cost criterion*);

3) The number of instructions in the programs having the shortest maximal computation duration (*relative cost criterion*).

As in parts I and II of this text we shall associate P-functions to instruction labels.

Let us consider the transformation of a binary instruction into an equivalent conditional program.

Theorem (Theorem on relative cost criterion)

If we consider the relative cost criterion as optimality criterion :

1. *Any (non-simple) optimal conditional program (equivalent to a binary instruction) has its instructions associated to prime P-functions.*
2. *Any simple optimal conditional program (equivalent to a binary instruction) has its instructions associated to reduced prime P-functions.*
3. *Any optimal conditional tree (equivalent to a binary instruction) has its instructions associated to prime P-cubes.*

Proof

Consider the binary decision instruction :

$$N \ [\ \bar{f}(\underline{x}) \qquad f(\underline{x}) \ ]$$
$$M'_1 \qquad M'_2$$

1.-To the label N we associate the prime P-function $<1;f>$ which is a total description of f ;

–To the labels M'_1 and M'_2 we associate the prime P-functions $<\bar{f};0>$ and $<f;1>$ respectively which constitute another total description of f.

–We know (theorem 4 of section 12.1) that starting with the prime P-functions $\{<\bar{f};0> \ , \ <f;1>\}$ an iterative generation of P-functions by means of composition laws t_x produces in at least one way the total description $<1;f>$ of f. To each of the intermediate P-functions can be associated an instruction of a conditional program equivalent to the binary instruction.

-The conditional programs so obtained are optimal with respect to the time criterion. Indeed, the maximal computation duration of a program is reflected by the maximal number of instructions between N and M_1' or M_2' i.e. also by the maximal number of intermediate P-functions from $<f;1>$ or from $<\bar{f};0>$ to $<1;f>$. This number is necessarily minimal when starting with prime P-functions since they are characterized by a maximal domain function so that the domain "1" is reached after a minimal number of intermediate steps.

-The conditional programs satisfying moreover the relative cost criterion are necessarily obtained by the above proposed transformation. We indeed know that the set of prime P-functions is closed for the composition law t_x (see theorem 1 of section 12.1). Among all the programs satisfying the time criterion those whose intermediate instructions are associated with prime P-functions are also optimal with respect to the relative cost criterion. These programs have indeed a minimum number of instructions since all the possible reconvergent instructions are detected (it can easily be verified that the fan-in of an instruction is reflected by the size of its domain function).

2.-If we use the law t_x^r instead of the law t_x, only some non-simple programs may not be detected : indeed the elimination of the variable x in the domain function eliminates the possibility of testing this variable again in a next step. Besides this since the set of reduced prime P-functions is closed for the law t_x^r (see theorem 2 of section 12.2) similar arguments as those developed above allow us to prove that the simple optimal programs are formed by means of instructions whose associated P-functions are reduced prime P-functions.

3.-Let us now prove the third point of the theorem. The synthesis of conditional trees may be performed as the synthesis of conditional programs : the only modification lies in starting the iterative computations with P-cubes instead of with P-functions. Let $p_i, \bar{q}_j$ be the prime implicants of f and of $\bar{f}$; the binary decision instruction is equivalent to the following program :

$$
\begin{array}{l}
N \left[\begin{array}{cc} \{\bar{q}_j\} & \{p_i\} \end{array} \right] \\
\qquad \{M_{1j}'\} \quad \{M_{2i}'\} \\
\{M_{1j}'\} \left[\begin{array}{c} 1 \\ \vdots \\ 1 \end{array} \right] \\
\qquad M_1' \\
\{M_{2j}'\} \left[\begin{array}{c} 1 \\ \vdots \\ 1 \end{array} \right] \\
\qquad M_2'
\end{array}
$$

Let us associate the prime P-cube <1;f> to N and the prime P-cubes $\{<\bar{q}_j;0>$, $<p_i;1>\}$ to the labels $\{M'_{1j}, M'_{2i}\}$ respectively. We know (see theorem 4 of section 12.1) that starting with the prime P-cubes $\{<\bar{q}_j;0>$, $<p_i;1>\}$ an iterative generation of P-functions by means of composition laws t_x^r produces in at least one way the total description <1;f> of f. The domain functions of the intermediate P-functions are cubes : we indeed verify that when starting with cube domain functions, the use of the law t_x^r produces only P-functions whose domains are cubes. Mo reover the instructions of a binary tree have associated P-functions which are P-cubes. Similar arguments as those developed for binary programs allow us to state that the optimal binary trees have instructions which are associated to prime P-cubes obtained from the transformation process described above.

The statement of the theorem is schematically represented in the entries of figure 58

Initial total description	Composition laws t_x	t_x^r
prime P-functions	conditional programs	conditional simple programs
prime P-cubes		conditional trees

Figure 58 : Generation of optimal conditional programs

Lattices associated with (prime) P-functions are lattices having the (prime) P-functions as vertices. The ordering relation is the Boolean inclusion (denoted $\leq$) acting on the domain function of the prime P-function ; their usefulness is twofold. First, they provide us with a simple graphical display showing how the prime P-functions are obtained from each other by the iterative process. Second, they constitute a representation of the connection of instructions required to realize the optimal conditional programs.

A sublattice of the lattice of prime P-functions of the example of figure 56 is drawn in figure 59. At the vertex D we may choose either x_4 or x_3 as decision variable. Therefore the lattice of figure 59 generates two optimal condition programs which are equivalent to the binary instruction

$$N \ [\ \bar{f}(\underline{x}) \qquad f(\underline{x}) \ ]$$
$$M'_1 \qquad M'_2$$

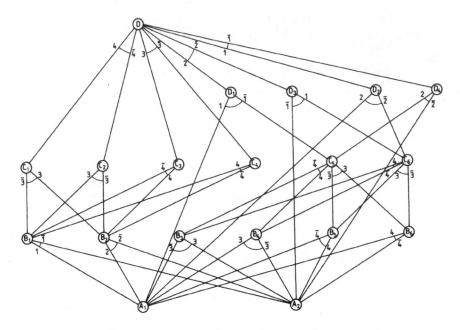

<u>Figure 59</u> : Sublattice of the lattice of prime P-functions
for the example of figure 56.

Using the notations (7,67) these optimal programs are :

       (a)   (b)

$$D(\bar{x}_3 C_4 \ , \ x_3 C_3)$$

$$C_4(\bar{x}_4 B_2 \ , \ x_4 B_1)$$

$$C_3(\bar{x}_4 B_1 \ , \ x_4 B_2)$$

$$B_2(\bar{x}_2 M_1' \ , \ x_2 M_2')$$

$$B_1(\bar{x}_1 M_1' \ , \ x_1 M_2')$$

$$D(\bar{x}_4 C_2 \ , \ x_4 C_1)$$

$$C_2(\bar{x}_3 B_2 \ , \ x_3 B_1)$$

$$C_1(\bar{x}_3 B_1 \ , \ x_3 B_2)$$

$$B_2(\bar{x}_2 M_1' \ , \ x_2 M_2')$$

$$B_1(\bar{x}_1 M_1' \ , \ x_1 M_2')$$

Optimal programs may evidently be written by simple examination of the list of P-functions without resorting to the constructions of the lattice of P-functions

        We easily verify that the prime cubes computed in section 12.1 (for the example of figure 56) produce the optimal tree of figure 60a while the prime P-functions evaluated in section 12.1 (for the example of figure 57) produce the optimal non-simple program of figure 60b. Let us note that the Boolean function of figure 57 is the simplest Boolean function for which an optimal non-simple progra having a lower cost than any optimal simple program may be found.

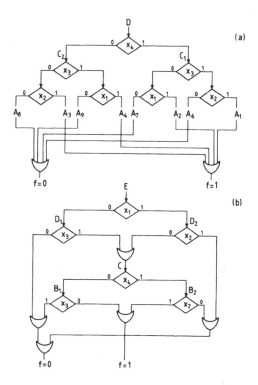

Figure 60a : Optimal tree for the example of figure 56

60b : Optimal non-simple program for the example of figure 57.

13.3. P-functions associated with Boolean functions; decomposition laws

The synthesis methods developed in section 12.2 for obtaining (optimal) conditional programs equivalent to a binary instruction may be summarized as follows : starting with a complete description of f by means of P-functions : $\{<g_j;h_j> \mid \vee g_j \equiv 1, h_j \in 0,1\}$ and using iteratively *composition laws* t_x^k acting on these P-functions, obtain the P-function $<1;f>$. The following synthesis method will be developed in this section : starting with the P-function $<1;f>$ and using iteratively a *decomposition law* d_x acting on the P-functions, obtain a complete description of f by means of P-functions · $\{<g_j;h_j> \mid \vee g_j \equiv 1, h_j \in 0,1\}$.

Definition 1 (Decomposition law d_x)

A decomposition law d_x is a law which when applied to a P-function $<g;h>$ produces the pair of P-functions :

$$d_x <g;h> = \{<\bar{x}g \; ; \; h(x=0)> \; , \; <xg \; ; \; h(x=1)>\}$$

Theorem 1 (Theorem on decomposition law d_x)

1) $<g;h> \nabla f \Rightarrow$

   $d_x <g;h> = \{<\bar{x}g; h(x=0)> \nabla f, <xg; h(x=1)> \nabla f\}$

2) *An iterative application of the laws* $d_{x_i} \forall x_i \in \underline{x}$ *to the P-function* $<1;f>$ *generates the total description of* $f : \{<g_j;h_j>| \ \forall g_j \equiv 1, h_j \in 0,1\}$.

Proof

1) $<g;h> \nabla f \Rightarrow fg = hg \Rightarrow f\bar{x}g = h \ (x=0) \ \bar{x}g \Rightarrow <\bar{x}g ; h(x=0> \nabla f$.

2) The proof of part 2 results from the fact that the application of the law d_x to $<g;h>$ introduces the variable x in the domain functions $\bar{x}g$ and xg while this variable disappears in the corresponding codomain functions $h(x=0)$ and $h(x=1)$ so that an iterated application of decomposition laws produces codomain functions which are constants.   □

The use of decomposition laws for generating conditional programs equivalent to a binary instruction is attractive since these laws are easy to handle ; they present however an important limitation since they generate only conditional trees. One verifies indeed that, when starting with the domain function 1, the iterative application of decomposition laws d_x produces only P-functions whose domain functions are cubes. We know that the P-cubes generate conditional trees only. This limitation may be circumvented by introducing a *union law* (or *merging law*) on the set of P-functions.

Definition 2. (Union law $\cup$)
A union law $\cup$ *is a law which when applied to a pair of P-functions* $<g_1;h_1> \nabla f$ *and* $<g_2;h_2> \nabla f$ *produces a P-function* :

$$<g_1 \vee g_2 ; h_1 \vee h_2> \nabla f.$$

We shall write : if $<g_1;h_1> \nabla f$ and $<g_2;h_2> \nabla f$, then :

$$<g_1;h_1> \cup <g_2;h_2> = <g_1 \vee g_2 ; h_1 \vee h_2>$$

iff $<g_1 \vee g_2 ; h_1 \vee h_2> \nabla f$.

Theorem 2 (Theorem on union law $\cup$)
$<g_1;h_1) \nabla f$ *and* $<g_2;h_2> \nabla f \Rightarrow$
$<g_1 \vee g_2 ; h_1 \vee h_2> \nabla f$ *iff*
$h_1g_1 \vee h_2g_2 \geqslant h_1g_2 \vee h_2g_1$ (150)

Proof

1) $\langle g_1;h_1\rangle \nabla f$ and $\langle g_2;h_2\rangle \nabla f \Rightarrow$

$\quad fg_1 = h_1 g_1$ and $fg_2 = h_2 g_2 \Rightarrow f(g_1 \vee g_2) = h_1 g_1 \vee h_2 g_2$

2) If (150) is satisfied then :

$\quad f(g_1 \vee g_2) = h_1 g_1 \vee h_2 g_2 \vee h_1 g_2 \vee h_2 g_1$

$\qquad\qquad = (h_1 \vee h_2)(g_1 \vee g_2) \Rightarrow$

$\langle g_1 \vee g_2 ; h_1 \vee h_2 \rangle \nabla f$ and the condition (150) is thus sufficient.

3) If $\langle g_1 \vee g_2 ; h_1 \vee h_2 \rangle \nabla f \Rightarrow$

$\quad f(g_1 \vee g_2) = (h_1 \vee h_2)(g_1 \vee g_2)$

$\qquad\qquad = h_1 g_1 \vee h_2 g_2 \vee h_1 g_2 \vee h_2 g_1 = h_1 g_1 \vee h_2 g_2$

$\Rightarrow h_1 g_1 \vee h_2 g_2 \geqslant h_1 g_2 \vee h_2 g_1$ and the condition (150) is thus necessary. $\qquad$ □

Observe that the condition (150) encompasses and generalizes the conditions on the union law that were introduced in section 3.3. (see (38)) : we indeed verify that (150) is satisfied either if $h_1 = h_2$ or if $g_1 = g_2$, i.e. :

$\quad \langle g;h_1\rangle \nabla f \cup \langle g;h_2\rangle \nabla f = \langle g; h_1 \vee h_2\rangle \nabla f$,

$\quad \langle g_1;h\rangle \nabla f \cup \langle g_2;h\rangle \nabla f = \langle g_1 \vee g_2 ; h\rangle \nabla f$.

We have seen that the iterative use of decomposition laws d_x applied to the initial P-function $\langle 1;f\rangle$ produces binary programs which are *binary trees* : the domain functions of the successive P-functions are cubes. The decomposition laws used together with the union law $\cup$ allow us to generate binary programs : we indeed verify that the union law produces domain functions which are disjunction of cubes. Moreover if all the merging possibilities are detected, the union of P-functions can necessarily produce P-functions having maximal domain functions, i.e. prime P-functions. Observe that the use of the union law requests that the merging condition (150) should be recognized. It may be difficult to recognize that P-functions $\langle g_1;h_1\rangle$ and $\langle g_2;h_2\rangle$ satisfy the condition (150). The less general conditions $h_1 = h_2$ or $g_1 = g_2$ are easier to detect ; if the only P-functions that are merged are those which satisfy these restricted conditions, then the use of the decomposition law together with the union law produces only simple programs ; indeed, the decomposition law and the (restricted) union law do not allow a variable x to be present simultaneously in the domain and codomain functions of the P-function. Hence, a variable already tested in the computation process may not be tested again.

Further on we shall use a *restricted union law*, denoted $\cup^r$ which is the union law using the restricted conditions :

$$h_1 = h_2 \text{ or } g_1 = g_2 \tag{151}$$

Example

Consider again the Boolean function described by the map of figure 56. Some of the P-functions evaluated below were already obtained when the composition laws were used ; these P-functions will keep their label.

$D = \langle 1 ; x_4x_3x_2 \vee x_4\bar{x}_3x_1 \vee \bar{x}_4\bar{x}_3x_2 \vee \bar{x}_4x_3x_1 \rangle = \langle 1; f \rangle$

$d_1(D) = \{\langle \bar{x}_1; x_2(x_4x_3 \vee \bar{x}_4\bar{x}_3) \rangle , \langle x_1 ; x_2 \vee \bar{x}_3 \vee x_4\bar{x}_3 \rangle\}$

$\quad = \{D_4, D_2\}$

$d_2(D) = \{\langle \bar{x}_2 ; x_1(\bar{x}_4x_3 \vee x_4\bar{x}_3) \rangle , \langle x_2 ; x_1 \vee x_3x_4 \vee \bar{x}_3\bar{x}_4 \rangle\}$

$\quad = \{D_3, D_1\}$

$d_3(D) = \{\langle \bar{x}_3 ; x_4x_1 \vee \bar{x}_4x_2 \rangle , \langle x_3 ; x_4x_2 \vee \bar{x}_4x_1 \rangle\}$

$\quad = \{C_4, C_3\}$

$d_4(D) = \{\langle \bar{x}_4 ; \bar{x}_3x_2 \vee x_3x_1 \rangle , \langle x_4 ; x_3x_2 \vee \bar{x}_3x_1 \rangle\}$

$\quad = \{C_2, C_1\}$

$d_2(D_4) = \{\langle \bar{x}_1\bar{x}_2 ; 0 \rangle , \langle \bar{x}_1x_2 ; \bar{x}_4\bar{x}_3 \vee x_4x_3 \rangle\} = \{A_2^1, C_5\}$

$d_1(D_1) = \{\langle \bar{x}_1\bar{x}_2 ; \bar{x}_4\bar{x}_2 \vee x_4x_2 \rangle , \langle x_1x_2 ; 1 \rangle\} = \{C_5, A_1^1\}$

$d_2(D_2) = \{\langle x_1\bar{x}_2 ; \bar{x}_4x_3 \vee x_4\bar{x}_3 \rangle , \langle x_1x_2 ; 1 \rangle\} = \{C_6, A_1^1\}$

$d_1(D_3) = \{\langle \bar{x}_1\bar{x}_2 ; 0 \rangle , \langle \bar{x}_2x_1 ; \bar{x}_4x_3 \vee x_4\bar{x}_3 \rangle\} = \{A_2^1 ; C_6\}$

$d_4(C_4) = \{\langle \bar{x}_4\bar{x}_3 ; x_2 \rangle , \langle x_4\bar{x}_3 ; x_1 \rangle\} = \{B_2^1 , B_1^1\}$

$d_4(C_3) = \{\langle \bar{x}_4x_3 ; x_1 \rangle , \langle x_4x_3 ; x_2 \rangle\} = \{B_1^2 , B_2^2\}$

$d_3(C_2) = \{\langle \bar{x}_4\bar{x}_3 ; x_1 \rangle , \langle \bar{x}_4x_3 ; x_1 \rangle\} = \{B_2^1 , B_1^2\}$

$d_3(C_1) = \{\langle x_4\bar{x}_3 ; x_1 \rangle , \langle x_4x_3 ; x_2 \rangle\} = \{B_1^1 , B_1^2\}$

$B_1 = B_1^1 \cup B_1^2 , \quad B_2 = B_2^1 \cup B_2^2$

$d_1(B_1) = \{\langle \bar{x}_1(x_4\bar{x}_3 \vee \bar{x}_4x_3); 0 \rangle , \langle x_1(x_4\bar{x}_3 \vee \bar{x}_4x_3) ; 1 \rangle\}$

$\quad = \{A_2^2 , A_1^2\}$

$d_2(B_2) = \{\langle \bar{x}_2(x_4x_3 \vee \bar{x}_4\bar{x}_3) ; 0 \rangle , \langle x_2(x_4x_3 \vee \bar{x}_4\bar{x}_3) ; 1 \rangle\}$

$\quad = \{A_2^3 , A_1^3\}$

$A_1 = A_1^1 \cup A_1^2 \cup A_1^3 = \langle f; 1 \rangle$

$A_2 = A_2^1 \cup A_2^2 \cup A_2^3 = \langle \bar{f}; 0 \rangle$

These P-functions allow us again to derive lattice of P-functions and programs. The lattice showing us how the P-functions are derived from each other is depicted in figure 59 ; optimal programs may be deduced either from this lattice, or directly from the list of P-functions (see section 12.2).

In summary, (optimal) realizations for Boolean functions and hence (optimal) realizations for conditional programs may be obtained either by means of composition laws acting iteratively on the initial P-functions $\{<\bar{f};0>\ ,\ <f;1>\}$ or by means of decomposition and merging laws acting iteratively on the initial P-function $<1;f>$. The possible realizations in terms of the initial systems of P-fun tions and of the transformation laws are given in figure 61 ; the final systems of P-functions are also indicated. The entries of figure 61 encompass those of figure 58.

The synthesis of a conditional program may be stated in either of the following forms :

1) Starting from the output instruction labels M_1', M_2' represented by their P-functions $\{<\bar{f};0>\ ,\ <f;1>\}$ respectively, use a composition law t_x or t_x^r which, when acting on pairs of P-functions generates a new P-function. It is requested that an iterative use of this composition law produces finally the P-function $<1;f>$ and that the intermediate P-functions are in one-to-one correspondence with the intermediate instructions.

2) Starting from the input instruction label N, represented by its P-function $<1;f>$, use a decomposition law d_x which,when acting on a P-function, generates two new P-functions. It is requested that an iterative use of this law d_x produces finally the P-functions $\{<\bar{f};0>\ ,\ <f;1>\}$ and that the intermediate P-functions are in one-to-one correspondence with the intermediate instructions.

A synthesis method of the type 1) is called a *leaves-to-root* algorithm since it star from the leaves M_1', M_2' of the program and comes to its root N. Similarly, a synthesis method of the type 2) will be called a *root-to-leaves* algorithm (observe that the calling "leaves" is generally used when the program to be synthesized is a tree)

The synthesis methods using either a composition law or a decomposition law and a union law present the following respective advantages and drawbacks.

The reconvergent nodes (degenerate join-or nodes) are automatically detected by the composition laws ; in order to detect reconvergent nodes a merging or union law must be added to the decomposition laws.

Algorithms based on composition laws need the evaluation of the first component of the P-function (domain function), while algorithms based on decomposition and merging laws need the evaluation of the two components of the P-function the merging criteria (150, 151) use the domain and codomain functions.

It is easier to perform decomposition of P-functions than composition of P-functions.

	Initial system	Transformation laws	Final system
Conditional	$\{<f;1>,<\bar{f};0>\}$	composition : t_x	$<1;f>$
programs	$<1;f>$	decomposition : d_x union : U	$\{<f;1> , <\bar{f};0>\}$
Simple conditional programs	$\{<f;1>,<\bar{f};0>\}$	composition : t_x^r	$<1;f>$
	$<1;f>$	decomposition : d_x union : U^r	$\{<f;1> , <\bar{f};0>\}$
Conditional	$\{<p_i;1>,<\bar{q}_j;0>\}$	composition : t_x^r	$<1;f>$
trees	$<1;f>$	decomposition : d_x	$\{<p_i;1>,<\bar{q}_j;0>\}$

Figure 61 : Synthesis of programs in terms of transformation
laws and of initial and final systems.

        In summary if the decomposition technique seems to be easier to handle when conditional trees are searched for, the composition technique is surely more appropriate for the obtention of conditional programs.

        Note finally that a general decomposition law d_x^k can be defined in the same way as the general composition law t_x^k (see definition 3 of section 12.1):

Definition 3 (Decomposition law)

A decomposition law d_x^k is a law acting on P-functions and satisfying the two following conditions :

(1) $d_x^k <g;h> \nabla f = \{<g_1^k ; h(x=0)> \nabla f , <g_2^k ; h(x=1)> \nabla f\}$

(2) *An iterated use of the law d_x^k, $\forall x \in \underline{x}$, acting on $<1;f>$ produces in at least one way the P-functions $\{<g_j;h_j> \mid \underset{j}{\vee} g_j \equiv 1, h_j \in 0,1\}$.*

The following theorem 3 is similar to the theorem 3 (on composition law t_x^k) of section 12.1.

Theorem 3 (Theorem on decomposition law d_x^k)

A decomposition law d_x^k associates to a P-function $<g;h>$ the pair of P-functions $<g_1^k;h_1>$, $<g_2^k;h_2>$ with :

$$d_x^k<g;h> = \{<\bar{x}g \leqslant g_1^k \leqslant f \oplus h(x=0) ; h(x=0> ,$$

$$<xg \leqslant g_2^k \leqslant f \oplus h(x=1) ; h(x=1)\}$$

The proof of this theorem is left to the reader.

13.4. Lattices of P-functions and logical design

Lattices of P-functions $P(f)$ are lattices whose vertices are associated to P-functions of f and whose edges are directed from $P_j(f)$ and $P_k(f)$ to $P_\ell(f)$ if $P_\ell(f)$ is generated by composition of $P_j(f)$ and $P_k(f)$, i.e. if

$$P_\ell(f) = P_j(f) \; t_i \; P_k(f) \tag{152}$$

The edges of the lattices are marked as follows ; whenever the P-functions P_ℓ, P_j and P_k are related by (152), the edge from P_j to P_ℓ will be marked "$\bar{i}$" while the edge from P_k to P_ℓ will be marked "i".

Theorem 1 (Synthesis by means of multiplexers)

If a logical network is deduced from the lattice of P-functions of f in the following way :

1) *to each vertex of the lattice corresponds a multiplexer and to the edges of the lattice correspond the connections between the multiplexers ;*

2) *if the edges "i" and "$\bar{i}$" are incident to the P-function $\langle g_\ell;h_\ell \rangle$, the multiplexer corresponding to that P-function has x_i as condition variable ;*

3) *the edges issued from the P-function(s) $\langle g_j;1 \rangle$ (with $\underset{j}{\vee} \, g_j = f$) are connected to the Boolean constant 1, while the edges issued from the P-function(s) $\langle g'_k;0 \rangle$ (with $\underset{k}{\vee} \, g'_k = \bar{f}$) are connected to the Boolean constant 0.*

Then it realizes the function f and, more generally, the multiplexer corresponding to the P-function $\langle g_\ell;h_\ell \rangle$ realizes h_ℓ as output function.

Theorem 2 (Synthesis by means of demultiplexers and of or-gates)

If a logical network is deduced from the lattice of P-functions of f in the following way :

1) *to each vertex of the lattice corresponds a demultiplexer whose input terminal is connected to the output terminal of an or-gate ;*

2) *the in-edges "i" and "$\bar{i}$" to this vertex are connected to the outputs of the demultiplexer with condition variable x_i, while the out-edges of this vertex are connected to the inputs of the or-gate ;*

3) *the input of the initial demultiplexer corresponding to the P-function $\langle 1;f \rangle$ is connected to the Boolean constant 1.*

Then it realizes the functions f and $\bar{f}$, and the or-gates corresponding to the P-function $\langle g_\ell;h_\ell \rangle$ realiz $g'_\ell \subseteq g_\ell$ as output function so that the connected demultiplexer realizes the functions $x_i g'_\ell$ and $\bar{x}_i g'_\ell$.

Both theorems may be gathered in the following proposition .

Theorem 3

Consider a sublattice of the lattice of P-functions obtained by choosing for each value $<g_\ell;h_\ell>$ a variable x_i in the set of the possible condition variables for this vertex ; to this sublattice corresponds two logical realizations :

1) *a realization with multiplexers; these multiplexers are connected as the vertices of the sublattice, and the multiplexer corresponding to the vertex $<g_\ell;h_\ell>$ produces h_ℓ as output function ; and*

2) *a realization with demultiplexers and or-gates ; these demultiplexers -or-gates are connected as the vertices of the considered sublattice and the demultiplexer corresponding to the vertex $<g_\ell;h_\ell>$ has the function $g'_\ell \subseteq g_\ell$ as input function.*

To the sublattice of the lattice of prime P-functions correspond optimal logical realizations.

The proofs of these theorems are quite self-evident and are left to the reader.

13.5. Boolean and pseudo-Boolean notations for P-functions

The transformation laws acting on P-functions are expressed in terms of Boolean operations such as the disjunction $\vee$ and the conjunction $\wedge$. The synthesis of the Boolean function f is obtained by performing the following transformation:

$$\left.\begin{array}{c}<\bar{f};0>\\<f;1>\end{array}\right\}\quad\begin{array}{c}\{t_x\}\\ \xrightarrow{\quad}\\ \{d_x,U\}\end{array}\quad <1;f> = <1 \; ; \; f.1 \vee \bar{f}.0> \tag{153}$$

with

$$<g_1;h_1> t_x <g_2;h_2> = <g_1\bar{x} \vee g_2x \; ; \; h_1\bar{x} \vee h_2x>$$
$$<g; h_1> U <g;h_2> = <g \; ; \; h_1 \vee h_2> \tag{154}$$

In this formulation both domain and codomain functions of any P-function are Boolean functions.

The Boolean function f may also be considered as the decision tool in the binary instruction :

$$\begin{array}{ccc} N & [\; \bar{f} & f\;] \\ & \sigma_1 & \sigma_2 \\ & M_1 & M_2 \end{array}$$

and the transformation associated to the synthesis of this instruction is :

$$\left.\begin{array}{c} <\bar{f}; \sigma_1> \\ <f; \sigma_2> \end{array}\right\} \quad \xrightarrow[\{d_x, U\}]{\{t_x\}} \quad <1 \; ; \; \bar{f}\sigma_1 + f\sigma_2> \tag{155}$$

The coefficients σ_1 and σ_2 which are present in the codomain functions are not Boolean quantities : the codomain of the P-functions are *pseudo-Boolean functions* instead of Boolean functions. Consequently it is formally more appropriate to express the codomain transformations in terms of the pseudo-Boolean addition "+" instead of in terms of the Boolean disjunction "v" , i.e. :

$$<g_1; h_1> \; t_x \; <g_2; h_2> \; = \; <g_1\bar{x} \lor g_2 x \; ; \; h_1\bar{x} + h_2 x>$$
$$<g; h_1> \; U \; <g; h_2> \quad = \; <g; h_1 + h_2> \tag{156}$$

The replacement of the disjunction "v" by the addition "+" is clearly of formal nature : it does not affect the theorems and the computations using the transformation laws. The law "+" allows us to introduce an interpretation : the codomain function $h_1 + h_2$ may e.g. be interpreted as a *parallel execution* of h_1 and h_2 or as a *nondeterministic execution* of h_1 or h_2. Besides this the use of the symbol "+" is classical in the transformation of pseudo-Boolean expressions (Hammer and Rudeanu [1968], Davio, Deschamps and Thayse [1978]).

13.6. <u>P-functions associated with incompletely specified Boolean functions</u>

Assume that the domains where a Boolean function take the values 1, 0 and - (indeterminate) are characterized by the solutions of the Boolean equations :

$$f_1 = 1 \;, \; f_2 = 0 \text{ and } f_3 = 1$$

respectively; we have :

$$f_1 \lor f_2 \lor f_3 \lor 1 \text{ and } f_i f_j \equiv 0 \quad \forall i, j \in \{1, 2, 3\} \;.$$

The maximal domains where the Boolean function may take the values 1 and 0 are characterized by the solutions of the Boolean equations :

$$f_1 \lor f_3 = 1 \text{ and } f_2 \lor f_3 = 1$$

respectively.

A Boolean function compatible with an incompletely specified Boolean function has values 1 and 0 on the domains characterized by $f_1 = 1$ and $f_2 = 1$ respectively.

A Boolean function g compatible with an incompletely specified Boolean function (f_1, f_2, f_3) is synthesized by performing the following transformation on P-functions :

$$\left. \begin{array}{c} <f_2 \lor f_3; 0> \\ <f_1 \lor f_3; 1> \end{array} \right\} \xrightarrow[\{d_x, U\}]{\{t_x\}} \quad <1; g>$$

The theorems and laws that were stated in the preceding sections of this chapter remain true provided the following substitutions are made :

$$f \to f_1 \lor f_3 \quad \text{and} \quad \bar{f} \to f_2 \lor f_3$$

Example

Consider the incompletely specified Boolean function described by means of the Karnaugh map of figure 62.

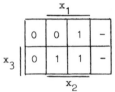

Figure 62 : Karnaugh map

We have :

$$f_1 = x_1 x_2 \lor x_1 x_3$$
$$f_2 = \bar{x}_1 \bar{x}_2 \lor \bar{x}_2 \bar{x}_3$$
$$f_3 = \bar{x}_1 x_2$$
$$f_1 \lor f_3 = x_2 \lor x_1 x_3$$
$$f_2 \lor f_3 = \bar{x}_1 \lor \bar{x}_2 \bar{x}_3$$

From the initial system of P-functions :

$$A_1 = <\bar{x}_1 \lor \bar{x}_2 \bar{x}_3 \; ; \; 0>$$
$$A_2 = <x_2 \lor x_1 x_3 \; ; \; 1>$$

we successively deduce :

$$B_1 = A_1 t_1^r A_2 = <x_2 \lor x_3 \; ; \; x_1>$$
$$B_2 = A_1 t_2^r A_2 = <\bar{x}_1 \lor \bar{x}_3 \; ; \; x_2>$$
$$B_3 = A_1 t_3^r A_2 = <x_2 \bar{x}_1 \lor \bar{x}_2 x_1 \; ; \; x_3>$$

$$C_1 = B_2 t_3^r B_1 = <1; \; x_2 x_3 \vee x_2 \bar{x}_3>$$

$$C_2 = A_1 t_1^r B_3 = <\bar{x}_2; \; x_3 x_1>$$

$$C_3 = B_3 t_2^r A_2 = <x_1 \; ; \; x_3 \vee x_2>$$

$$D_1 = A_1 t_1^r C_3 = <1 \; ; \; x_1(x_2 \vee x_3)>$$

$$D_2 = C_2 t_2^r A_2 = <1 \; ; \; x_3 x_1 \vee x_2>$$

From these P-functions we deduce the realizations of three functions compatible with the incompletely specified Boolean function of figure 62. These three functions are the codomains of P-functions whose domains are 1, i.e. :

$$x_1 x_3 \vee x_2 \bar{x}_3 \; , \; x_1(x_2 \vee x_3), \; x_2 \vee x_3 x_1.$$

The realizations of these functions in terms of *if then else* instructions are depicted in figure 63. The three programs of figure 63 satisfy the *cost criterion* while the program with entry C_1 satisfies moreover the *time criterion*.

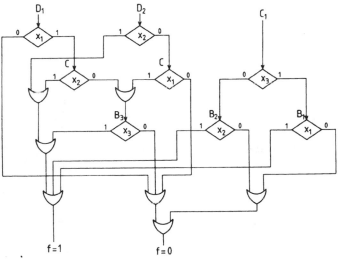

Figure 63 : Realizations of an incompletely defined Boolean function.

Multivalued or *discrete functions*, i.e. functions having finite domain and codomain, play an increasing role in various fields of computer science.
Most often, handled and transmitted information is of binary nature and it could
be argued that Boolean algebra is probably one of the only forms of discrete mathe-
matics endowed with fitting technical applications. Other forms of discrete mathema
tics also have found a useful place in everyday computer science : think of finite
automata theory, that applies to the design of sequential switching circuits and to
the description of microprogrammed systems, of the combinatorial algebra and of its
impact on reliable communication and on econometrics, and also of the numerous appl
cations of graph theory and pseudo-Boolean methods.

Various reasons motivate an ever-increasing use of multivalued logic
and of multivalued circuitry. A first argument is that a discrete function may be r
presented in multivalued logics much more concisely than it could be in binary logics : in this sense, multivalued logics already appears as an adequate tool for
coping with problems of higher size or complexity and it is clear that the appearan
ce of highly complex systems is a typical characteristic of today's technical trends
On the other hand, the relative cost of the connections indeed becomes the most si-
gnificant part of the overall system cost and multivalued logic appears as a mean
of increasing the information density over these connections and thus their efficie
cy. Similarly, technology imposes severe limitations on the number of connections
of an integrated circuit with the external world. This argument again favours multivalued logics.

The present chapter attempts to give a generalization of the theory
of P-functions and, as such, it hopefully can provide the computer scientist with
some multivalued sights of program design.

Section 14.1 is devoted to the algebraic extension of the theory of
P-functions : P-functions associated to discrete functions are defined and the laws
acting on discrete P-functions are stated. A discrete or multivalued-constant can
be coded by a vector of binary constants $\{0,1\}$. Since the laws acting on Boolean
P-functions have been extended componentwise for dealing with vector domain functio
in Part I of this text, the theory developed in chapter 3 allows us already to deal
with P-functions associated with discrete functions of binary variables, i.e. mappings

$$f : \{0,1\}^n \rightarrow \{0,1, \ldots, m-1\} \quad .$$

The theory that will be developed in the present chapter allows us moreover to deal
with discrete functions of discrete variables, i.e. mappings :

$$f : \{0,1, \ldots , m-1\}^n \rightarrow \{0,1, \ldots , m-1\} .$$

The transformations of P-functions associated with these discrete functions are performed by generalizing the transformation laws t_x, d_x and U.

Section 14.2 is devoted to the treatment of an example and to the interpretation of P-functions associated with discrete functions in terms of program synthesis and of its implementation. In particular we propose a microprogrammed implementation for programs using multivalued instructions as decision instructions. These decision instructions correspond to the *switch* instruction in *algol* and to the *case* instruction in *pascal*.

14.1. General theory

Let $\underline{x}=(x_1,x_2,\ldots,x_n)$ be a set of n variables ; a *discrete* or *multivalued function* $f(\underline{x})$ is a mapping $f : S^n \rightarrow S$ with $S = \{0,1,\ldots,m-1\}$.
The *lattice exponentiation* $x_i^{(C_i)}$ is defined as follows :

$$x_i^{(C_i)} = m-1 \text{ iff } x_i \in C_i \text{ with } C_i \subseteq S ,$$
$$x_i^{(C_i)} = 0 \quad \text{otherwise} .$$

The following operation symbols are used :

$\vee$ stands for the disjunction, i.e. $a \vee b = \max(a,b)$; $a,b \in S$.

$\wedge$ or absence of symbol stands for the conjunction, i.e. :
$$a \wedge b = \min(a,b).$$

A *cube function* is a discrete function of the form :

$$\ell \wedge \bigwedge_{i=1}^{n} x_i^{(C_i)} , \quad \ell \in \{0,1,\ldots,m-1\} . \quad C_i \subseteq S \; \forall i .$$

An *implicant* of a discrete function f is a cube smaller than f ; a *prime implicant* of f is an implicant which is not smaller than any other implicant.

Let $g(\underline{x})$ be a binary function, i.e. a function :

$$g : \{0,1,\ldots,m-1\} \rightarrow \{0,m-1\}^n$$

Definition 1 (P-function)
The pair of functions $\langle g;h \rangle$ is a P-function of f (one will write $\langle g;h \rangle \nabla f$) if and only if if the m-valued functions f,h : $S^m \rightarrow S$ and the binary function g : $S \rightarrow \{0,m-1\}$ satisfy the relation :

$$fg = hg \qquad (157)$$

The relation (157) means that f reduces to h in the domain characterized by g=1.
The set of P-functions $\{<g_i;h_i>\nabla f \mid \underset{i}{\vee}\, g_i \equiv m-1\}$ is a *total description* of f :
we have indeed :

$$\underset{i}{\vee}\, h_i g_i = f(\underset{i}{\vee}\, g_i) = f$$

The propositions and theorems that were stated in chapter 13 with
respect to P-functions associated to Boolean functions remain true with respect to
P-functions associated to discrete functions. The formal proof of these theorems
will be left to the reader ; we shall only give the multivalued extension of the
main definitions and computation algorithms.

A straightforward generalization of the lemma of section 13.1 allows
us to state that the set :

$$\{g_i \mid <g_i;h> \mid \nabla f\}$$

is closed for the operations of conjunction and of disjunction so that it constitutes
a sublattice of the lattice of discrete functions and has consequently a maximum element denoted $[f,h]$; we have :

$$[f,h] = m-1 \quad \forall\, \underline{x} : f(\underline{x}) = h(\underline{x}) ,$$

$$= 0 \quad \forall\, \underline{x} : f(\underline{x}) \neq h(\underline{x}) .$$

Theorem 1 (Theorem on composition law t_x ; theorem 1 of 13.1).
$<g_i;h_i>\nabla f$, $0 \leqslant i \leqslant m-1 \Rightarrow$

$$t_x\,(<g_i;h_i>) = < \overset{m-1}{\underset{i=0}{\vee}}\, g_i\, x^{(i)} \; ; \; \overset{m-1}{\underset{i=0}{\vee}}\, h_i\, x^{(i)} > \nabla f . \qquad (158)$$

Moreover $g_i = [f;h_i]$ $\forall i \Rightarrow$

$$\overset{m-1}{\underset{i=0}{\vee}}\, g_i x^{(i)} = [f , \overset{m-1}{\underset{i=0}{\vee}}\, h_i\, x^{(i)}] \quad .$$

Theorem 2 (Theorem on composition law t_x^r ; theorem 2 of 13.1)

$<g_i;h_i> \nabla f$, $0 \leqslant i \leqslant m-1 \Rightarrow$

$$t_x^r(<g_i;h_i>) = < \overset{m-1}{\underset{i=0}{\wedge}}\, g_i(x=i) \; ; \; \overset{m-1}{\underset{i=0}{\vee}}\, h_i\, x^{(i)} > \nabla f . \qquad (159)$$

Moreover $g_i = [f;h_i]$ $\forall i$

$\overset{m-1}{\underset{i=0}{\wedge}}\, g_i(x=i)$ *is the greatest function independent of x and contained in* $[f, \overset{m-1}{\underset{i=0}{\vee}}\, h_i x^{(i)}]$

Theorem 3 (Theorem on decomposition law d_x ; theorem 1 of 13.3)

1) $<g;h> \quad \forall f \Rightarrow$

$$d_x <g;h> = \{<g \ x^{(i)} \ ; \ h \ (x=i)> \forall f\} \qquad 0 \leqslant i \leqslant m-1 \qquad (160)$$

2) *An iterative application of the laws* $d_{x_i} \in \underline{x}$ *to the P-function* $<m-1;f>$
   generates the total description of $f : \{<g_j;h_j>| \lor g_j \equiv m-1 , h_j \in S\}$.

      We verify that the concepts of prime P-function, P-cubes, prime P-cu-
bes, total description and union laws that were defined in chapter 13 with respect
to Boolean functions are extended without any modification to discrete functions.
All the theorems of chapter 13 such as e.g. the theorem 2 of section 13.3 on the
union law U also hold in the multivalued case .

      General composition laws t_x^k and decomposition laws d_x^k could be defin-
ed in the same way. Their straightforward statement is left to the reader.

      Two total descriptions of a discrete function

$$f : S^n \rightarrow S$$

in terms of prime P-functions are : $\{<f^{(i)};i> , \ 0 \leqslant i \leqslant m-1\}$ and $<m-1;f>$. The
synthesis of this discrete function f may be viewed as the transformation between
these two total descriptions obtained by using the laws t_x or d_x and U , i.e. :

$$\left. \begin{array}{l} <f^{(0)} \ ; \ 0> \\ <f^{(1)} \ ; \ 1> \\ \quad \vdots \\ <f^{(m-1)};m-1> \end{array} \right\} \quad \begin{array}{c} \{t_x\} \\ \xleftarrow{\hspace{1.5cm}} \\ \{d_x,U\} \end{array} \quad <m-1;f> \qquad (161)$$

      The multivalued function f can also be considered as the decision
tool in the row-instruction :

$$N \left[\begin{array}{cccc} f^{(0)} & f^{(1)} & \cdots & f^{(m-1)} \\ \sigma_0 & \sigma_1 & & \sigma_{m-1} \\ M_0 & M_1 & \cdots & M_{m-1} \end{array} \right]$$

The multivalued function : $f = \lor f^{(i)}_i$ and its total description $\{<f^{(i)};i>\}$ are
thus written respectively : $f = \sum_i f^{(i)} \sigma_i$ and $\{<f^{(i)};\sigma_i>\}$; the transformation
(161) becomes accordingly :

$$\left.\begin{array}{c} <f^{(0)} ; \sigma_0> \\ <f^{(1)} ; \sigma_1> \\ \vdots \\ <f^{(m-1)};\sigma_{m-1}> \end{array}\right\} \quad \xrightarrow[\{d_x,U\}]{\{t_x\}} \quad <m-1;f> \qquad (162)$$

with :

$$t_x(<g_i;h_i>, 0 \leqslant i \leqslant m-1) = < \underset{i}{\vee} g_i \; x^{(i)} ; \underset{i}{\sum} h_i \; x^{(i)}> \qquad (163)$$

$$<g;h_1> \; U \; <g;h_2> = <g; h_1 + h_2>$$

The transformations (161) and (162) are **straightforward** extensions of the transformations (154) and (155) respectively.

Assume now that f is an incompletely specified discrete function and
that the unspecified domain is characterized by the solutions of $f^* =(m-1)$. We
easily verify that a discrete function g compatible with an incompletely specified
discrete function f is synthesized by performing the following transformation on P-
functions :

$$\left.\begin{array}{c} <f^{(0)} \vee f^* ; \sigma_0> \\ <f^{(1)} \vee f^* ; \sigma_1> \\ \vdots \\ <f^{(m-1)} \vee f^*;\sigma_{m-1}> \end{array}\right\} \quad \xrightarrow[\{d_x,U\}]{\{t_x\}} \quad <m-1;f> \qquad (164)$$

In the transformations (161, 162), the binary function $f^{(i)}$ represent
the domain where the discrete function f takes the value i ; the left P-functions
of (161,162) have thus disjoint domain-functions, i.e. :

$$f^{(j)} \; f^{(k)} \equiv 0 \quad \forall j \neq k$$

Consider the transformation (165) where the domain functions f_j are binary functions $f_j : S \rightarrow \{0,m-1\}$ which are not necessarily disjoint

$$\left.\begin{array}{c} <f_0 ; \sigma_0> \\ <f_1 ; \sigma_1> \\ \vdots \\ <f_{m-1};\sigma_{m-1}> \end{array}\right\} \quad \begin{array}{l} \xrightarrow{\{t_x\}} <m-1 ; f' = \underset{j}{\sum} g_i \; \sigma_i> \quad , \\ \xrightarrow{\{t_x,U\}} <m-1 ; f = \underset{i}{\sum} f_i \; \sigma_i > \end{array} \qquad (165)$$

We know that an iterative use of the laws $\{t_x\}$ produces a P-function having $(m-1)$ as domain and $f' = \sum_i g_i \sigma_i$ as codomain with :

$$g_i \subseteq f_i \ \forall i \ , \quad g_j g_k \equiv 0 \quad \forall j \neq k \ .$$

If we use the laws $\{t_x, U\}$ it is possible to obtain a P-function having $(m-1)$ as domain and $f = \sum_i f_i \sigma_i$ as codomain (see the theorem of section 5.1.). This last transformation may be interpreted with respect to the synthesis of a row-instruction :

$$N \begin{bmatrix} f_0 & f_1 & \cdots & f_{m-1} \\ \sigma_0 & \sigma_1 & \cdots & \sigma_{m-1} \\ M_0 & M_1 & \cdots & M_{m-1} \end{bmatrix}$$

in terms of elementary multivalued decision instructions :

$$N' \begin{bmatrix} x_i^{(0)} & x_i^{(1)} & \cdots & x_i^{(m-1)} \\ M_0' & M_1' & \cdots & M_{m-1}' \end{bmatrix} \tag{166}$$

This last row-instruction (166) has the meaning :
when reaching N' go to the next instruction label M_j' iff $x_i = j$; it corresponds to the *switch* instruction in algol or to the *case* instruction in pascal (see also the example in section 14.2).

      Observe finally that the componentwise extensions of the transformation laws that were defined in part I (see e.g. the transformation (34)) for Boolean laws are extended without any difficulty to the discrete transformation laws of theorems 1,2 and 3.

      The simultaneous synthesis of q discrete functions $\{f_j\}$ is obtained by performing the transformation (167) :

$$
\left.\begin{array}{l}
\langle f_1^{(0)} , \quad f_2^{(0)} , \ldots , f_q^{(0)} \ ; m-1 \rangle \\
\langle f_1^{(1)} , \quad f_2^{(1)} , \ldots , f_q^{(1)} \ ; m-1 \rangle \\
\qquad \cdots \\
\langle f_1^{(m-1)}, \ f_2^{(m-1)} , \ldots , f_q^{(m-1)} ; m-1 \rangle
\end{array}\right\}
\begin{array}{c} \xrightarrow{\{t_x\}} \\[2pt] \xleftarrow{\{d_x, U\}} \end{array}
\left\{\begin{array}{l}
\langle m-1, \ - \ , \ldots , \ - \ ; f_1 = \sum_i f_1^{(i)} i \rangle \\
\langle - , \ m-1 , \ldots , \ - \ ; f_2 = \sum_i f_2^{(i)} i \rangle \\
\qquad \cdots \\
\langle - , \ - \ , \ldots , m-1 ; f_q = \sum_i f_q^{(i)} i \rangle
\end{array}\right.
$$

$$\tag{167}$$

which is the composition extension of (161). More general componentwise extensions of P-functions will be studied in chapter 15.

14.2. Example and interpretations

Example

Consider the discrete function :

$$f : \{0,1,2\}^3 \rightarrow \{0,1,2\}$$

defined either by the table of figure 64 or by the expression (168).

2	2	2	2	0	0	0	2	2	2
x_2 1	2	2	2	2	1	0	2	2	2
0	2	1	0	2	1	0	2	1	0

Figure 64 :
Truth table

x_1 0   1   2   0   1   2   0   1   2

x_3 0   0   0   1   1   1   2   2   2

$$f = 0 \; [x_1^{(2)} \; (x_2^{(0)} \vee x_3^{(1)}) \vee x_2^{(2)} \, x_3^{(1)}] \vee$$
$$1 \; [x_1^{(1)} \; (x_3^{(1)} \, x_2^{(0,1)} \vee x_2^{(0)})] \vee$$
$$2 \; [x_1^{(0)} \; (x_2^{(0,1)} \vee x_3^{(0,2)}) \vee x_2^{(1,2)} \, x_3^{(0,2)}] \qquad (168)$$

If we choose the reduced law t_x^r a straightforward extension of the computational methods developed for Boolean functions allows us first to obtain the transformation (169) on P-functions from which we deduce the combinatorial realizations of figure 65.

Since :

$$(m-1) \bigwedge_i x_i^{(c_i)} = x_i^{(c_i)}$$

the coefficient (m-1) may be dropped in the expression of discrete functions.

$$\left. \begin{array}{l} A_1 = \langle x_1^{(2)} \; (x_2^{(0)} \vee x_3^{(1)}) \vee x_2^{(2)} \, x_3^{(1)} \; ; \; 0 \rangle \\[6pt] A_2 = \langle x_1^{(1)} \; (x_3^{(1)} \, x_2^{(0,1)} \vee x_2^{(0)}) \; ; \; 1 \rangle \\[6pt] A_3 = \langle x_1^{(0)} \; (x_2^{(0,1)} \vee x_3^{(0,2)}) \vee x_2^{(1,2)} \, x_3^{(0,2)} \; ; \; 2 \rangle \end{array} \right\} \begin{array}{c} \text{Initial} \\ \text{system} \end{array} \qquad (169a)$$

$$B = t_1^r \, (A_3, A_2, A_1) = \langle x_2^{(0)} \vee x_3^{(1)} \, x_2^{(0,1)} \; ; \; x_1^{(0)} \vee 1x_1^{(1)} \vee 0 \, x_1^{(2)} \rangle$$

$$C_1 = t_2^r \, (B, B, A_1) = \langle x_3^{(1)} \; ; \; 0 \, x_2^{(2)} \vee x_2^{(0,1)} \, (x_1^{(0)} \vee 1x_1^{(1)} \vee 0x_1^{(2)}) \rangle$$

$$C_2 = t_2^r \, (B, A_3, A_3) = \langle x_3^{(0,2)}; \; x_2^{(1,2)} \vee x_2^{(0)} (x_1^{(0)} \vee 1x_1^{(1)} \vee 0 \, x_1^{(2)}) \rangle$$

$$D = t_3^r \, (C_2, C_1, C_2) = \langle 2; f \rangle \; : \; \text{Final P-function} \qquad (169b)$$

The combinatorial realizations of figures 65 are made
lued multiplexers, demultiplexers and or-gates which are straightforward generaliza-
tions of the corresponding binary gates, and of the discrete constants 0, 1 and 2.

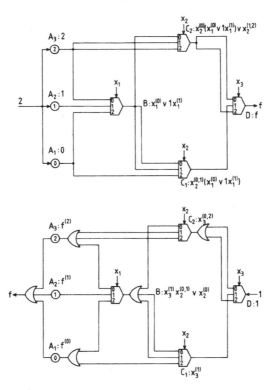

Figure 65 : Hardware realizations of discrete functions.

Clearly in the above expressions and realizations, the coefficients
of the discrete constant "0" could be dropped. If the transformation (169) represents an instruction instead of a discrete function the constants "i" have to be
replaced by the orders "σ_i" the coefficients of which may evidently no longer be
dropped. In order to remain as general as possible we shall explicitly write the
coefficients of "0". Observe that this reduces to writing a Boolean function f in
the following form :

$$f = 1.f \vee 0.\bar{f} \ .$$

As noted above the synthesis of a discrete function

$$f : S^n \to S$$

can be interpreted with respect to the synthesis of an instruction.

Consider an elementary decision instruction of the row-type :

$$N \; [x^{(0)} \quad x^{(1)} \quad \ldots \quad x^{(m-1)}]$$
$$M_0 \qquad M_1 \quad \ldots \quad M_{m-1}$$

$$(170)$$

The transformation (161) on P-functions can be interpreted as the realization of a row-instruction :

$$N \; [\; f^{(0)} \qquad f^{(1)} \quad \ldots \quad f^{(m-1)} \;]$$
$$M_0 \qquad M_1 \quad \ldots \quad M_{m-1}$$

$$(171)$$

in terms of the elementary instructions (170) where the variables x are the elementary predicates of the problem.

The synthesis of the decision instruction :

$$D \; [\; f^{(0)} \qquad f^{(1)} \qquad f^{(2)} \;]$$
$$A_0 \qquad A_1 \qquad A_2$$

where f is given either by the truth table 64 or by the expression (168) in terms of elementary decision instructions is deduced from the transformation (169a) → (169b) ; using the notation (169) we have :

$$D \; [\; x_3^{(0)} \qquad x_3^{(1)} \qquad x_3^{(2)} \;]$$
$$C_2 \qquad C_1 \qquad C_2$$

$$C_1 \; [\; x_2^{(0)} \qquad x_2^{(1)} \qquad x_2^{(0)} \;]$$
$$B \qquad B \qquad A_1$$

$$C_2 \; [\; x_2^{(0)} \qquad x_2^{(1)} \qquad x_2^{(2)} \;]$$
$$B \qquad A_3 \qquad A_3$$

$$(172)$$

$$B \; [\; x_1^{(0)} \qquad x_1^{(1)} \qquad x_1^{(2)} \;]$$
$$A_3 \qquad A_2 \qquad A_1$$

$$A_i \; : \; f = i \; , \; 1 \leqslant i \leqslant 3 \; .$$

Clearly, the transformation (169a) (169b) and consequently the program (172) can be interpreted with respect to a factorization of a matrix of discrete functions as a product of matrices of discrete variables. To the transformation (169) corresponds the following factorization :

$$\left[f^{(0)}(x_1,x_2,x_3) \quad f^{(1)}(x_1,x_2,x_3) \quad f^{(2)}(x_1,x_2,x_3) \right] =$$

$$\left[x_3^{(1)} \quad x_3^{(0,2)} \right] \begin{bmatrix} x_2^{(0,1)} & x_2^{(2)} & 0 \\ x_2^{(0)} & 0 & x_2^{(1,2)} \end{bmatrix} \begin{bmatrix} x_1^{(2)} & x_1^{(1)} & x_1^{(0)} \\ 2 & 0 & 0 \\ 0 & 0 & 2 \end{bmatrix} \quad (173)$$

It turns out that the theory developed in part I of this text and dealing with matrix-instruction, (and)-and (or)-interpretations, duality principles, transposition principles etc. could be extended without any difficulty from the Boolean domain to the multivalued or discrete domain. The reader will verify that in most cases the definitions, theorems, propositions of part I remain true when the term *Boolean function* is replaced by the term *discrete function*.

As long as the hardware implementation is concerned, all the logical devices have their multivalued counterpart (see e.g. Davio, Deschamps and Thayse [1978], Vranesic and Smith [1974], Preparata and Yeh [1973], Allen and Givone [1968]) so that the combinatorial syntheses proposed in part I for Boolean functions are extended without any modification to discrete functions. For example, the realizations of figure 65 are made of multiplexers and of demultiplexers whose general input-output relationships are given by the following equations respectively :

$$z = \bigvee_{i=0}^{m-1} a_i \, x^{(i)} \qquad (174a)$$

$$z_i = a \, x^{(i)} \qquad , \quad 0 \leqslant i \leqslant m-1 \qquad (174b)$$

Equation (174a) provides us with the multiplexer output z in terms of the multiplexers inputs a_i, $0 \leqslant i \leqslant m-1$ and of the multivalued control variable x ; similarly equations (174b) provide us with the m demultiplexers outputs z_i, $0 \leqslant i \leqslant m-1$ in terms of the demultiplexer input a and of the multivalued control variable x.

Finally the programmed and microprogrammed realization of discrete functions by means of safe programs and of integrated elements are obtained from a straightforward extension of the concepts developed in part II of this text. Consider e.g. the program (172). Its implementation by means of ternary Read-Only-Memories, address decoders and registers is only a matter of encoding the instruction labels into a ternary code. Let us choose the following encoding :

D	C_2	C_1	B	A_3	A_2	A_1
00	01	02	10	20	21	22

The network of figure 66 realizes a microprogrammed implementation of the program (172). The behaviour of this network can be briefly explained as follows

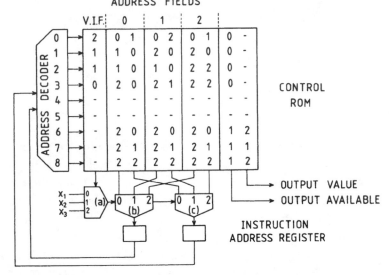

Figure 66 : Multivalued microprogrammed implementation of the program (172).

- The address presently contained in the instruction address register selects one of the rows of the control ROM by means of the address decoder.
- The variable identification field (V.I.F.) of the selected row selects one of the variables x_1, x_2 and x_3 by means of the multiplexer a.
- The value of the selected input variable selects one of the three address fields and determines the next instruction address by means of the multiplexers b and c ; this new address is stored in the instruction address register.
- Once the computation is completed, a "1" appears on the output available wire and $f(x_1, x_2, x_3)$ is available on the output value wire (the symbol "-" in figure 66 stands for the don't care condition).

In the general case of a multivalued algorithm computing an n-variable m-valued discrete function in p steps (or instructions), a row of the control memory must contain the following informations :

- A variable identification field (1 out of n) ;
- m next addresses fields m×(1 out of p) ;
- an Output-Available field and an Output-Value field.

Chapter 15.   The vectorial extension of P-functions and of their laws

         We have seen in section 3.2 that the description and the synthesis
of matrix-instructions requested the introduction of P-functions having *vector
domain functions*. In section 15.1 we first recall the properties of the vectorial
extension of the domain functions and we extend it to multivalued P-functions. We
show that a system of m P-functions whose domain has the dimension p generates ei‐
a matrix of (m×p) boolean functions or a column matrix of p m-valued discrete fun‐
tions.

         In section 15.2 we introduce P-functions whose *codomain is a vecto:
of functions*. We show that the treatment of P-functions with vectorial codomains
leads to an interesting interpretation in terms of instruction synthesis : these :
functions generate *safe programs* which can immediately be implemented in a progra:
med or in a microprogrammed way.

         Section 15.3 is devoted to the analysis of P-functions having simu‐
taneously a *vector domain* and a *vector codomain*. We show that systems of P-functi‐
having q-ary domains and p-ary codomains generate a matrix of (p×q) discrete func
tions. We also show that these P-functions may be interpreted with respect to the
synthesis of safe programs equivalent to matrix-instructions

         A general survey of transformations between P-functions and of the
interpretation in terms of program synthesis is made in section 15.4.

15.1. The vectorial extension of the domain function

         Consider the p discrete functions :

$$\{f_j\} : S^n \to S , \quad 1 \leqslant j \leqslant p ;$$

these functions are represented by the system of P-functions :

$$\{<f_1^{(i)}, f_2^{(i)} , \ldots , f_p^{(i)} ; i>\} , \quad 0 \leqslant i \leqslant m-1 \qquad (175$$

where the domain function is a vector of binary functions :

$$\{f_j^{(i)}\} : S^n \to \{0,m-1\} , \quad 1 \leqslant j \leqslant p .$$

The transformation laws t_x, d_x and $\cup$ are the componentwise extension of the laws
defined in chapter 14 for discrete functions. In particular it is clear that an
iterative application of the laws t_x to the set of p P-functions (175) can in any

case produce a "m-1" at the j-th component of the domain vector $(1 \leqslant j \leqslant p)$; to the "m-1" value of the j-th component necessarily corresponds a codomain function f_j, i.e. a P-function of the form (176) :

$$< \bar{}_1 , \bar{}_2 , \ldots , (m-1)_j , \ldots , \bar{}_p ; f_j > \qquad (176)$$

As usual the dash "-" means an indeterminate discrete function. The synthesis of p discrete functions is reflected by the transformation (177) between systems I and II of P-functions. We can either perform the transformation from system I to system IIb (leaves-to-root synthesis) or perform the transformation from system IIa to system I of (177) (root-to-leaves synthesis).

System I

$$\{< f_1^{(i)}, f_2^{(i)}, \ldots , f_j^{(i)}, \ldots , f_p^{(i)} ; i> , \quad 0 \leqslant i \leqslant m-1\}$$

$\uparrow \{d_x, U\}$ $\qquad\qquad$ $\downarrow \{t_x\}$

$$\{< g_1', g_2', \ldots , g_j', \ldots , g_p' ; h>\} \quad \{< g_1, g_2, \ldots , g_j, \ldots , g_p ; h>\}$$

$\uparrow \{d_x, U\}$ $\qquad\qquad$ $\downarrow \{t_x\}$

$$\{< 0_1, 0_2, \ldots, (m-1)_j, \ldots , 0_p ; f_j >\} \quad \{< \bar{}_1, \bar{}_2, \ldots, (m-1)_j, \ldots, \bar{}_p ; f_j >$$

$$(1 \leqslant j \leqslant p)$$

System IIa   System IIb

$$(177)$$

The dash "$-_k$" at the k-th place of the j-th P-function of system IIb represents any discrete function g_k such that :

$$g_k \, f_k = f_j \; .$$

Since this information is useless for any transformation process, the two transformations (leaves-to-root and root-to-leaves) represented by (177) will unambiguously be written :

| System I | | System II |

$$\{<f_1^{(i)},\ f_2^{(i)},\ldots,f_p^{(i)};i>\} \underset{\{d_x,\cup\}}{\overset{\{t_x\}}{\rightleftarrows}} \{<O_1,O_2,\ldots,(m-1)_j,\ldots,\ O_p\ ;\ f_j = \sum_i f_j^{(i)}i>\}$$

$$0 \leqslant i \leqslant m-1 \qquad\qquad\qquad\qquad 1 \leqslant j \leqslant p$$

$$(178)$$

Example

Consider the synthesis of four Boolean functions of four variables ; assume that f_2 is partially defined, i.e. : $f_{2M} \geqslant f_2 \geqslant f_{2m}$; the functions (f_1,f_2,f_3,f_4) are either characterized by the Karnaugh map of figure 67 or by the expressions (179).

$$x_1$$

(f_1,f_2,f_3,f_4)

1 1 0 0	1 1 1 1	1 1 1 1	1 0 0 1
0 0 0 0	0 0 1 1	0 - 1 1	1 0 1 1
0 1 0 0	1 1 1 0	1 1 1 1	1 1 1 1
1 1 1 1	1 1 1 1	1 1 1 1	1 1 1 1

x_3 (left label), x_4 (right label), x_2 (bottom label)

Figure 67 : Karnaugh map.

$$f_1 = \bar{x}_3 \vee x_1 x_4 \vee x_2 x_4 \vee \bar{x}_1 x_2 \ ,$$

$$f_{2M} = x_4 \vee \bar{x}_2 \bar{x}_3 \vee x_1 \bar{x}_3 \vee x_1 x_2 \ ; \ f_{2m} = x_4 \vee \bar{x}_2 \bar{x}_3 \vee x_1 \bar{x}_3 \ ,$$

$$f_3 = x_1 \vee \bar{x}_3 x_4 \vee x_2 x_4 \vee x_2 x_3 \ ,$$

$$f_4 = x_2 \vee x_1 \bar{x}_4 \vee \bar{x}_3 x_4 \vee x_1 \bar{x}_3 \ .$$

$$(179)$$

We shall use the transformation scheme from system I (178) to system II (178) with the reduced law t_x^r ; the two P-functions of system I are :

$$A_1 = <x_3(\bar{x}_1\bar{x}_2 \vee \bar{x}_2\bar{x}_4 \vee x_1 x_4),\ x_4(\bar{x}_1 x_2 \vee x_3)\ ,$$

$$\bar{x}_1(\bar{x}_2 x_3 \vee \bar{x}_2 x_4 \vee \bar{x}_3 x_4),\ \bar{x}_2(\bar{x}_1 \bar{x}_4 \vee \bar{x}_1 x_3 \vee x_3 x_4)\ ;\ 0>$$

$$A_2 = <\bar{x}_3 \vee x_1 x_4 \vee x_2 x_4 \vee \bar{x}_1 x_2,\ x_4 \vee \bar{x}_2\bar{x}_3 \vee x_1\bar{x}_3 \vee x_1 x_2\ ,$$

$$x_1 \vee \bar{x}_3 x_4 \vee x_2 x_4 \vee x_2 x_3,\ x_2 \vee x_1\bar{x}_3 \vee \bar{x}_3 x_4 \vee x_1\bar{x}_3\ ;\ 1>$$

The computation process starting from system I and producing system II :

$$\{<1,-,-,-; f_1> \ , \ <-,1,-,-; f_2> \ , \ <-,-,1,-; f_3> \ , \ <-,-,-,1; f_4>\}$$

is detailed below (see (180a) → (180b)).

$$\left.\begin{array}{l} A_1 = <\bar{f}_1, \ \bar{f}_{2m}, \ \bar{f}_3, \ \bar{f}_4 \ ; \ 0> \\[2mm] A_2 = <f_1, \ f_{2M}, \ f_3, \ f_4 \ ; \ 1> \end{array}\right\} \qquad \text{System I} \qquad\qquad (180a)$$

$$B_1 = A_1 t_2^r A_2 = <\bar{x}_1 x_3, \ x_1 x_3 \bar{x}_4, \ \bar{x}_1(x_3 \vee x_4), \ \bar{x}_1 \bar{x}_4 \vee \bar{x}_1 x_3 \vee x_3 x_4 \ ; \ x_2>$$

$$B_2 = A_1 t_4^r A_2 = <x_1 x_3, \ \bar{x}_1 x_2 \vee x_1 x_3 \vee \bar{x}_2 x_3, \ \bar{x}_1 \bar{x}_3, \ \bar{x}_1 \bar{x}_1 \bar{x}_3; \ x_4>$$

$$C_1 = B_1 t_1^r A_2 = <x_3 x_4, \ 0, \ x_3 \vee x_4, \ \bar{x}_4 \ ; \ x_1 \vee x_2)$$

$$C_2 = B_2 t_1^r A_2 = <0, \ x_2, \ \bar{x}_3, \ \bar{x}_2 \bar{x}_3 \ ; \ x_1 \vee x_4>$$

$$C_3 = A_2 t_3^r B_1 = <\bar{x}_1, \ x_1 \bar{x}_4, \ \bar{x}_1 x_4, \ x_4 \ ; \ x_2 \vee \bar{x}_3>$$

$$C_4 = A_2 t_3^r B_2 = <x_1, \ x_1 \vee \bar{x}_2, \ 0, \ 0 \ ; \ \bar{x}_3 \vee x_4>$$

$$\left.\begin{array}{l} D_1 = C_3 t_1^r C_4 = <1, \ 0, \ 0, \ 0 \ ; \ f_1> \\[2mm] D_2 = C_4 t_2^r C_2 = <0, \ 1, \ 0, \ 0 \ ; \ f_2> \\[2mm] D_3 = C_2 t_3^r C_1 = <0, \ 0, \ 1, \ 0 \ ; \ f_3> \\[2mm] D_4 = C_1 t_4^r C_3 = <0, \ 0, \ 0, \ 1 \ ; \ f_4> \end{array}\right\} \qquad \text{System II} \qquad (180b)$$

If the Boolean functions $\{f_1, f_2, f_3, f_4\}$ are the decision functions for the (or)-interpreted matrix instruction :

$$\begin{array}{c c c} & \sigma_0 & \sigma_1 \\ D_1 & \bar{f}_1 & f_1 \\ D_2 & \bar{f}_2 & f_2 \\ D_3 & \bar{f}_3 & f_3 \\ D_4 & \bar{f}_4 & f_4 \\[2mm] & \sigma_0 & \sigma_1 \\ & M_1 & M_2 \end{array}$$

it is more appropriate to use a pseudo-Boolean formalism for the transformation :
(180a) → (180b), i.e. :

$$\left.\begin{array}{l} A_1 = <\bar{f}_1, \bar{f}_2, \bar{f}_3, \bar{f}_4 \ ; \sigma_0> \\[6mm] A_2 = <f_1, f_2, f_3, f_4 \ ; \sigma_1> \end{array}\right\} \xrightarrow{\{t_i^r\}} \left\{\begin{array}{l} <1,0,0,0; \ \bar{f}_1 \sigma_0 + f_1 \sigma_1> \\[2mm] <0,1,0,0; \ \bar{f}_2 \sigma_0 + f_2 \sigma_1> \\[2mm] <0,0,1,0; \ \bar{f}_3 \sigma_0 + f_3 \sigma_1> \\[2mm] <0,0,0,1; \ \bar{f}_4 \sigma_0 + f_4 \sigma_1> \end{array}\right.$$

$$\text{(181a)} \qquad\qquad\qquad\qquad \text{(181b)}$$

Using the notations (67), the program (182) resulting from the transformation
(180a) → (180b) (or equivalently (181a) → (181b)) is written in the following way :

$$
\begin{aligned}
\rightarrow \quad & D_1 \quad (\bar{x}_1 C_3 \ , \ x_1 C_4) \\
\rightarrow \quad & D_2 \quad (\bar{x}_2 C_4 \ , \ x_2 C_2) \\
\rightarrow \quad & D_3 \quad (\bar{x}_3 C_2 \ , \ x_3 C_1) \\
\rightarrow \quad & D_4 \quad (\bar{x}_4 C_1 \ , \ x_4 C_3) \\
& C_1 \quad (\bar{x}_1 B_1 \ , \ x_1 A_2) \\
& C_2 \quad (\bar{x}_1 B_2 \ , \ x_1 A_2) \\
& C_3 \quad (\bar{x}_3 A_2 \ , \ x_3 B_1) \\
& C_4 \quad (\bar{x}_3 A_2 \ , \ x_3 B_2) \\
& B_1 \quad (\bar{x}_2 A_1 \ , \ x_2 A_2) \\
& B_2 \quad (\bar{x}_4 A_1 \ , \ x_4 A_2) \\
& A_1 \quad \sigma_0 \quad M_1 \\
& A_2 \quad \sigma_1 \quad M_2
\end{aligned}
$$

(182)

A flowchart representation of the program (182) is given in figure 68.

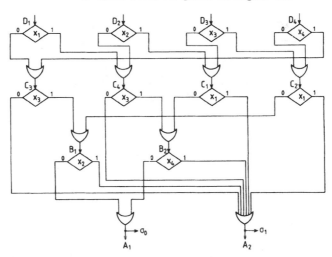

Figure 68 : Flowchart representation of the program (182).

Note finally that to the transformation (178) correspond the network schemes of figure 69. In the multiplexer synthesis the discrete functions
$\{f_1, f_2, \ldots, f_p\}$ are obtained simultaneously. In the demultiplexer synthesis, the
functions $\{f_1, f_2, \ldots, f_p\}$ are obtained one at a time according to the value 0 or 1

of the binary parameters e_i : the demultiplexer synthesis is a programmable synthesis.

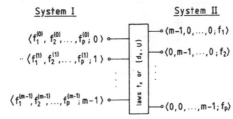

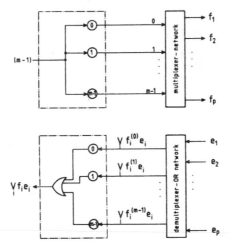

Figure 69 : Network schemes corresponding to the transformation (178).

15.2. The vectorial extension of the codomain function

Consider the p discrete functions :

$$\{f_j\} : S^n \to S \quad , \quad 1 \leqslant j \leqslant p \ .$$

these functions are represented by the system of P-functions :

$$\{<f_1^{(i_1)} f_2^{(i_2)} \dots f_p^{(i_p)} ; i_1, i_2, \dots, i_p>\}, \quad 0 \leqslant i_j \leqslant m-1 \quad , \tag{183}$$

where the codomain function is a vector of functions. Indeed, since :

$$f_j(f_1^{(i_1)} f_2^{(i_2)} \dots f_p^{(i_p)}) = i_j(f_1^{(i_1)} f_2^{(i_2)} \dots f_p^{(i_p)})$$

the elements of (183) are P-functions of $\{f_1, f_2, \ldots, f_p\}$; moreover, since

$$\underset{i_1, \ldots, i_p}{\vee} \quad f_1^{(i_1)} f_2^{(i_2)} \ldots f_p^{(i_p)} \equiv m-1$$

the system of P-functions (183) is a total description of $\{f_j\}$. Hence, the laws t_x, d_x and U being defined componentwise for the codomain function, an iterative application of the laws t_x to the set of P-functions (183) produces the P-function

$$<m-1 \; ; \; f_1, \; f_2, \ldots, f_p>$$

so that the synthesis processes are schematized by the two transformations System I → System II and System II → System I :

$$\{<f_1^{(i_1)} \ldots f_p^{(i_p)} \; ; \; i_1, \ldots, i_p>\} \; \underset{\{d_x, U\}}{\overset{\{t_x\}}{\rightleftarrows}} \; <m-1; \; f_1, \; \ldots \; , \; f_p> \tag{184}$$

$$(0 \leqslant i_j \leqslant m-1)$$

$$\text{System I} \qquad\qquad \text{System II}$$

Example

We continue the example of section 15.1; in order to synthesize the same functions as in section 15.1 we shall take $f_2 = f_{2M}$.

$$\left.\begin{array}{l}
A_1 = <\bar{x}_1 \bar{x}_2 x_3 \bar{x}_4 \; ; \; 0, \; 0, \; 0, \; 0> \\[4pt]
A_2 = <\bar{x}_1 \bar{x}_2 x_3 x_4 \; ; \; 0, \; 1, \; 0, \; 0> \\[4pt]
A_3 = <\bar{x}_1 \bar{x}_2 \bar{x}_3 \bar{x}_4 \; ; \; 1, \; 1, \; 0, \; 0> \\[4pt]
A_4 = <\bar{x}_1 \bar{x}_2 x_3 \bar{x}_4 \; ; \; 0, \; 0, \; 1, \; 1> \\[4pt]
A_5 = <\bar{x}_1 x_2 \bar{x}_3 \bar{x}_4 \; ; \; 1, \; 0, \; 0, \; 1> \\[4pt]
A_6 = <x_1 x_2 x_3 \bar{x}_4 \; ; \; 0, \; 1, \; 1, \; 1> \\[4pt]
A_7 = <\bar{x}_1 x_2 x_3 \bar{x}_4 \; ; \; 1, \; 0, \; 1, \; 1> \\[4pt]
A_8 = <x_1 \bar{x}_2 x_3 x_4 \; ; \; 1, \; 1, \; 1, \; 0>
\end{array}\right\} \qquad \text{System I} \tag{185a}$$

$$A_9 = <x_2 x_4 \vee x_1 \bar{x}_3 \vee \bar{x}_3 x_4 \; ; \; 1, \; 1, \; 1, \; 1>$$

$$B_1 = A_1 t_1^r A_4 = <\bar{x}_2 x_3 \bar{x}_4 \; ; \; 0, \; 0, \; x_1, \; x_1>$$

$$B_2 = A_2 t_1^r A_8 = <\bar{x}_2 x_3 x_4 \; ; \; x_1, \; 1, \; x_1, \; 0>$$

$$B_3 = A_3 t_1^r A_9 = <\bar{x}_2 \bar{x}_3 \bar{x}_4 \; ; \; 1, \; 1, \; x_1, \; x_1>$$

$$B_4 = A_5 t_1^r A_9 = <x_2 \bar{x}_3 \bar{x}_4 \; ; \; 1, \; x_1, \; x_1, \; 1>$$

$$B_5 = A_5 t_1^r A_6 = <x_2 x_3 \bar{x}_4 \; ; \; \bar{x}_1, \; x_1, \; 1, \; 1>$$

$$C_1 = B_1 t_4^r B_2 = \langle \bar{x}_2 x_3 \; ; \; x_1 x_4, \; x_4, \; x_1, \; x_1 \bar{x}_4 \rangle$$

$$C_2 = B_3 t_4^r A_9 = \langle \bar{x}_2 \bar{x}_3 \; ; \; 1, \; 1, \; x_1 \vee x_4, \; x_1 \vee x_4 \rangle$$

$$D_1 = C_2 t_3^r C_1 = \langle \bar{x}_2; \; \bar{x}_3 \vee x_1 x_4, \; \bar{x}_3 \vee x_4, \; x_1 \vee \bar{x}_3 x_4, \; x_1 \bar{x}_3 \vee \bar{x}_3 x_4 \vee x_1 \bar{x}_4 \rangle$$

$$D_2 = C_3 t_4^r A_9 = \langle x_2; \; x_4 \vee \bar{x}_3, \; x_4 \vee x_1, \; x_4 \vee x_1 \vee x_3, 1 \rangle$$

$$E = D_1 t_2^r D_2 = \langle 1; \; f_1, \; f_2, \; f_3, \; f_4 \rangle : \qquad \text{System II} \qquad \qquad (185b)$$

The transformation (184) has an interesting interpretation in terms of instruction synthesis. Assume that the f_j are Boolean functions and that they constitute the decision functions for a row instruction :

$$N \begin{bmatrix} f_1 & f_2 & \cdots & f_p \end{bmatrix}$$
$$\sigma_1 \quad \sigma_2 \quad \cdots \quad \sigma_p$$
$$M \quad M \quad \cdots \quad M$$

We know (see section 10.5, program (143) and figure 48b) that a safe program equivalent to this row instruction is given by :

$$N \begin{bmatrix} \bar{f}_1 & f_1 & \bar{f}_2 & f_2 & \cdots & \bar{f}_p & f_p \end{bmatrix}$$
$$\lambda \quad \sigma_1 \quad \lambda \quad \sigma_2 \quad \cdots \quad \lambda \quad \sigma_p$$
$$M_1 \quad M_1' \quad M_2 \quad M_2' \quad \cdots \quad M_p \quad M_p'$$

$$M_i' \quad \tau_i \quad M_i \qquad 1 \leqslant i \leqslant p \qquad\qquad\qquad (186)$$

$$\begin{matrix} M_1 \\ M_2 \\ \vdots \\ M_p \end{matrix} \begin{bmatrix} 1 \\ 1 \\ \vdots \\ 1 \end{bmatrix}$$
$$M$$

The synthesis of the first instruction of (186) is obtained by performing the transformation (187) which is nothing but an interpreted form of the transformation (184) for Boolean functions :

$$\{<f_1^{(i_1)}...f_p^{(i_p)} \; ; \; \lambda\bar{i}_1+\sigma_1 i_1 \;,...,\; \lambda\bar{i}_p+\sigma_p i_p> \;,\qquad 0 \leqslant i_j \leqslant 1\}$$

$$\{t_x\}\downarrow \qquad \uparrow\{d_x, \; U\}\qquad\qquad\qquad (187)$$

$$<1; \; \bar{f}_1\lambda + \; f_1\sigma_1 \;,\; ...,\; \bar{f}_p\lambda + \; f_p\sigma_p>$$

Using the interpretation (187), the transformation (185) is written in the following way (the domain function of the P-function A_j of (185a) is denoted g_j) :

$$
\left.\begin{aligned}
A_1 &= <g_1 \; ; \; \lambda, \; \lambda, \; \lambda, \; \lambda>\\
A_2 &= <g_2 \; ; \; \lambda,\sigma_2, \; \lambda, \; \lambda>\\
A_3 &= <g_3 \; ; \; \sigma_1,\sigma_2, \; \lambda, \; \lambda>\\
A_4 &= <g_4 \; ; \; \lambda, \; \lambda,\sigma_3,\sigma_4>\\
A_5 &= <g_5 \; ; \; \sigma_1, \; \lambda, \; \lambda,\sigma_4>\\
A_6 &= <g_6 \; ; \; \lambda,\sigma_2,\sigma_3,\sigma_4>\\
A_7 &= <g_7 \; ; \; \sigma_1, \; \lambda,\sigma_3,\sigma_4>\\
A_8 &= <g_8 \; ; \; \sigma_1,\sigma_2,\sigma_3, \; \lambda>\\
A_9 &= <g_9; \; \sigma_1,\sigma_2,\sigma_3,\sigma_4>
\end{aligned}\right\} \longrightarrow
\begin{aligned}
&<1; \; \bar{f}_1\lambda + f_1\sigma_1 \;,\; \bar{f}_2\lambda + f_2\sigma_2 \;,\\
&\quad \bar{f}_3\lambda + f_3\sigma_3 \;,\; \bar{f}_4\lambda + f_4\sigma_4 >
\end{aligned}
\qquad (188)
$$

To the transformation (188) corresponds the safe program of figure 70.

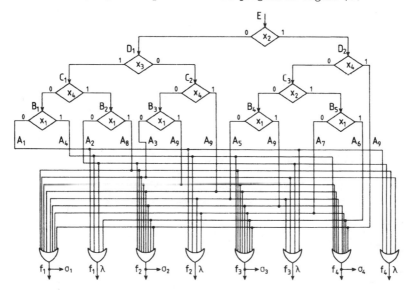

Figure 70 : Safe program corresponding to the transformation (188).

Note finally that to the transformation (184) correspond the network schemes of figure 71. In the demultiplexer synthesis the discrete functions $\{f_1, f_2, \ldots, f_p\}$ are obtained simultaneously while in the multiplexer synthesis these functions are obtained one at a time ; the syntheses of figures 69 and 71 constitute thus dual syntheses.

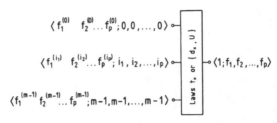

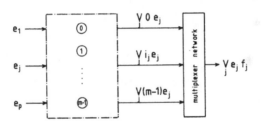

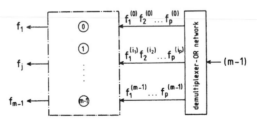

Figure 71 : Network schemes corresponding to the transformation (184).

15.3. The vectorial extension of the domain and of the codomain functions

The P-functions considered in sections 15.1 a,d 15.2 can be considered as particular cases of a more general type of P-functions having both a domain and a codomain which are vectors of functions.

We shall consider P-functions of the type :

$$\langle g_1, g_2, \ldots, g_q \; ; \; h_1, h_2, \ldots, h_p \rangle \; . \tag{189}$$

We first show that an appropriate system of P-functions of the type (189) can represent a set of p×q discrete functions.

Be the P-functions :

$$\{<g_1^i, g_2^i, \ldots , g_q^i ; h_1^i, h_2^i, \ldots , h_p^i>\} \tag{190}$$

with $g_j^{(i)}$ binary functions $S^n \to \{0,m-1\}$ satisfying the relations :

$$\underset{i}{\vee} \; g_j^i \equiv m-1 , \qquad 1 \leqslant j \leqslant q .$$

The P-functions (190) can represent the p×q discrete functions

$$\{f_{11}, \ldots , f_{ij}, \ldots , f_{pq}\} \quad : \quad S^n \to S.$$

In this respect, we choose the domain and the codomain functions as follows :

$$
\begin{aligned}
f_{11}g_1^i = h_1^i g_1^i \; ; \; f_{12}g_2^i = h_1^i g_2^i \; ; \; \ldots \; ; \; f_{1q}g_q^i = h_1^i g_q^i \\
f_{21}g_1^i = h_2^i g_1^i \; ; \; f_{22}g_2^i = h_2^i g_2^i \; ; \; \ldots \; ; \; f_{2q}g_q^i = h_2^i g_q^i \\
\vdots \qquad\qquad \vdots \qquad\qquad\qquad \vdots \\
f_{p1}g_1^i = h_p^i g_1^i \; ; \; f_{p2}g_2^i = h_p^i g_2^i \; ; \; \ldots \; ; \; f_{pq}g_q^i = h_p^i g_p^i
\end{aligned}
\tag{191}
$$

Each of the functions f_{jk}, $1 \leqslant j \leqslant p$, $1 \leqslant k \leqslant q$ is uniquely determined by the P-functions (190) ; we have indeed :

$$\underset{i}{\vee} \; h_j^i \; g_k^i = \underset{i}{\vee} \; f_{jk} \; g_k^i = f_{jk} \tag{192}$$

and the system (190) of P-functions is a complete description of the functions $\{f_{jk}\}$ if the P-functions satisfy the conditions (191). In view of the equalities (191), the system (190) of P-functions can be expressed in terms of the functions f_{jk} as follows :

$$\{<f_{11}^{(i_1)} f_{21}^{(i_2)} \ldots f_{p1}^{(i_p)} , f_{12}^{(i_1)} f_{22}^{(i_2)} \ldots f_{p2}^{(i_p)} , \ldots , f_{1q}^{(i_1)} f_{2q}^{(i_2)} \ldots f_{pq}^{(i_p)} \; ;$$

$$i_1, i_2, \ldots , i_p> \; ; \; 0 \leqslant i_j \leqslant m-1\} \tag{193}$$

Taking (193) as the system I of P-functions, an iterative use of the laws t_x allows us to transform (193) into a P-function having a "m-1" at the j-th place of the domain function ; we obtain the following type of transformation which generalizes both transformations (178) and (184) (as in (178), the dashes "-" of system II are replaced by "0") :

<u>System I</u>

$$\{<f_{11}^{\;(i_1)}\; f_{21}^{\;(i_2)}\; \ldots f_{p1}^{\;(i_p)}\;,\ldots,\; f_{1q}^{\;(i_1)}\; f_{2q}^{\;(i_2)}\; \ldots f_{pq}^{\;(i_p)}\; ;\; i_1,i_2,\ldots,i_p>\}$$

$$\{t_x\} \Big\downarrow \qquad \Big\uparrow \{d_x,\mathbf{U}\} \qquad\qquad (194)$$

$$\{<m-1\;,\; 0\;,\;\ldots\;,0\;;\; f_{11},\; f_{21},\;\ldots,\; f_{p1}>\;,$$

$$<\;0\;\;,m-1,\;\ldots\;,0\;;\; f_{12},\; f_{22},\;\ldots,\; f_{p2}>\;,$$

$$\cdot\quad\cdot\quad\cdot\quad\cdot\quad\cdot\quad\cdot\quad\cdot\quad\cdot\quad\cdot\quad\cdot\quad\cdot$$

$$<\;0\;\;,\; 0\;,\;\ldots\;,m-1;\; f_{1q},\; f_{2q},\;\ldots,\; f_{pq}>\}$$

<u>System II</u>

From the transformation (194) we deduce that a multiplexer network produces simultaneously all the discrete functions of a row of matrix (195) while the row considered is chosen by an adequate programmation of the network inputs ; dually, a demultiplexer network produces simultaneously all the functions of a column of matrix (195) while the considered column is chosen by an adequate arrangement of the network inputs.

$$\begin{bmatrix} f_{11} & f_{12} & \cdots & f_{1q} \\ f_{21} & f_{22} & \cdots & f_{2q} \\ \cdots & \cdots & \cdots & \cdots \\ f_{p1} & f_{p2} & \cdots & f_{pq} \end{bmatrix} \qquad (195)$$

The transformation (194) and the corresponding networks are schematized in figure 72.

<u>Example</u>

We continue the example of sections 15.1 and 15.2 : we consider the synthesis of the functions f_1, f_2, f_3 and f_4 arranged in the following matrix form :

$$\begin{bmatrix} f_1 & f_3 \\ f_2 & f_4 \end{bmatrix}.$$

The multiplexer synthesis will produce a simultaneous realization of either the functions f_1 and f_3 or the functions f_2 and f_4 while the demultiplexer synthesis will produce a simultaneous synthesis of either the functions f_1 and f_2 or the functions f_3 and f_4.

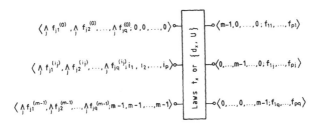

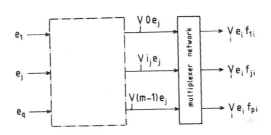

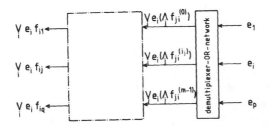

<u>Figure 72</u> : Network schemes corresponding to the transformation (194).

The successive P-functions of the transformation are the following ones.

$$A_1 = \langle \bar{f}_1\bar{f}_2, \bar{f}_3\bar{f}_4 ; 0, 0\rangle$$
$$= \langle \bar{x}_2 x_3 \bar{x}_4, \bar{x}_1\bar{x}_2(x_3 \vee \bar{x}_4); 0, 0\rangle$$
$$A_2 = \langle \bar{f}_1 f_2, \bar{f}_3 f_4 ; 0, 1\rangle$$
$$= \langle x_3(\bar{x}_1\bar{x}_2 x_4 \vee x_1 x_2\bar{x}_4), \bar{x}_1 x_2\bar{x}_3\bar{x}_4; 0,1\rangle$$
$$A_3 = \langle f_1\bar{f}_2, f_3\bar{f}_4; 1, 0\rangle$$
$$= \langle \bar{x}_1 x_2\bar{x}_4, x_1\bar{x}_2 x_3 x_4; 1, 0\rangle$$
$$A_4 = \langle f_1 f_2, f_3 f_4; 1, 1\rangle$$
$$= \langle \bar{x}_3 x_4 \vee \bar{x}_3\bar{x}_2 \vee x_1 x_4 \vee x_2 x_4,$$
$$\bar{x}_3 x_4 \vee x_1\bar{x}_3 \vee x_1\bar{x}_4 \vee x_1 x_2 \vee x_2 x_4 \vee x_2 x_3; 1,1\rangle$$

System I   (196a)

$$B_1 = A_2 t_3^r A_4 = <0, \ \bar{x}_1 x_2 \bar{x}_4; \ x_3, \ 1>$$

$$B_2 = A_4 t_3^r A_1 = <\bar{x}_2 \bar{x}_4, \ \bar{x}_1 \bar{x}_2 x_4; \ \bar{x}_3, \bar{x}_3>$$

$$B_3 = A_4 t_3^r A_2 = <\bar{x}_1 \bar{x}_2 x_4 \lor x_1 x_2 \bar{x}_4, 0 \ ; \ \bar{x}_3, 1>$$

$$B_4 = A_4 t_3^r A_3 = <0, \ x_1 \bar{x}_2 x_4; \ 1, \ \bar{x}_3>$$

$$C_1 = B_3 t_1^r A_4 = <\bar{x}_2 x_4, \ 0 \ ; \ \bar{x}_3 \lor x_1, 1>$$

$$C_2 = A_3 t_1^r B_4 = <x_2 \bar{x}_4, 0 \ ; \ \bar{x}_1 \lor \bar{x}_3, \ x_1>$$

$$C_3 = B_2 t_1^r B_4 = <0, \ \bar{x}_2 x_4; \ \bar{x}_3 \lor x_1, \ \bar{x}_3>$$

$$C_4 = A_1 t_2^r B_1 = <0, \ \bar{x}_1 \bar{x}_4 \ ; \ x_2 x_3, \ x_2>$$

$$D_1 = C_1 t_2^r A_1 = <x_4, 0 \ ; \ x_2 \lor \bar{x}_3 \lor x_1, \ 1>$$

$$D_2 = B_2 t_2^r C_2 = <\bar{x}_4, 0 \ ; \ \bar{x}_3 \lor \bar{x}_1 x_2, \ \bar{x}_2 \bar{x}_3 \lor x_1 x_2>$$

$$D_3 = C_3 t_2^r A_4 = <0, \ x_4 \ ; \ x_1 \lor \bar{x}_3 \lor x_2, \ \bar{x}_3 \lor x_2>$$

$$D_4 = C_4 t_1^r A_4 = <0, \ \bar{x}_4; \ x_1 \lor x_2 x_3, \ x_1 \lor x_2>$$

$$\left.\begin{array}{l} E_1 = D_2 t_4^r D_1 = <1, \ 0; \ f_1, \ f_2> \\[2mm] E_2 = D_4 t_4^r D_3 = <0, \ 1; \ f_3, \ f_4> \end{array}\right\} \qquad \text{System II} \qquad (196b)$$

The transformation (194) has an interesting interpretation in terms of instruction synthesis. Assume that the f_{jk} are Boolean functions and that they constitute the decision functions for the (or)-interpreted matrix-instruction :

$$\begin{array}{c} N_1 \\ N_2 \\ \vdots \\ N_p \end{array} \left[\begin{array}{cccc} f_{11} & f_{12} & \cdots & f_{1q} \\ f_{21} & f_{22} & \cdots & f_{2q} \\ \vdots & \vdots & & \vdots \\ f_{p1} & f_{p2} & \cdots & f_{pq} \end{array} \right]$$

$$\begin{array}{cccc} \sigma_1 & \sigma_2 & \cdots & \sigma_q \\ M & M & \cdots & M \end{array}$$

From (186) we deduce that a safe program equivalent to this matrix instruction is given by :

$$
\begin{array}{c}
N_1 \\
N_2 \\
\vdots \\
N_p
\end{array}
\left[
\begin{array}{cccccccc}
\bar{f}_{11} & f_{11} & \bar{f}_{12} & f_{12} & \cdots & \bar{f}_{1q} & f_{1q} \\
\bar{f}_{21} & f_{21} & \bar{f}_{22} & f_{22} & \cdots & \bar{f}_{2q} & f_{2q} \\
 & & & & & & \\
\bar{f}_{p1} & f_{p1} & \bar{f}_{p2} & f_{p2} & \cdots & \bar{f}_{pq} & f_{pq} \\
\lambda & \sigma_1 & \lambda & \sigma_2 & & \lambda & \sigma_q
\end{array}
\right]
$$

$$
\begin{array}{ccccccc}
M_1 & M_1' & M_2 & M_2' & \cdots & M_q & M_Q'
\end{array}
\tag{197}
$$

$$
M_i' \quad \tau_i \quad M_i \qquad 1 \leqslant i \leqslant q
$$

$$
\begin{array}{c}
M_1 \\
M_2 \\
\vdots \\
M_p
\end{array}
\left[
\begin{array}{c}
1 \\
1 \\
\vdots \\
1
\end{array}
\right]
$$

$$
M
$$

The synthesis of the decision matrix instruction of (197) is obtained by performing the transformation (198) which is nothing but an interpreted form of the transformation (194) for Boolean functions :

$$
\{ <f_{11}^{(i_1)} \cdots f_{p1}^{(i_p)} , \ldots, f_{1q}^{(i_1)} \cdots f_{pq}^{(i_p)} ; \lambda \bar{i}_1 + \sigma_1 i_1, \ldots, \lambda \bar{i}_p + \sigma_p i_p > , \ 0 \leqslant i_j \leqslant 1 \}
$$

$$
\{t_x\} \Big\downarrow \quad \Big\uparrow \{d_x, U\}
\tag{198}
$$

$$
\{ < 1 , 0 , \ldots, 0 ; \bar{f}_{11} \lambda + f_{11} \sigma_1 , \ldots , \bar{f}_{p1} \lambda + f_{p1} \sigma_p > ,
$$

$$
< 0 , 1 , \ldots, 0 ; \bar{f}_{12} \lambda + f_{12} \sigma_1 , \ldots , \bar{f}_{p1} \lambda + f_{p2} \sigma_p > ,
$$

$$
\cdot \quad \cdot \quad \cdot \quad \cdot \quad \cdot \quad \cdot \quad \cdot \quad \cdot \quad \cdot \quad \cdot \quad \cdot \quad \cdot \quad \cdot \quad \cdot
$$

$$
< 0 , 0 , \ldots, 1 ; \bar{f}_{1q} \lambda + f_{1q} \sigma_1 , \ldots , \bar{f}_{pq} \lambda + f_{pq} \sigma_p > \}
$$

Using the interpretation (198), the transformation (196) is written in the following way :

$$
\left.
\begin{array}{l}
A_1 = < \bar{f}_1 \bar{f}_2, \ \bar{f}_3 \bar{f}_4 \ ; \ \lambda \ , \ \lambda > \\
A_2 = < \bar{f}_1 f_2, \ \bar{f}_3 f_4 \ ; \ \lambda \ , \ \sigma_2 > \\
A_3 = < f_1 \bar{f}_2, \ f_3 \bar{f}_4 \ ; \ \sigma_1, \ \lambda > \\
A_4 = < f_1 f_2, \ f_3 f_4 \ ; \ \sigma_1, \ \sigma_2 >
\end{array}
\right\}
\begin{array}{c}
\{t_x\} \\
\xrightleftharpoons{} \\
\{d_x, U\}
\end{array}
\left\{
\begin{array}{l}
< 1, 0 \ ; \ \bar{f}_1 \lambda + f_1 \sigma_1, \ \bar{f}_2 \lambda + f_2 \sigma_2 > \\
< 0, 1 \ ; \ \bar{f}_3 \lambda + f_3 \sigma_1, \ \bar{f}_4 \lambda + f_4 \sigma_2 >
\end{array}
\right.
$$

$$
\tag{199}
$$

To the transformation (199) corresponds the safe program of figure 73.

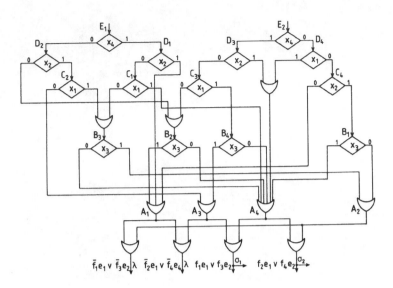

$\bar{f}_1e_1 \vee \bar{f}_3e_2]\lambda \quad \bar{f}_2e_1 \vee \bar{f}_4e_4]\lambda \quad f_1e_1 \vee f_3e_2]^{\sigma_1} \quad f_2e_1 \vee f_4e_2]^{\sigma_2}$

Figure 73 : Safe program corresponding to the transformation (199)

15.4. Generalized transformations on P-functions and their interpretation

We consider the following transformation between systems of P-functions :

$$
\left.
\begin{array}{l}
\langle f_{11}, f_{12}, \cdots, f_{1p} ; \sigma_{11}, \sigma_{12}, \cdots, \sigma_{1q}\rangle \\[4pt]
\langle f_{21}, f_{22}, \cdots, f_{2p} ; \sigma_{21}, \sigma_{22}, \cdots, \sigma_{2q}\rangle \\[4pt]
\quad\cdot\quad\cdot\quad\cdot\quad\cdot\quad\cdot\quad\cdot\quad\cdot\quad\cdot\quad\cdot\quad\cdot\quad\cdot \\[4pt]
\langle f_{r1}, f_{r2}, \cdots, f_{rp} ; \sigma_{r1}, \sigma_{r2}, \cdots, \sigma_{rq}\rangle
\end{array}
\right\} \text{System I}
$$

$$
T = \{t_i, U\} \Big\downarrow \quad \Big\uparrow T^{-1} = \{d_i, U\} \tag{200}
$$

$$
\left.
\begin{array}{l}
\langle m-1, 0, \cdots, 0 ; \ \sum f_{i1}\sigma_{i1}, \ \sum f_{i1}\sigma_{i2}, \cdots, \ \sum f_{i1}\sigma_{iq}\rangle \\[4pt]
\langle 0, m-1, \cdots, 0 ; \ \sum f_{i2}\sigma_{i1}, \ \sum f_{i2}\sigma_{i2}, \cdots, \ \sum f_{i2}\sigma_{iq}\rangle \\[4pt]
\quad\cdot\quad\cdot\quad\cdot\quad\cdot\quad\cdot\quad\cdot\quad\cdot\quad\cdot\quad\cdot\quad\cdot\quad\cdot\quad\cdot\quad\cdot\quad\cdot\quad\cdot \\[4pt]
\langle 0, 0, \cdots, m-1; \ \sum f_{ip}\sigma_{i1}, \ \sum f_{ip}\sigma_{i2}, \cdots, \ \sum f_{ip}\Sigma_{iq}\rangle
\end{array}
\right\} \text{System II}
$$

The functions f_{ij} $(1 \leqslant i \leqslant r, 1 \leqslant j \leqslant p)$ are binary functions :

$$
f_{ij} : \{0, 1, \ldots, m-1\}^n \to \{0, m-1\}
$$

satisfying the relations :

$$\underset{i}{\vee} f_{ij} \equiv m-1 \quad \forall j \quad .$$

The transformation (200) can be considered as a generating transformation which synthesizes a matrix of $p \times q$ discrete functions

$$F_{jk} = \underset{1 \leqslant i \leqslant r}{\sum} f_{ij} \, \sigma_{ik} \, , \, 1 \leqslant j \leqslant p, \, 1 \leqslant k \leqslant q \quad . \tag{201}$$

The matrix of discrete functions :

$$\begin{bmatrix} F_{11} & F_{12} & \cdots & F_{1q} \\ F_{21} & F_{22} & \cdots & F_{2q} \\ \cdot & \cdot & \cdot \cdot \cdot & \cdot \\ F_{p1} & F_{p2} & \cdots & F_{pq} \end{bmatrix} \tag{202}$$

can be realized as an interconnection of multiplexers, fanout connections and or-gates; a transpose realization can be derived by replacing the multiplexers by de-multiplexers and by interchanging the fanout connections and the or-gates. If the multiplexer synthesis evaluates simultaneously all the discrete functions of any row of a $p \times q$ matrix of functions, the different rows being available in a programmable way, then the demultiplexer synthesis evaluates simultaneously all the discrete func-tions of any column of this matrix, the different columns being available in a pro-grammable way.

Assume that the discrete functions of (202) are m-valued functions, i.e. functions :

$$F_{jk} : \{0,1,\ldots,m-1\}^n \rightarrow \{0,1,\ldots,m-1\} \tag{203}$$

The matrix (202) can then be considered as the decision part of a discrete matrix-instruction that we write :

$$\begin{matrix} N_1 \\ N_2 \\ \vdots \\ N_p \end{matrix} \begin{bmatrix} F_{11} & F_{12} & \cdots & F_{1q} \\ F_{21} & F_{22} & \cdots & F_{2q} \\ \vdots & \vdots & & \\ F_{p1} & F_{p2} & \cdots & F_{pq} \end{bmatrix}$$

$$\begin{bmatrix} \sigma_{01}=\lambda & \sigma_{02}=\lambda & \cdots & \sigma_{0q}=\lambda \\ \sigma_{11} & \sigma_{12} & \cdots & \sigma_{1q} \\ \vdots & \vdots & & \vdots \\ \sigma_{(m-1)1} & \sigma_{(m-1)2} & \cdots & \sigma_{(m-1)q} \end{bmatrix}$$

$$\begin{matrix} M_1 & M_2 & \cdots & M_q \end{matrix} \tag{204}$$

This (or)-interpreted matrix-instruction can be described as follows :

- While reaching one of the input labels N_j we first evaluates the values of all the discrete functions F_{jk}, $1 \leqslant k \leqslant q$

- We perform the command $\sigma_{\ell k}$ if the value of the function F_{jk} is ℓ ($1 \leqslant j \leqslant q$, $\ell \in \{0,1,\ldots,m-1\}$).

We verify that the hardware realizations of the matrix (202) and that the software realizations of the instruction (204) encompass and generalize the hardware and software implementations considered in this book respectively.

Chapter 16 : <u>Finite automata, matrix-instructions and speech recognition</u>

The purpose of this chapter is to introduce some possible extensions of the theory of matrix-instructions. The material will be presented in an unfinished and tentative form and must rather be considered as a preliminary draft of a future research work.

Attention will first be paid to some problems evolving from the speech recognition environment : we show that the description and the treatment of these problems induce a generalization of the concept of matrix-instruction. This is not surprising since we know that binary trees and programs have widespread applications in speech (and pattern) recognition and that matrix-instructions and binary programs are equivalent concepts (see part I).

Section 16.1 is an introductory section where we present the speech recognition problems that will be considered in the sequel.

We show in sections 16.2 and 16.3 how an elementary speech recognition problem, namely the recognition of isolated words based on demisyllable segmentation without repetition or omission, can be formulated in terms of matrix-instructions whose entries are finite generators and finite recognizers (which are particular cases of finite automata). More elaborated speech recognition problems can be handled by considering matrix-instructions having finite automata as entries ; this is discussed in section 16.4.

16.1 Introduction to speech recognition

The speech recognition problem to be considered is the isolated word recognition based on a demisyllable segmentation. There is experimental evidence that the maxima and minima of the smoothed intensity curve are suitable cutting points for a segmentation in demisyllables. Recognition is performed first by matching the segments with demisyllable reference prototypes and next by recognizing isolated words as legal sequences of demisyllables. In its simplest form, the recognition procedure can be formulated in the following way :

- The recognition system receives a string of demisyllables as input. For convenience the demisyllables will be designated by letters : $a, b, \ldots, q$ so that a single word will be represented as a sequence of letters.

- The aim of the algorithm is to recognize (or equivalently to accept) the legal strings and to reject the others.

In more elaborate forms of the isolated word recognition problem the input-output behaviour of the recognition algorithm has to be modified in various ways.

- Due to noise, difference in pronunciation, the inputs of the algorithm are not exactly the expected letters (demisyllables) $a, b, \ldots, q$, but signals $\alpha, \beta, \ldots,$

γ which are to be identified with these prototypes.

- The identification of a signal α with a given letter depends on the distance between α and each of the letters $a, b, \dots, q$ of the vocabulary ; in a more elaborate model it will also depend on the relative positions of α in the input string and of the letters actually present in the expected string(s). For example if α appears at the beginning of the input string while a appears at the end of the expected string one will try to identify α with the other letters $b, \dots, q$ of the vocabulary even of the distance between α and a is smaller than the distances between α and $b, \dots,$α and q.

- Some repetition of letters must be tolerated ; e.g. if :

$$a \quad b \quad c \quad b \quad a$$

is a legal sequence, an input sequence of the form :

$$a \quad a \quad b \quad b \quad b \quad c \quad b \quad b \quad a$$

should be accepted and identified with the legal sequence.

- Some omission of letters must be tolerated ; for the same expected sequence of letters as above, an input sequence of the form :

$$a \quad c \quad b \quad a$$

should be accepted in some circumstances.

The purpose of this chapter is the formulation of algorithms for isolated word recognition in terms of *finite-state models*. The finite-state tools that will be used for the design of algorithms are the finite automaton and the matrix-instruction. One will show that a generalization of the concept of matrix-instruction allows us to formulate isolated word recognition algorithms by means of one matrix-instruction having finite automata and Boolean functions in its entries. Since matrices of Boolean functions and finite automata are equivalent to flowcharts (see part I of this book and Wulf [1981], p. 53), this matrix-instruction can be transformed by means of straightforward computations into a conditional program, i.e. a program made-up of conditional instructions of the type *if then else* and of execution instructions of the type *do*.

16.2. Recognition of letter strings without repetition or omission

Let $\sum = \{\alpha, \beta, \dots\}$ be the set of signals (which are the possible inputs of the recognition algorithm) and S = $\{a, b, \dots, q\}$ the set of letters. Assume that $\sum$ is the union of subsets $\sum_i$ defined as follows :

$$\sigma \in \textstyle\sum_i \text{ iff } \sigma \text{ is recognized as } i \; \forall \, \sigma \in \textstyle\sum \quad , \forall \, i \in S \quad ;$$

$$\textstyle\sum = \bigcup_{i \in S} \textstyle\sum_i \quad .$$

This definition does not necessarily require that the sets $\sum_i$ are disjoint : if the signal σ can be recognized both as the letters i and j , then :

$$\sigma \in \textstyle\sum_i \text{ and } \sigma \in \textstyle\sum_j \quad .$$

We define binary functions $f_i \; \forall \; i \in S$ from $\sum$ to $\{0,1\}$:

$$f_i(\sigma) = 1 \text{ iff } \sigma \in \textstyle\sum_i \; ,$$

$$= 0 \text{ otherwise.}$$

$$\textstyle\sum = \bigcup_{i \in S} \textstyle\sum_i \Rightarrow \bigvee_{i \in S} f_i \equiv 1 \; ,$$

$$\text{if } \textstyle\sum_i \cap \textstyle\sum_j = \emptyset \Rightarrow f_i f_j \equiv 0 \quad \forall \, i \neq j \; .$$

In the sequel we shall assume that the elements of $\sum$ and of S are represented (or encoded) by means of a vector $\underline{x}$ of n Boolean variables x_j : $\underline{x} = (x_1, x_2, \dots, x_n)$; consequently the $f_i(\sigma)$ are Boolean functions $f_i(\underline{x})$:

$$f_i : \{0,1\}^n \to \{0,1\} \quad .$$

Assume that the algorithm has to recognize a string of m letters $\in S = \{a, \dots, q\}$. Since repetition and omission of letters are forbidden, the algorithm will receive as input a string of m signals $\{\underline{x}_1, \underline{x}_2, \dots, \underline{x}_m\}$, $\underline{x}_i \in \sum \; \forall \, i$; $\underline{x}_i$ represents the i-th value of $\underline{x}$.

Let us show that isolated word recognition algorithms can be described by means of products of matrices having Boolean functions, finite generators and finite recognizers as entries.

Remember that *finite generators* belong to a class of finite automata that take no input but write a fixed sequence of outputs while *finite recognizers* belong to a class of finite automata that produces no output : if after running through the input tape, the recognizer is in a *final state*, it is said to have accepted or recognized its input. A finite generator and a finite recognizer are dual concepts.

Proposition 1

The isolated word recognition algorithm can be described by means of one matrix-instruction made of :

- one finite generator ;

- *a row-matrix of Boolean functions ;*
- *an (and)-interpreted column-matrix of recognizers.*

This instruction is written and interpreted as follows :

$$N \ \tau \ [G_{\underset{m}{1}}] \ [f_a(\underline{x}_i) \ \dots \ f_q(\underline{x}_i)] \begin{bmatrix} R_a \\ \vdots \\ R_q \end{bmatrix} \qquad (205)$$
$$(1 \leqslant i \leqslant m)$$
$$\sigma$$
$$M$$

1) While starting the execution of N the finite generator G_1 produces a sequence of m 1's which yields m successive evaluations of the Boolean functions $f_j(\underline{x})$ for the successive values $\underline{x}_i$ $(1 \leqslant i \leqslant m)$ of $\underline{x}$;

2) The binary sequences $\{f_j(\underline{x}_1), \ f_j(\underline{x}_2), \dots, f_j(\underline{x}_m)\}$ constitute the respective input tapes for the recognizers R_j, $a \leqslant j \leqslant q$;

3) The order σ for accepting the input sequence $\{\underline{x}_1, \dots, \underline{x}_m\}$ is executed iff all the finite recognizers are in their final state.

It can be verified that instruction (205) describes an isolated word recognition algorithm which recognizes a given sequence of m demisyllabes iff the R_j's are defined as follows :

R_j is a finite recognizer which accepts the binary sequence (made of 0's and 1's) of length m whose i-th term is 1 iff the i-th letter of the sequence to be recognized is j.

The recognition of p strings of letters can be described by the following instruction :

$$N \ \tau \ [G_{\underset{m}{1}}] \ [f_a(\underline{x}_i)\dots f_q(\underline{x}_i)] \begin{bmatrix} R_{a1} & \dots & R_{ap} \\ \vdots & & \\ R_{q1} & \dots & R_{qp} \end{bmatrix} \qquad (206)$$
$$(1 \leqslant i \leqslant m)$$
$$\sigma_1 \ \dots \ \sigma_p$$
$$M_1 \ \dots \ M_p$$

The rectangular matrix of (206) is a matrix-instruction whose rows are (and)-interpreted; its meaning is :

The order σ_k $(1 \leqslant k \leqslant p)$ for accepting the k-th sequence of letters is enabled iff each of the R_{jk}'s, $a \leqslant j \leqslant q$, is in a final state.

An isolated word recognition algorithm based on demisyllable segmentation can be represented by instruction (206). The j-th output $(1 \leqslant j \leqslant p)$ of instruction (206) is reached iff the received sequence coincides with the j-th expected sequence. To instruction (206) is associated a *transpose instruction* which is written :

$$
\begin{matrix} M_1 \\ \vdots \\ M_p \end{matrix}
\quad
\begin{matrix} \tau_1 \\ \vdots \\ \tau_p \end{matrix}
\quad
\begin{bmatrix} G_{a1} & \cdots & G_{q1} \\ \vdots & & \vdots \\ G_{qp} & \cdots & G_{qp} \end{bmatrix}
\begin{bmatrix} f_a(\underline{x}_i) \\ \vdots \\ f_q(\underline{x}_i) \end{bmatrix}
\begin{bmatrix} R_{1_{\!\!-m}} \\ N \end{bmatrix}
\qquad (207)
$$

$$(1 \leqslant i \leqslant m)$$

Instruction (207) is deduced from instruction (206) by transposing the matrix product and by interchanging the concepts of finite generator and of finite recognizer. This derives from the fact that the operation of transposition interchanges the instruction inputs (i.e. the rows of the matrix) and the instruction outputs (i.e. the columns of the matrix).

It can be verified that the enabling of input M_j in (207) produces as a result the acceptance of the input sequence $(\underline{x}_i)$, $1 \leqslant i \leqslant m$, iff it coincides with the j-th expected sequence.

In summary we see that the matrix-instruction (206) represents a 1-input, p-outputs algorithm which simultaneously compares a received sequence of letters with p expected sequences of letters ; the matrix-instruction (207) represents a p-inputs, 1-output algorithm which compares a received sequence of letters with one sequence which is taken from a set of p sequences. Algorithms represented by (206) and (207) can schematically be described as follows : (the s_j's represent sequences of letters) :

$$
(206) := \text{input} \rightarrow \begin{bmatrix} s_1 & s_2 & \cdots & s_p \end{bmatrix}
\qquad (208a)
$$
$$
\downarrow \qquad \downarrow \qquad \qquad \downarrow
$$
$$
\text{outputs}
$$

$$
(207) := \text{inputs} \;\;\rightarrow \begin{bmatrix} s_1 \\ s_2 \\ \vdots \\ s_p \end{bmatrix}
\qquad (208b)
$$
$$
\downarrow
$$
$$
\text{output}
$$

The algorithms represented by (208a, 208b) can be considered as particular cases of a more general type of algorithm having a row and a column-component.

Assume that the sequences $s_1, s_2, \ldots, s_p$ are arranged in a rectangular matrix $(p = v \times w)$:

$$\text{inputs} \quad \begin{array}{c} \rightarrow \\ \vdots \\ \rightarrow \end{array} \left[\begin{array}{ccc} s_{11} = s_1 & \cdots & s_{1w} \\ \vdots & & \vdots \\ s_{v1} & \cdots & s_{vw} = s_p \\ & \cdots & \end{array} \right] \qquad (209)$$

$$\text{outputs}$$

We first show that an appropriate type of matrix-instruction represents an algorithm which matches a given input sequence simultaneously with all the sequences $(s_{i1},\ldots, s_{iw})$ of a row of matrix (209). In this respect we define generators $G_{i(jk)}$ and recognizers $R_{i(jk)}$ $(a \leqslant i \leqslant q, 1 \leqslant j \leqslant v, 1 \leqslant k \leqslant w)$ which play with respect to the sequences s_{jk} the same role as the generators G_{ij} and the recognizers R_{ij} with respect to the sequences s_j. Moreover we define parallel compositions of generators and of recognizers, i.e. :

$$G_{ij}^* = \bigcup_k G_{i(jk)} \quad ,$$
$$\hspace{4cm} a \leqslant i \leqslant q, \ 1 \leqslant j \leqslant v, \ 1 \leqslant k \leqslant w \qquad (210)$$
$$R_{ik}^* = \bigcup_j R_{i(jk)} \quad .$$

Remember that for the parallel composition of automata it is assumed that the inputs to each automaton are the same and that the output of the composite automaton is formed by logically combining the outputs of all the automata. In the present case the logical combination will be performed by means of the disjunction. The generator G_{ij}^* will thus produce a sequence which is the disjunction of the sequences produced by the $G_{i(jk)}$, $1 \leqslant k \leqslant w$ while the recognizer R_{ik}^* will accept any sequence which is accepted by one of the recognizers $R_{i(jk)}$, $1 \leqslant j \leqslant w$.

The following proposition holds.

Proposition

The recognition algorithm which is described by the matrix-instruction :

$$\begin{array}{c} N_1 \\ \vdots \\ N_v \end{array} \quad \begin{array}{c} \tau_1 \\ \vdots \\ \tau_v \end{array} \quad \left[\begin{array}{ccc} G_{a1}^* & \cdots & G_{q1}^* \\ \vdots & & \vdots \\ G_{av}^* & \cdots & G_{qv}^* \end{array} \right] \left[\begin{array}{ccc} f_a(\underline{x}_i) & & 0 \\ & \ddots & \\ 0 & & f_q(\underline{x}_i) \end{array} \right] \left[\begin{array}{ccc} R_{a1}^* & \cdots & R_{aw}^* \\ \vdots & & \vdots \\ R_{q1}^* & \cdots & R_{qw}^* \end{array} \right] \qquad (211)$$

$$(1 \leqslant i \leqslant m) \quad \begin{array}{ccc} \sigma_1 & \cdots & \sigma_w \\ M_1 & \cdots & M_w \end{array}$$

compares a given input sequence $(\underline{x}_1, \underline{x}_2, \ldots, \underline{x}_m)$ with all the sequences $(s_{j1}, \ldots, s_{jw})$ of the j-th row of the matrix :

$$
\begin{bmatrix}
s_{11} & \cdots & s_1 w \\
\vdots & & \vdots \\
s_{v1} & \cdots & s_{vw}
\end{bmatrix}
$$

The algorithm accepts the sequences of $\{s_{j1},\ldots,s_{jw}\}$; *the j-th row of the matrix is selected by imposing the value :* $\tau_j=1$, $\tau_k=0$ $\forall$ $k\neq0$ *to the input parameters.*

Proof

The algorithms represented by the instruction (206, 207) are also described by means of the matrix-instructions (212a, 212b) respectively :

$$
N \quad \tau \quad [G_a \ \ldots \ G_q]
\begin{bmatrix}
f_a(\underline{x}_i) & & 0 \\
 & \ddots & \\
0 & & f_q(\underline{x}_i)
\end{bmatrix}
\begin{bmatrix}
R_{a1} & \cdots & R_{ap} \\
\vdots & & \vdots \\
R_{q1} & \cdots & R_{qp} \\
\sigma_1 & \cdots & \sigma_p \\
M_1 & \cdots & M_p
\end{bmatrix}
\tag{212a}
$$

with : $G_k = \underset{j}{U} \ G_{kj}$

$$
\begin{matrix}
M_1 \\ \vdots \\ M_p
\end{matrix}
\quad
\begin{matrix}
\tau_1 \\ \vdots \\ \tau_p
\end{matrix}
\begin{bmatrix}
G_{a1} & \cdots & G_{q1} \\
\vdots & & \vdots \\
G_{ap} & \cdots & G_{qp}
\end{bmatrix}
\begin{bmatrix}
f_a(\underline{x}_i) & & 0 \\
 & \ddots & \\
0 & & f_q(\underline{x}_i)
\end{bmatrix}
\begin{bmatrix}
R_a \\ \vdots \\ R_q \\ \sigma \\ M
\end{bmatrix}
\tag{212b}
$$

with : $R_k = \underset{j}{U} \ R_{kj}$

The announced result is then obtained by performing : either an induction on the number of rows of the first factor of (212a), or an induction on the number of columns of the last factor of (212b).

At this point it is necessary to define the behaviour of a matrix instruction with generators and recognizers in a more precise way.

Definition

A matrix-instruction is represented as a product of three matrices having generators, Boolean functions and recognizers as entries, respectively :

$$
\begin{array}{cc}
N_1 & \tau_1 \\
\vdots & \vdots \\
N_p & \tau_p
\end{array}
\begin{bmatrix}
G_{11} & \cdots & G_{1q} \\
\vdots & & \vdots \\
G_{p1} & \cdots & G_{pq}
\end{bmatrix}
\begin{bmatrix}
f_{11}(\underline{x}) & \cdots & f_{1r}(\underline{x}) \\
\vdots & & \\
f_{q1}(\underline{x}) & \cdots & f_{qr}(\underline{x})
\end{bmatrix}
\begin{bmatrix}
R_{11} & \cdots & R_{1s} \\
\vdots & & \vdots \\
R_{r1} & \cdots & R_{rs} \\
\sigma_1 & \cdots & \sigma_s \\
M_1 & \cdots & M_s
\end{bmatrix}
\qquad (213)
$$

It is interpreted as follows :

1) While starting the execution of the instruction and for $\tau_i = 1$, $\tau_k = 0$ $\forall k \neq i$, one activates the generators $\{G_{i1}, \ldots, G_{iq}\}$ of the i-th row of the (or)-interpreted matrix instruction $[G_{ij}]$; each of the generators G_{ij}, $1 \leqslant j \leqslant q$ produces a binary sequence of length m which is denoted : $\{G_{ij}^k\}$, $1 \leqslant k \leqslant m$.

2) One evaluates the m successive values of the Boolean functions $f_{ij}(\underline{x})$, i.e. : $f_{ij}(\underline{x}_1), \ldots, f_{ij}(\underline{x}_m)$; at the k-th instant the r outputs of the matrix of Boolean functions are :

$$
\{F_{i\ell}^k = \sum_j G_{ij}^k \; f_{j\ell}(\underline{x}_k)\} \;, \qquad 1 \leqslant \ell \leqslant r \;.
$$

3) The binary sequences $\{F_{i\ell}^1, \ldots, F_{i\ell}^m\}$, $1 \leqslant \ell \leqslant r$ constitute the respective input tapes for the recognizers $R_{\ell h}$, $1 \leqslant h \leqslant s$; the order σ_h is executed iff all the recognizers $\{R_{1h}, \ldots, R_{rh}\}$ are in their final state, i.e. iff the r binary sequences $\{F_{i\ell}^k\}$ are accepted by the r recognizers $\{R_{\ell h}\}$, $1 \leqslant \ell \leqslant r$ respectively.

16.3 <u>Recognition of letters using a relative distance measure</u>

Until now we have assumed that the identification of a signal $\underline{x}$ with a given letter depends only on the distance between $\underline{x}$ and each of the letters a, b, $\ldots, q$ of the vocabulary. We shall now introduce a more elaborate model where this identification will also depend on the relative positions of $\underline{x}$ in the input string and the letters in the expected string(s).

Assume that the set $\sum$ of signals is the union of subsets $\sum_{ij}$ defined as follows :

$\sigma \in \sum_{ij}$ iff σ is recognized as the word j at an instant where it is the letter i which is expected (in the sequence of letters) ;

$\sum = \underset{j}{\cup} \sum_{ij}$ $\qquad \forall i \in \{a, b, \ldots, q\}$

We define binary functions f_{ij} $\forall i, j \in S$ from $\sum$ to $\{0, 1\}$:

$$f_{ij}(\sigma) = 1 \text{ iff } \sigma \in \Sigma_{ij} ,$$
$$= 0 \text{ otherwise.}$$

Similar arguments as those developed for deriving the instruction (205) allow us to state that an isolated word recognition algorithm which has to match a string of m signals $\{\underline{x}_1, \underline{x}_2, \dots, \underline{x}_m\}$ with an expected string of m letters $\in$ S can be described by the following matrix-instruction :

$$N \quad \tau \quad [G_a \quad G_b \quad \dots \quad G_q] \begin{bmatrix} f_{aa}(\underline{x}_i) & f_{ab}(\underline{x}_i) & \dots & f_{aq}(\underline{x}_i) \\ f_{ba}(\underline{x}_i) & f_{bb}(\underline{x}_i) & \dots & f_{bq}(\underline{x}_i) \\ \vdots & & & \vdots \\ f_{qa}(\underline{x}_i) & f_{qb}(\underline{x}_i) & \dots & f_{qq}(\underline{x}_i) \end{bmatrix} \begin{bmatrix} R_a \\ R_b \\ \vdots \\ R_q \\ \sigma \\ M \end{bmatrix} \qquad (214)$$

It can be verified that the comparison of a string of m signals with p expected strings of m letter in S can be described by the matrix-instruction (215) :

$$\begin{matrix} N_1 & \tau_1 \\ \vdots & \vdots \\ N_p & \tau_p \end{matrix} \begin{bmatrix} G_{a1} & \dots & G_{q1} \\ \vdots & & \vdots \\ G_{ap} & \dots & G_{qp} \end{bmatrix} \begin{bmatrix} f_{aa}(\underline{x}_i) & \dots & f_{aq}(\underline{x}_i) \\ \vdots & & \vdots \\ f_{qa}(\underline{x}_i) & \dots & f_{qq}(\underline{x}_i) \end{bmatrix} \begin{bmatrix} R_{a1} & \dots & R_{ap} \\ \vdots & & \vdots \\ R_{q1} & \dots & R_{qp} \\ \sigma_1 & \dots & \sigma_p \\ M_1 & \dots & M_p \end{bmatrix} \qquad (215)$$

From (215) we deduce that algorithms of the form (212a) and (212b) (but where the identification of a signal $\underline{x}_i$ with a letter j depends on the relative positions of $\underline{x}_i$ in the input string and of j in the expected string) are represented by means of the matrix-instructions (216a) and (216b) respectively :

$$N_1 \quad \tau \quad [G_a \quad \dots \quad G_1] \begin{bmatrix} f_{aa}(\underline{x}_i) & \dots & f_{aq}(\underline{x}_i) \\ \vdots & & \vdots \\ f_{qa}(\underline{x}_i) & \dots & f_{qq}(\underline{x}_i) \end{bmatrix} \begin{bmatrix} R_{a1} & \dots & R_{ap} \\ \vdots & & \vdots \\ R_{q1} & \dots & R_{qp} \\ \sigma_1 & \dots & \sigma_p \\ M_1 & \dots & M_p \end{bmatrix} \qquad (216a)$$

$$M_1 \quad \tau_1 \quad \begin{bmatrix} G_{a1} & \cdots & G_{q1} \\ \vdots & & \vdots \\ G_{ap} & \cdots & G_{qp} \end{bmatrix} \begin{bmatrix} f_{aa}(\underline{x}_i) & \cdots & f_{aq}(\underline{x}_i) \\ \vdots & & \vdots \\ f_{qa}(\underline{x}_i) & \cdots & f_{qq}(\underline{x}_i) \end{bmatrix} \begin{bmatrix} R_a \\ \vdots \\ R_q \end{bmatrix} \qquad (216b)$$

$$\sigma$$
$$M$$

with : $G_i = \underset{j}{\cup} G_{ij}, \ R_i = \underset{j}{\cup} R_{ij}$.

The type of algorithm represented by (215) can schematically be described as follows :

$$\text{inputs} \quad \begin{array}{c} \rightarrow \\ \rightarrow \\ \vdots \\ \rightarrow \end{array} \begin{bmatrix} s_1 & - & - \\ - & s_2 & - \\ & & \ddots \\ - & - & s_p \end{bmatrix} \qquad (217)$$
$$\downarrow \quad \downarrow \quad \cdots \quad \downarrow$$
$$\text{outputs}$$

If the j-th input is chosen, the j-th output accepts or rejects the sequence s_j; the result of the other outputs is meaningless.

As a result of sections 16.2 and 16.3 we can state the following trans-position principle.

If a letter-recognition algorithm with $p=v \times w$ reference-sequences is described as a matrix product of generators, Boolean functions and recognizers, then a transpose algorithm is obtained by transposing the matrix product and by interchanging genera-tors and recognizers.If the initial algorithm compares simultaneously the input se-quence with all the sequences of any row of a $(v \times w)$ matrix of sequences, the diffe-rent rows being available in a programmable way, then the transpose algorithm compa-res simultaneously the input sequence with all the sequences of any column of this matrix, the different columns being available in a programmable way.

We have shown in part I that any matrix-instruction whose decision part has Boolean functions as entries can be represented by an equivalent flowchart made of decision instructions (of the type *if then else*) and of execution instruc-tions (of the type *do*). Since for any finite automaton, there is an input-output equivalent finite flowchart (see Wulf [1981] , p.53), for any matrix-instruction of the type (213) there is an equivalent finite flowchart. Accordingly, the methods which transform matrices of Boolean functions and finite automata into equivalent flowcharts can be used to transform the matrix-instruction (213) into an equivalent flowchart. Hence the interest of formulating algorithms such as the isolated word recognition algorithm in terms of the matrix-instruction (213).

16.4 Recognition of isolated words with repetition of letters

We shall assume that some repetition of letters with respect to the expected sequence must be tolerated in the accepted sequences. For example if :

$$a \quad b \quad c \quad b \quad a$$

is an expected sequence, an input sequence of the form

$$a \quad a \quad b \quad b \quad b \quad c \quad b \quad b \quad a$$

should be accepted by the recognition algorithm and identified with the expected sequence.

The algorithms proposed in sections 16.2 and 16.3 can be schematically represented as follows :

$$\underset{(x_i)}{\downarrow}$$
$$\underline{N} \quad \underline{\tau} \; [\underline{G}] \; [\underline{f}(\underline{x})][\underline{R}] \; \underline{\sigma} \; \underline{M} \tag{218}$$

These algorithms work as follows

- The generators $\underline{G}$ are enabled by the signals $\underline{\tau}$;
- The output sequences of G are produced in a synchronous way with the successive evaluations $\underline{f}(\underline{x}_i)$ of $\underline{f}$;
- The recognizers $\underline{R}$ receive in a synchronous way the results of the matrix product $[\underline{G}][\underline{f}]$ and accept these results iff they match the sequences recognized by $[\underline{R}]$; the orders σ are then enabled.

We show that, in order to take into account some possible repetition of letters in the input tape, the algorithm scheme (218) has to be replaced by the scheme (219) :

$$\underset{(x_i)}{\downarrow}$$
$$\underline{N} \quad \underline{\tau} \; [\underline{G}] \; [\underline{f}(\underline{x})] \; [\underline{R}] \quad \underline{\sigma} \; \underline{M} \tag{219}$$
$$\underset{\underline{\sigma}_G \quad \quad \underline{\sigma}_R}{}$$
$$\underline{A}$$

The scheme (219) works as follows :

- The generators $\underline{G}$ are enabled by the signals $\underline{\tau}$; they produce repetitively the same element of their sequence until the receipt of an order σ_G issued from an automaton of $\underline{A}$: the generators produce then (repetitively) the next element of their sequence.
- The recognizers $\underline{R}$ keep the results of the matrix product $[\underline{G}] \; [\underline{f}]$ as input at the receipt of an order σ_R issued from an automaton of $\underline{A}$;
- The outputs of the matrix product $[\underline{G}][\underline{f}]$ constitute the input-alphabet of a set

$\underline{A}$ of automata which has as many elements as the number of columns of $[\underline{f}]$; the commands $\underline{\sigma}_G$ and $\underline{\sigma}_R$ constitute the output alphabet of $\underline{A}$.

To each output (i.e. to each column) of the matrix $[\underline{f}(\underline{x})]$ there is associated an automaton A ; the role of these automata can be depicted as follows .

- The recognizers of $\underline{R}$ accept sequences of m letters ; due to repetition of letters the length of the sequences of signals $\underline{x}_i$ is larger than m. Thus only a part of the sequence of outputs of $[f(\underline{x})]$ has to be sent to the recognizers : it is that part which occurs when σ_R is enabled.

- The generators $\underline{G}$ generate sequences of m letters ; due to repetition of letters, at some moments the generators $\underline{G}$ have to produce repetitively the same element of the sequence : the next element will be produced at the receipt of an order σ_G.

Repetition of letters can be detected by comparing the present value of the functions $f_{ij}(\underline{x})$ to their preceding value. Hence the past and the present values of $f_{ij}(\underline{x})$ characterize the state of the automaton associated to the j-th column of the matrix $[\underline{f}]$. Since $f_{ij}(\underline{x})$ are Boolean functions, the automaton A has four states denoted as follows :

(present/past) values of $f_{ij}(\underline{x})$ = {(0/0), (0/1), (1/0), (1/1)} .

- The state (1/1) of the automaton associated to the j-th column of $[\underline{f}]$ characterizes the repetition of the letters j in the sequence : neither the command σ_G, nor the command σ_R has to be enabled.

- The state (0/0) of the automaton associated to the j-th column of $[\underline{f}]$ characterizes the absence of the letters j from the sequence : this automaton does not have to enable the commands σ_G or σ_R.

- The state (0/1) of the automaton associated to the j-th column of $[\underline{f}]$ characterizes the disappearence of the letter j from the sequence : the command σ_R has to be enabled and the past values of all the outputs of $[\underline{f}]$ are to be sent to the recognizers.

- The state (1/0) of the automaton associated to the j-th column of $[\underline{f}]$ characterizes the appearence of the letter j in the sequence : the command σ_G has to be enabled.

Accordignly the transition diagram for the automaton A can be represented as in Figure 74.

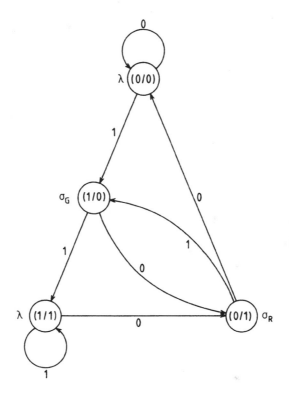

Figure 74 : Transition diagram for the automaton A

The general organization of the algorithm (219) is depicted in Figure 75.

Example

Assume that we have to detect the expected sequence of three letters a,b,c :

$$a \quad b \quad c \quad b \quad a$$

The generators and recognizers have to generate or to recognize respectively the following sequences :

$$G_a \rightarrow \{1 \quad 0 \quad 0 \quad 0 \quad 1\} \rightarrow R_a$$
$$G_h \rightarrow \{0 \quad 1 \quad 0 \quad 1 \quad 0\} \rightarrow R_b$$
$$G_c \rightarrow \{0 \quad 0 \quad 1 \quad 0 \quad 0\} \rightarrow R_c$$

The matrix of Boolean function is :

$$\begin{bmatrix} f_{aa} & f_{ab} & f_{ac} \\ f_{ba} & f_{hh} & f_{bc} \\ f_{ca} & f_{cb} & f_{cc} \end{bmatrix}$$

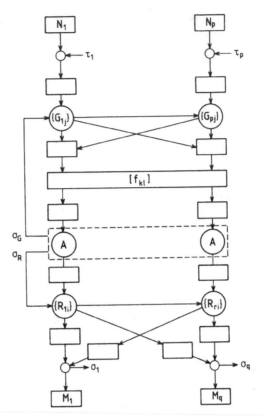

Figure 75 : General organization of the algorithm (219)

To each column of this matrix is associated an automaton A ; assume that the received sequence is

$$a \quad a \quad b \quad b \quad b \quad c \quad b \quad a \quad a \qquad (220)$$

$$t = 1 \quad 2 \quad 3 \quad 4 \quad 5 \quad 6 \quad 7 \quad 8 \quad 9$$

The sequences of states of the automata A associated to the columns a, b, c are
respectively :

$$t = \quad 0 \quad 1 \quad 2 \quad 3 \quad 4 \quad 5 \quad 6 \quad 7 \quad 8 \quad 9 \quad 10$$

$$a : \text{state} = \begin{array}{l} \text{present output} \\ \\ \text{past output} \end{array} = \begin{bmatrix} 0 & 1 & 1 & 0 & 0 & 0 & 0 & 0 & 1 & 1 & 0 \\ 0 & 0 & 1 & 1 & 0 & 0 & 0 & 0 & 0 & 1 & 1 \end{bmatrix}$$

$$\sigma_G \qquad \sigma_R \qquad\qquad \sigma_G \qquad \sigma_R$$

b : state $=$ $\begin{matrix}\text{present output} \\ \\ \text{past output}\end{matrix}$ $=$ $\begin{bmatrix} 0 & 0 & 0 & 1 & 1 & 1 & 0 & 1 & 0 & 0 & 0 \\ 0 & 0 & 0 & 0 & 1 & 1 & 1 & 0 & 1 & 0 & 0 \end{bmatrix}$

$$\quad\quad\quad\quad\quad\quad \sigma_G \quad\quad \sigma_R\ \sigma_G\ \sigma_R$$

c : state $=$ $\begin{matrix}\text{present output} \\ \\ \text{past output}\end{matrix}$ $=$ $\begin{bmatrix} 0 & 0 & 0 & 0 & 0 & 0 & 1 & 0 & 0 & 0 & 0 \\ 0 & 0 & 0 & 0 & 0 & 0 & 0 & 1 & 0 & 0 & 0 \end{bmatrix}$

$$\quad\quad\quad\quad\quad\quad\quad\quad \sigma_G\ \sigma_R$$

We verify that the commands occur at the following time instants :

$$\sigma_G = 1,\ 3,\ 6,\ 7,\ 8\ ;$$

$$\sigma_R = 3,\ 6,\ 7,\ 8,\ 10\ .$$

Accordingly the recognizers R_a, R_b, R_c receive the expected sequence $(a\ b\ c\ b\ a)$ and the sequence (220) is accepted.

The transition diagrams for the recognizers R_a, R_b and R_c are depicted in Figures 76a,b and c respectively.

a) $R_a = R(10001)$

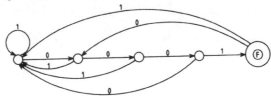

b) $R_b = R(01010)$

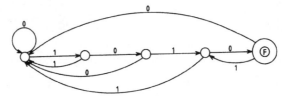

c) $R_c = R(00100)$

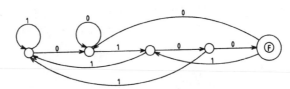

Figure 76 : Transition diagrams for the recognizers R_a, R_b and R_c.

Bibliography

S. B. Akers [1978]

Binary decision diagrams, IEEE Trans. Comput., vol. C-27, pp. 509-516, June 1978.

C. Allen and D. Givone [1968]

A minimization technique for multiple-valued logic systems, IEEE Trans. Comput., vol. C-17, pp. 182-184,   1968.

S. Baranov and A. Keevallik [1981]

Transformations of graph-schemes of algorithms, Digital Processes, vol. 6, pp. 127-147, 1981.

M. Blanchard and J. Gillon [1977]

Réalisations logiques programmées des réseaux de Petri, Journées d'étude : Logique câblée ou logique programmée, Lausanne, pp. 51-57, March 1977.

C. Böhm and G. Jacopini [1966]

Flow diagrams : Turing machines and languages with only two formation rules, Com. ACM, vol. 9, p 366-371, May 1966.

E. Cerny, D. Mange and E. Sanchez [1979]

Synthesis of minimal binary decision trees, IEEE Trans. Comput., vol. C-28, pp. 472-482, July 1979.

C. Clare [1973]

Designing logic systems using state machines, Mc Graw-Hill, New York, 1973.

L. Dadda [1976]

On the simulation of Petri nets as a control tool, Euromicro News letter, vol. 2, pp. 38-45, January 1976.

M. Davio and A. Thayse [1978]

Optimization of multivalued decision algorithms, Philips Journal of Research, vol. 33, pp. 31-65, 1978.

M. Davio and A. Thayse [1980]

Implementation and transformation of algorithms based on automata, Part I : Introduction and elementary optimization problems, Philips Journal of Research, vol. 35, pp. 122-144, 1980.

M. Davio, J.P. Deschamps and A. Thayse [1978]

Discrete and switching functions, Mc Graw-Hill, New York, 1978.

Acknowledgement

This book would probably never have been written without the kind invitation of Professor Daniel Mange (Ecole Polytechnique Fédérale of Lausanne) : most of this text has been written during my stay as invited Professor in his department.

Professor Vitold Belevitch, Director of the Philips Research Laboratory (Brussels) gave me the possibility of undertaking this research within the framework of the Philips Research Laboratory activities.

Professor Sheldon Akers (University of Syracuse and General Electrics) kindly accepted to preface the text.

Professor Sheldon Akers, Professor Marc Davio (University of Louvain and Philips Research Laboratory), Professor Daniel Mange and Professor Michel Sintzoff influenced with their suggestions the intellectual lines of development that led to this book.

My colleagues of the Philips Research Laboratory, Dr Philippe Delsarte, Dr Pierre Devijver and Dr Yves Kamp read the manuscript and suggested numerous improvements and corrections.

Mrs Edith Moës typed the manuscript with amability and competence. Mr Claude Semaille executed the numerous drawings with his usual care and Mrs Ingeborg Mayer provided me with her kind editorial assistance.

M. Davio, J.P. Deschamps and A. Thayse [1983a]
Digital systems with algorithm implementation, John Wiley, New York, 1983

M. Davio, J.P. Deschamps and A. Thayse [1983b]
Machines algorithmiques, Presses polytechniques Romandes, Lausanne, 1983.

S. Ghosh [1977]
Some comments on timed Petri nets, Journées d'étude AFCET, Réseaux de Petri, Paris,
pp. 151-163, March 1977.

V. Glushkov and A. Letichevskii [1964]
Theory of algorithms and discrete processors, Advances in information systems scien-
ces, vol. 1, Ed. Julius T. Tou, 1964.

V. Glushkov [1965]
Automata theory and formal microprogram transformation, Kibernetika, vol. 1, pp. 1-9
1965.

V. Glushkov [1966]
Introduction to Cybernetics, Academic Press, New York, 1966.

V. Glushkov [1970]
Some problems in the theories of automata and artificial intelligence, Kibernetica,
vol. 6, p.2, 1970.

M. Hack [1975]
Decision problems for Petri nets and vector addition systems, MAC Techn. Memo. 59,
M.I.T., March 1975.

V. Hamacher, Z. Vranesic and S. Zaky [1978]
Computer organization, Mc Graw-Hill, New York, 1978.

P. Hammer and S. Rudeanu [1968]
Boolean methods in operations research, Springer Berlin, 1968.

M. Harrison [1965]
Introduction to switching and automata theory, Mc Graw-Hill, New York, 1975.

J. Hartmanis and R. Stearns [1966]
Algebraic structures theory of sequential machines, Prentice-Hall, Englewood Cliffs,
1966.

B. Howard [1975a]
Determinacy of computation schemata for both parallel and simultaneous operations,
Electronic letters, vol. 11, pp. 485-487, 1975.

B. Howard [1975b]

Parallel computation schemata and their hardware implementation, Digital processes, vol. 1, pp. 183-206, 1975.

A. Holt and F. Commoner [1970]

Events and conditions, Record of the project MAC Conference on concurrent systems and parallel computation, ACM, New York, pp. 3-52, 1970.

K. Hwang [1979]

Computer arithmetic, John Wiley, New York, 1979.

R. Jump and P. Thiagarajan [1975]

On the interconnection of asynchronous control structures, J. ACM, vol. 22, pp. 596-612, October 1975.

R. Karp and R. Miller [1969]

Parallel program schemata, J. Comput. Syst. Sci., vol. 3, pp. 147-195, May 1969.

R. Keller [1970]

On maximally parallel schemata, Eleventh annual symposium on switching and automata theory, pp. 32-50, October 1970.

R. Keller [1973a]

Parallel program schemata and maximal parallelism, Part I : Fundamental results, J. Assoc. Comput. Mach., vol. 20, pp. 514-537, July 1973.

R. Keller [1973b]

Parallel program schemata and maximal parallelism, Part II : Construction of closures, J. Assoc. Comput. Mach., vol. 20, pp. 696-710, October 1973.

R. Keller [1974]

Toward a theory of universal speed independent modules, IEEE Trans. Comput., vol. C-23, pp. 21-23, January 1974.

K. Leung, C. Michel and P. Lebeux [1977]

Logical systems design using PLA's and Petri nets. Programmable hardwired systems, IFIP Congress, Toronto, pp. 607-611, 1977.

L. Logrippo [1972]

Renamings in program schemata, Thirteenth annual symposium on switching and automata theory, pp. 62-67, October 1972.

D. Mange [1978]

Analyse et synthèse des systèmes logiques, Presses polytechniques Romandes, Lausanne, Suisse, 1978.

D. Mange [1979]
Compteurs microprogrammés, Bulletin de l'association suisse des électriciens, vol. 70, pp. 1087-1095, 1979.

D. Mange [1980]
Microprogrammation structurée, Le nouvel automatisme, vol. 25, pp. 45-54, 1980.

D. Mange [1981]
Programmation structurée, Bulletin de l'association suisse des électriciens, vol. 72, pp. 1087-1095, 1981.

D. Mange, E. Sanchez and A. Stauffer [1982]
Systèmes logiques programmés, Presses polytechniques romandes, Lausanne, 1982.

Z. Manna [1964]
Mathematical theory of computation, Mc Graw-Hill, New York, 1964.

M. Mano [1979]
Digital logic and computer design, Prentice-Hall, Englewood-Cliffs, 1979.

S. Meisel and D. Michalopoulos [1973]
A partitioning algorithm with application in pattern classification and the optimization of decision trees, IEEE Trans. Comput., vol. C-22, pp. 93-103, January 1973.

A. Mishchenko [1967]
Transformations of microprograms, Cybernetics, vol. 3, pp. 7-13, 1967.

A. Mishchenko [1968a]
The formal synthesis of an automaton by a microprogram, Cybernetics, vol. 4, pp. 20-26, 1968.

A. Mishchenko [1968b]
Formal synthesis of an automaton by a microprogram, part II, Cybernetics, vol. 4, pp. 17-22, 1968.

M. Moalla, J. Sifakis et M. Zachariades [1976]
MAS : Un outil d'aide à la description et à la conception des automatismes logiques, Colloque ADEPA-AFCET : Automatismes logiques, Recherches et applications industrielles, Paris, décembre 1976.

M. Moalla, J. Sifakis et M. Silva [1980]
A la recherche d'une méthodologie de conception sûre des automatismes logiques basés sur l'utilisation des réseaux de Petri; dans : Sûreté de fonctionnement des systèmes informatiques, pp. 133-167, Monographies d'informatique de l'AFCET, Editions hommes et techniques, Paris, 1980.

M. Moalla, J. Pulou and J. Sifakis [1978]
Réseaux de Petri synchronisés, vol. 12, n°2, pp. 103-130, 1978.

B. Moret [1980]
The representation of discrete functions by decision trees : aspects of complexity
and problems of testing, Ph. D. Dissertation, Univ. of Tennessee, Knoxville, 1980.

B. Moret, M. Thomason and R. Gonzalez [1980]
The activity of a variable and its relation to decision trees, ACM Trans. Program.
Lang. Syst., vol. 2, pp. 580-595, October 1980.

H. Payne and W. Meisel [1977]
An algorithm for constructing optimal binary decision trees, IEEE Trans. Comput.,
vol. C-26, pp. 905-916, 1977.

Y. Perl and Y. Breitbart [1976]
Optimal sequential arrangement of evaluation trees for Boolean functions, Inf. Sci.,
pp. 1-12, 1976.

J. Peterson [1977]
Petri nets, ACM Comp. Surveys, vol. 9, pp. 223-251, September 1977.

J. Peterson [1982]
Petri net theory and the modeling of systems, Prentice Hall, 1981

C. Petri [1962]
Communication with automata ; Supplement 1 to the technical report RADC-TR-65-377,
vol. 1, New York 1966 (Translated from "Kommunication mit Automaten", University
of Bonn, 1962).

F. Preparata and R. Yeh [1973]
Introduction to discrete structures, Addison-Wesley, Reading, Massachussets, 1973.

C. Ramchandani [1973]
Analysis of asynchronous concurrent systems by timed Petri nets, Ph. D. Thesis,
M.I.T., September 1973.

S. Rudeanu [1974]
Boolean functions and equations, North-Holland, Amsterdam, 1973.

E. Sanchez and A. Thayse [1981]
Implementation and transformation of algorithms based on automata, Part II : Optimization of evaluation programs, Philips Journal of Research, vol. 36, pp. 159-172,
1981.

J. Savage [1976]
The complexity of computing, Wiley, New York, 1976.

H. Sholl [1974]
Direct transition memory and its application in computer design, IEEE Trans. Comp.,
vol. 23, pp. 1048-1061, October 1974.

H. Sholl [1975]
Design of asynchronous sequential network using ROM, IEEE Trans. Comp., vol. 24,
pp. 195-206, February 1975.

J. Sifakis [1977a]
Use of Petri nets for performance evaluation, in : Measuring, modelling and evaluating computer systems, North-Holland, pp. 75-93, 1977.

J. Sifakis [1978]
Structural properties of Petri nets, 7th Symp. on math. foundations of computer Sci.,
Zakopane, Pologne, September 1978.

A. Stauffer [1980]
Méthode de synthèse des systèmes digitaux, Bulletin de l'association suisse des électriciens, vol. 71, pp. 143-150, 1980.

A. Thayse [1978]
Meet and join derivatives and their use in switching theory, IEEE Trans. Comp.,
vol. C-27, pp. 713-720, August 1978.

A. Thayse [1979]
Encoding of parallel program schemata by vector addition systems, Int. J. of Comput.
and Inf. Sci., vol. 8, pp. 209-218, June 1979.

A. Thayse [1980]
Implementation and transformation of algorithms based on automata, Part II : Synthesis of evaluation programs, Philips Journal of Research, vol. 35, pp. 190-216, 1980.

A. Thayse [1981a]
P-functions : A new tool for the analysis and synthesis of binary programs, IEEE
Trans. Comp., vol. C-30, pp. 698-705, 1981.

A. Thayse [1981b]
Programmable and hardwired synthesis of discrete functions, Part I : One-level addres-
sing networks, Philips Journal of Research, vol. 36, pp. 40-73, 1981.

A. Thayse [1981c]
Programmable and hardwired synthesis of discrete functions, Part II : Two-level ad-
dressing networks, Philips Journal of Research, vol. 36, pp. 140-158, 1981.

A. Thayse [1981d]
Boolean calculus of differences, Lecture notes in Computer Science, Springer-Verlag,
New York, 1981.

A. Thayse [1982]
Synthesis and optimization of programs by means of P-functions, IEEE Trans. Comp.,
vol. C-31, pp. 34-40, 1982.

A. Thayse [1984a]
A matrix formalism for asynchronous implementation of algorithms, IEEE Trans. Comp.,
to appear , April 1984.

A. Thayse [1984b]
A computation method for factorizing Boolean matrices : application to asynchronous
implementation of algorithms, IEEE Trans. Comp., to appear.

A. Thayse [1984c] , Anwendung der theorie Boolescher funktionen auf den entwurf von
algorithmen, in : Boolesche Gleichungen-Theorie, Anwendungen, Algorithmen, Editors :
Profs D. Bochmann and Ch. Posthoff (Karl-Marx-Stadt), Prof. A. Zakrevskij, Minsk;
V.E.B. Verlag Tecknik, Berlin and Springer-Verlag, Berlin, New York, 1984

A. Thayse [1984 d]
Synchronous and asynchronous implementations of algorithms, to appear.

A. Thayse, M. Davio and J.P. Deschamps [1978]
Optimization of multi-valued decision algorithms, 8-th International symposium on
multiple-valued logic, pp. 171-178, Chicago, 1978.

Z. Vranesic and K. Smith [1974]
Engineering aspects of multi-valued logic systems, Computer, vol. 7, pp. 34-41,
1974.

M. Wilkes [1951]
The best way to design an automatic calculating machine, Manchester university inau-
gural conference, 1951.

W. Wulf, M. Shaw, P. Hilfinger and L. Flon [1981]
Fundamental structures of computer Science, Addison-Wesley, Reading, Massachusetts,
1981.

P. Zsombor-Murray, L. Vroomen, R. Hudson, T. Le-Ngoc, P. Holck [1983]
Binary-decision-based programmable controllers, IEEE Micro, vol. 3, pp. 67-83, 1983.

Index

List of symbols, of notations and of conventions

Conjunction : No symbol or $\wedge$

Disjunction : $\vee$

Negation of a : $\bar{a}$

Ring sum or addition modulo 2 : $\oplus$

Uninterpreted addition law : +

　　$((\sigma_1 + \sigma_2)$ can among others be interpreted as : perform the operations σ_1 and σ_2, or as : perform the operations σ_1 or $\sigma_2)$

Implication : $\Rightarrow$

Equivalence : $\Longleftrightarrow$

$\in$　means is an element of

Inclusion relation : $\leqslant$ or $<$ (strict inclusion)

Binary or discrete constants are denoted by lower-case letters like a,...,e,...,k.

Binary or discrete variables are denoted by lower-case letters like x,y,z.

Underlined lower-case letters like $\underline{e}$ are used to denote either the vector of constants : $(e_1, e_2, \ldots, e_n)$ or the conjunction of constants : $\bigwedge_{i=1,n} e_i$

Underlined lower-case letters like $\underline{x}$ are used to denote either the vector of variables : $(x_1, x_2, \ldots, x_n)$ or the conjunction of variables : $\bigwedge_{i=1,n} e_i$

Lattice exponentiation : for a fixed integer $m \geqslant 2$, a discrete variable $x \in S = \{0, 1, \ldots, m-1\}$ and a subset C of S, the lattice exponentiation

$$x^{(C)}$$

is defined as follows :

$$x^{(C)} = m-1 \text{ iff } x \in C$$
$$= 0 \quad \text{otherwise}$$

The lattice exponentiation $\underline{x}^{(\underline{C})}$ is used to denote either the vector of exponentiations : $(x_1^{(C_1)}, x_2^{(C_2)}, \ldots, x_4^{(C_4)})$ or the conjunction of exponentiations : $\bigwedge_{i=1,n} x_i^{(C_i)}$

For m=2 the definition of the lattice exponentiation allows us to write :

$$x^{(0,1)} = 1$$
$$x^{(1)} = x$$
$$x^{(0)} = \bar{x}$$

$\langle g; h \rangle$: P-function

t_x, t_x^r, t_x^k : composition laws acting on P-functions

d_x, d_x^r, d_x^k : decomposition laws acting on P-functions

U, U^r : Union laws acting on P-functions

σ : command, λ : empty command

τ : end of execution signal

Low-level instructions : see figure 26

High-level matrix-instructions : see figure 27

      The present text is divided into 15 chapters and each chapter is divided into sections. The equations and the figures are continuously numbered. The definitions and theorems are numbered per section. If a section contains only one definition or one theorem it will not be numbered. The references are defined by the author's name followed by the publication year.